Springer Series

FOCUS ON WOMEN

Violet Franks, Ph.D., Series Editor

Confronting the major psychological, medical, and social issues of today and tomorrow, *Focus on Women* provides a wide range of books on the changing concerns of women.

VOLUME 1

THE SAFETY OF FERTILITY CONTROL

Editor-in-Chief: Louis G. Keith, M.D.
Associate Editors: Deryck R. Kent, M.D., Gary S. Berger, M.D.,
and Janelle R. Brittain, M.B.A.
With contributors

VOLUME 2

THERAPY WITH WOMEN
A Feminist Philosophy of Treatment

Susan Sturdivant, Ph.D.

Forthcoming:
VOLUME 3

SHELTERING BATTERED WOMEN
A National Study and Service Guide

Albert R. Roberts, D.S.W.

Susan Sturdivant, Ph.D., is in private practice in Dallas, Texas, specializing in the treatment of women and adolescent girls. She received her doctorate in clinical psychology from The Fielding Institute, and has also studied at The University of Texas and Southern Methodist University. She is the author of numerous papers and seminar presentations on therapy for women, sex roles, and the psychology of women. She is an active member of the Association for Women in Psychology as well as the American Psychological Association and the American Academy of Psychotherapists. Dr. Sturdivant is listed in *Who's Who of American Women, Who's Who in the South and Southwest, Personalities of America,* and the *Dictionary of International Biography.*

Therapy with Women
A Feminist Philosophy of Treatment

Susan Sturdivant, Ph.D.

Springer Publishing Company
New York

Quoted material has been reproduced by special permission from *The Journal of Applied Behavioral Science,* "Male Power and the Women's Movement" by Barbara Bovee Polk, Vol. 10, No. 3, 1974, direct quotes and paraphrasing taken from pp. 415–431, NTL Institute for Applied Behavioral Science.

Material quoted from "A conceptual framework for the process of feminist therapy" by Beth Earnhart is used with permission.

Lines from "Revolucinations" from *Monster: Poems by Robin Morgan* © 1972 are reprinted with permission of Random House, Inc.

Material cited from "Feminist and non-feminist outpatients compared," "Therapeutic groups for women: Rationale, indications and outcome," and "Psychotherapists' biases towards women: Overt manifestations and unconscious determinants" is reprinted with permission of Teresa Bernardez-Bonesatti.

Extract from "Feminist concepts of therapy outcomes" by Marjorie Klein from *Psychotherapy: Theory, Research and Practice* is reprinted with permission.

Springer Publishing Company, Inc.
200 Park Avenue South
New York, New York 10003

84 / 10 9 8 7 6 5 4 3

Library of Congress Cataloging in Publication Data

Sturdivant, Susan
    Therapy with women.

    (Springer series, focus on women; 2)
    Includes bibliographical references and index.
    1. Feminist therapy.   2. Women--Mental Health.
I. Title. II. Series.
RC489.F45S78   616.89′14   79-27536
ISBN 0-8261-2880-7
ISBN 0-8261-2881-5 pbk.

Printed in the United States of America

Contents

Foreword by Jessie Bernard   *vii*
Preface   *xi*

◼ One

Theoretical Issues

1 Why Philosophy of Treatment?   3
2 Basic Assumptions of Philosophy of Treatment   10
3 The Questions   30

◼ Two

Historical Background

4 The Current Feminist Movement   39
5 The Women's Movement and Freud   49
6 The Feminist Critique of Psychotherapy   54
7 The Emergence of Feminist Therapy   67

◼ Three

A Feminist Philosophy of Treatment

8 The Value System of Feminist Therapy   75

9   The Nature of Woman   *85*
10 The Etiology of Psychological Distress in Women   *105*
11 Interpretation of Symptoms   *117*
12 The Focus of Therapeutic Interventions   *130*
13 The Role of the Therapist   *149*
14 Goals of Feminist Therapy   *161*

■ Four

Conclusions

15 The Impact of Feminist Therapy   *177*
16 New Directions   *182*

References   *187*

Index   *203*

Foreword

Although I am neither a practitioner nor a "consumer" of feminist therapy, I found Susan Sturdivant's description and analysis of it both useful and illuminating. I was especially interested in its message in light of the current preoccupation with the sociobiological point of view which, despite disavowals (Barash, 1977), is clearly sexist in orientation.

As interpreted by Daniel Freedman, for example, sociobiology finds an evolutionary rationale for male dominance in human societies: "It is apparently imperative for the male to feel superior to the female" (1979). Thus, he continues, "Males everywhere tend to demean women, belittle their accomplishments, and, in the vernacular (clearly laden with symbolism) 'put them down.' " Nor is this a quaint parochial practice in our own society, for Freedman goes on to say that: "I have not heard of a culture in which the males do not engage in this chauvinistic sport." In our society, Henley (herself a strong feminist) has documented how this male dominance is expressed in personal interaction or "body politics": showing how non-verbal behavior—demeanor, posture, touch, eye contact, facial and emotional expression—express male dominance (1977). Another sociobiologist, Dawkins (1976), has a neat explanation for all this: "The female sex is exploited, and the fundamental evolutionary basis for this exploitation is the fact that eggs are larger than sperms." And Barash (1977) sums it up by saying, "Mother Nature appears to be a sexist." Equally relevant is the sociobiological conclusion that women prefer it that way, for, as Freedman (1979) tells us "there appears to be something reflexive in young women that causes them to defer to men."

All, however, is not lost for we are not, according to the sociobiologists, entirely at the mercy of our biology. For, in the last analysis, it is culture that determines human behavior. Our genes may tell us to act one way, but we can teach ourselves to act another way. "We have the power to defy the selfish genes of our birth," according to Dawkins (1976) and even, by extension, our indoctrination. We are not, after all, at the mercy of our biology. Tiger and Shepher (1975) go even further by suggesting that feminist "perturbation" may even be a kind of species response to overpopulation!

I have presented the above ideas in order to explain why we need feminist therapy. Let me now speak more directly to the point. Women have been subjected to a kind of socialization which is not only nonfunctional for the actual world they live in but, in many cases, even profoundly dysfunctional. We have inherited from the nineteenth century a folk image of women who dedicated their lives to the rearing of children and the caring of a household, and who were fully protected from the harsh, outside world and taken care of by a watchful, conscientious, male provider. This female world was governed by a love and/or duty ethos: women were expected to devote their lives to selfless service to others (Deland, 1911).

In the nineteenth century, the "bonds of womanhood" (Cott, 1977) supplied the affectionate support that made the conditions of life bearable. In the twentieth century, however, these female friendships came under suspicion (Sahli, 1979), and fell into disrepute (Bernard, 1980). Only recently have there been strong efforts to relegitimatize them (Seiden and Bart, 1975; Bart, 1979) and to rejuvenate the idea of sisterhood.

These remarks should help to explain why feminist therapy is so important. There are so many services that have to be performed, so many women victimized by destructive socialization practices who need to be released. So many women who, as Freedman (1979) reminds us, have been demeaned, belittled, put down, and who have to be picked up again. So much deference has been demanded, whatever the psychological cost. So much guilt inculcated. So much depression generated. So much helplessness well taught and well learned (Seligman, 1974). It becomes clear why therapists who have not yet examined the processes or the contexts which have produced so many symptoms and needs are unable to cope with them. Certainly no therapist with a sociobiological orientation would be able to deal effectively with such symptoms and needs. It may well be true that many of the symptoms that women bring to the therapist are related to their sex, but not in the deterministic sociobiological sense. They are symptoms that can be produced in any-one given certain circumstances. It just happens that the conditions for producing them are commoner for women.

This welcome book performs an invaluable service for the nascent but growing profession of feminist therapy. It shows us the whole pic-ture—theoretical, historical, and philosophical—without losing sight of the individual woman. The woman herself is always there, front and center. It is her needs that must be met: mere "insight" or "understand-ing" is not enough. Self-directed growth is the watchword; emancipation from debilitating dependencies a major objective. Autonomy is the goal, not in a punitive or rejecting sense, but rather in an outgoing sense. All this means participation, community with other women, and connection with all humanity. It means political awareness and social action.

A tall order for feminist therapy, but nothing less will do. The author of this valuable book does not try to make it sound easy. It isn't easy, but it is possible. More power to her and to all the other partici-pants in this important revolution.

Jessie Bernard

References

Barash, David P. 1977. *Sociobiology and Behavior*. New York: Elsevier.

Bart, Pauline. 1979. Letter to Editor. *Chrysalis*, 8: 6–7.

Bernard, Jessie. 1980. *The Female World*. New York: Free Press.

Cott, Nancy. 1977. *The Bonds of Womanhood*. New Haven: Yale University Press.

Dawkins, Richard. 1976. *The Selfish Gene*. New York: Oxford University Press.

Freedman, Daniel G. 1979. *Human Sociobiology*. New York: Free Press.

Henley, Nancy. 1977. *Body Politics*. Englewood Cliffs: Prentice-Hall.

Sahli, Nancy. 1979. "Smashing, Smashing Women's Relationships before the Fall." *Chrysalis*, 8; 17–27.

Seiden, Ann M. and Bart, Pauline B. 1975. "Woman to Woman: Is Sisterhood Powerful?" in Nona Glazer, ed., *Old Family/New Family*, pp. 189–228. New York: D. Van Nostrand.

Seligman, M.E.P. 1974. "Depression and Learned Helplessness," in R.J.

Friedman and M.M. Katz, eds., *The Psychology of Depression*. pp. 83–113. Washington, D.C.: Winston and Sons.

Smith-Rosenberg, Carroll. 1975. "The Female World of Love and Ritual: Relations between Women in Nineteenth-Century America." *Signs, 1:* 1–28.

Tiger, Lionel and Shepher, Joseph. 1975. *Women in the Kibbutz*. New York: Harcourt, Brace, Jovanovich.

Preface

My interest in women and therapy began when, as a student in a traditionally oriented graduate program, I was assigned to do a report on "Minorities in Psychology." "Minorities" covered everyone except white males: Blacks, Chicanos, Indians—and women. I was given a group of papers from a recent American Psychological Association conference on the subject as a starting point. Among them was the now-classic Broverman (1970) study on sex-role stereotypes and judgments of mental health. A "click" resounded in my head when I read that the mentally healthy woman was described by therapists—the people supposedly helping her to fuller realization of her human potential— as "neurotic, flighty, easily upset," and so forth. At the same time, healthy men were described in much the same way as "healthy adult" and generally in much more positive and socially desirable terms. The implication seemed clear: one could either be female or a person, but not both!

When, in the early seventies, feminists began to write about a "feminist therapy," I read everything I could find on it (which was little enough). What I read was both fragmented and unified: fragmented in that each paper addressed only selected aspects of feminist therapy; unified in that all of the writers clearly held the same vision of a new approach to treating women in therapy. They talked about their own value system, a feminist value system; about their relationships to their clients; about their hopes for the development of a better treatment model for women. Over and over, whether criticizing traditional therapy or discussing feminist therapy, they seemed to be saying that the crucial factor in doing therapy with women was the therapist's attitudes, values, and beliefs about women and about therapy. Thus, therapists could utilize varying theories of personality to explain human behavior, could employ a variety of therapeutic techniques, but still be united in a common philosophical approach to treatment: a feminist approach. I began to think and talk about "philosophy of treatment," only to find that there was absolutely nothing written about the subject. I am, however, indebted to Erwin Singer's (1970) discussion of "Historical and Philosophical Roots of Psychotherapy," which at least validated my belief in the importance of the influence of philosophical concepts in shaping the process of therapy.

As a young graduate student, I often heard Quinn McNemar say that "You can assume anything you want to, as long as you remember that you've assumed it." The implication was that if things went awry later on you'd best go back and reexamine the validity of that initial assumption. Despite this, I knew that most therapists continued to cling to the myth that therapy could be value-free and that they themselves could be impartial, rational observers. It was also apparent from reading feminist criticisms of traditional psychotherapy that it was precisely this delusion that allowed sexist attitudes and practices to flourish within the profession. Clearly, the profession as a whole had forgotten that it had made many assumptions about women. Sigmund Koch of the University of Texas at Austin, also influenced my thinking. If he taught his students anything at all, it was to always look for and question the basic assumptions underlying any intellectual phenomenon.

The time seemed ripe for a critical analysis of the basic assumptions of psychotherapy, particularly of its beliefs about women, so that a new and more effective system of therapy could be developed. Putting these factors together, it seemed obvious to me that the nascent phenomenon called feminist therapy was, more than anything, a philosophy of treatment and that it was time to set forth its basic assumptions in a systematic and scholarly way, within the conceptual framework that I had begun to call "philosophy of treatment."

I am indebted to The Fielding Institute of Santa Barbara, California, for affording me the intellectual opportunity and educational freedom to do the theoretical dissertation that formed the basis for this book and for providing me with superb faculty, among them John Gladfelter, PhD. and Stan Caplan, EdD., to assist in the process. I also wish to thank Mary Hargrave, PhD., Pat Kurtz, M.S., and Flint Sparks, M.S.

for their emotional support and critical review of this work while in progress. My appreciation also goes to the feminist therapists all over the country who generously shared with me their unpublished papers and their expressions of support for my efforts.

■one
THEORETICAL ISSUES

1
Why Philosophy of Treatment?

> . . . no interventive theory is without its moral philosophy and some core assumptions about human nature.
>
> Saleebey (1975, p. 472)

In developing a new approach to conceptualizing and treating psychological distress in women, why select "philosophy of treatment"—a rather esoteric-sounding concept—as a starting point? There seem to be two answers to this question.

One is that the women's movement of the last decade has made a profound and lasting impact on the practice of psychotherapy. It has generated criticism of the theory and practice of traditional psychotherapy, exposed sexist biases in psychotherapy, and called for a reexamination of the basic assumptions and values of psychotherapy with regard to women. The response to these concerns has been the development of a new kind of therapy for women, based on an integration of feminist philosophy into therapeutic theory and practice. This new therapy stresses the importance of therapists' attitudes, values, and beliefs on the therapy process and outcome. These are primarily philosophical, not theoretical or technical, concerns.

Secondly, it seems logical that, if we are to build a new system of

3

therapy for women, we should begin with the basic philosophical assumptions that form the core of any approach to treatment. While modern psychology began as an extension of the scientific method of study into human behavior, the practice of psychotherapy will always be related as much to what we *believe* about people as to what we *know* about them.

Since conceptualization determines the standards used to judge the nature and extent of emotional illness (or mental health), it would seem to be extremely important to define the philosophical concepts underlying this new therapy. Defining the basic assumptions of a feminist therapy would form a system of meaning within which the "symptoms" of distress in women would become intelligible not only as individual problems but as cultural problems as well. In addition, exposition and definition are necessary precedents for later empirical validation of the theoretical propositions that grow out of the concepts of feminist therapy.

The Impact of Feminism on Psychotherapy

> What feminism promises is a world in which being a woman, no longer a wound, is also not a weapon.
>
> Suzanne Gordon (1976)

The current women's movement, which began in the 1960s, has touched virtually every aspect of American women's lives. The early feminist movement at the turn of the century mistook the right to vote as the symbol of full equality. While broader social and attitudinal reforms were also espoused, they were generally subordinated to the drive for suffrage. With the attainment of the vote for women, this movement was largely disbanded for want of consensus as to where next to focus their energies.

Recognizing that suffrage actually did little to improve women's status, the current movement has taken a broader approach, demanding equality for women in all areas of their lives. The breadth and scope of the current movement may be attributed in large part to the unifying effect of a common ideology. While the movement for suffrage had been labeled a feminist movement, in practice it was limited to being a political advocacy movement for females. With the movement of the 1960s, however, feminism came to be defined in a much broader way, encompassing social, cultural, and personal attitudes and values, as well as a political position.

In so doing, it has created a true cultural revolution that has affected every aspect of American society, including the professions. Although this movement also seeks economic equality for women through "equal pay for equal work" and increased participation of women in the legislative process, it is on the social and cultural levels that it has made both the greatest demands and the greatest impact, challenging the sexist attitudes and double standards that permeate our culture. This movement has demanded not only economic and political equality for women but also equalization of personal and social power in relationships between women and men. To this end, it has emphasized careful analysis of sex roles and power relationships, and through the development of consciousness-raising groups, has increased women's awareness of how they have internalized oppressive attitudes and beliefs.

As a result, feminism in the 1960s and 1970s has become a well-integrated and widespread ideology, as well as a social and political movement. Consequently, it is on the ideological level that it has made the greatest impact on the profession of psychotherapy; the result has been the emergence of what its practitioners call a feminist therapy.

What feminists criticize most frequently about traditional psychotherapy and psychotherapists are the sexist attitudes, beliefs, and practices that they harbor; what feminist therapists speak of most often in describing themselves and their work are their attitudes toward therapy, their beliefs about what therapy for women should be, and their vision of what women can be. In one of the earliest papers on feminist therapy Hannah Lerman (1974) noted that the specific techniques used by feminist therapists are less important than the philosophy that determines the attitudes with which the techniques are used. This was confirmed by Thomas (1975), who, after interviewing feminist therapists, concluded that feminist therapy must be understood less as a theoretical orientation in the traditional sense and more as a belief system and a series of ways in which that belief system is put into practice. She emphasized the congruency among the therapists she interviewed both in their commitment to a feminist value system and in the similar ways by which these beliefs were implemented in the therapy situation, despite widely disparate theoretical orientations.

The term "feminism," however, remains ill-defined and emotion laden, capable of eliciting surprisingly hostile reactions at times; even some people who agree with most of its tenets abhor the label. Since feminist ideology or philosophy is crucial to the treatment approach that will be presented here, it seems appropriate to briefly define this term before going further.

The core of feminism is simply the insistence that personal autonomy is essential for women. This means that women should have both the freedom and the responsibility to direct all important areas of their lives: emotional, intellectual, economic, and sexual. It means that women must decide for themselves what it means to be an adequate woman, instead of accepting the prevalent male definitions of womanhood. And it means that women must define themselves as independent persons, separate and apart from their relationships with others, be they husbands, parents, children, or lovers.

Like the Black movement, feminism also fosters a sense of pride in being female. It emphasizes the commonality of the female experience across cultural and socioeconomic lines and develops a sense of community among women, rather than the competition for male approval that female socialization traditionally teaches women.

Feminism holds that, in theory, all roles are open to all people; that every person is entitled to the opportunity to develop his/her potentials to the fullest, unhampered by the restraints of artificially dichotomous sex roles. Feminism assumes that women and men are more alike than they are different and insists that differences, where they do exist, no longer be conceptualized in terms of "inferiority" and "superiority."

Finally, feminism strives to equalize personal power between the sexes. While individual differences in status, due to education, intelligence, expertise, and socioeconomic level, are likely to persist indefinitely, feminism insists that people can and must have equity in their personal relationships with one another, both between and within the sexes. Feminism asserts that no person should have noncontractual dominion over another; it thus encourages egalitarian relationships between people, whether they be husband/wife, parent/child, friends, or lovers.

While feminism does not shrink from blaming men for our long history of female oppression, it places the majority of the responsibility for changing this injustice with women themselves. Thus, it is primarily an advocacy system for women, rather than a vendetta against men.

This belief system has been carried into the practice of psychotherapy by female professionals and paraprofessionals. Recognizing that traditional psychotherapy was not meeting women's needs and that it in fact at times furthered women's oppression, they turned to feminism to help them forge a new approach to treatment. The result has been not so much new theories of therapy or new treatment techniques as a shift in attitudes, in emphasis, in conceptualization of issues, in goals of treatment, and in beliefs about the nature and purpose of therapy.

The Importance of Philosophy of Treatment

> . . . in all therapies, explicitly or implicitly, there is an influencing of the patient toward a productive life philosophy. The particular kind of ideology is bound to reflect that which the therapist finds meaningful, and the values of the patient will be molded by this.
>
> Wolberg (1954, p. 277)

This brings us to the second answer to the question we pose in this chapter: "Why philosophy of treatment?" Central to every form of psychotherapeutic treatment are beliefs about what people are like and what they might become, as well as a conceptual framework within which to order and understand the data of human experience and behavior. In most cases, however, these assumptions remain implicit. They are not stated openly but are expressed indirectly through theory and techniques, both of which develop from the belief system or philosophy of treatment.

Modern psychotherapy began with Freud, who utilized a mechanistic, drive-reduction model of human nature and who attempted to adapt the interpretation of human behavior to the framework of empirical science. These views have since been proven by twentieth-century psychology and science to be fallacious and naive. Schafer (1974) summarizes the problem as follows:

> Freud was working within a nineteenth-century biological-medical tradition . . . . He merely applied and extended the conventions that constituted that tradition. That tradition was marked by a fusion of mechanistic and evolutionary modes of thought and patriarchal complacency. It based itself on ruling principles of nature such as survival; great natural polarities or dichotomies, such as activity-passivity and masculinity-femininity; and other broad generalizations designed to take nature by the throat. Additionally, it was a tradition of belief in the idea of value-free empiricism and of pride in the achievements of the utterly objective scientist, and so was philosophically immature to appreciate what is better established today— namely the pluralistic, relativistic, linguistic and inevitably valuative aspects of the various forms of knowledge. (p. 483)

It is time for the profession of psychotherapy to give up its mantle of pseudoscientism, to recognize the importance of philosophical questions to the practice of psychotherapy, and to state its answers to these questions openly. I will not argue here the thorny question of whether or not psychology is a science. It is clear to me that the practice of psychotherapy is not, because values and beliefs are not amenable to investigation and treatment by the scientific method. It is values and beliefs that form the foundation of psychotherapy, not empirical facts, and we must come to grips with this. I can only agree wholeheartedly with Fine (1974, p. 25), who says: "Pure empiricism without any philosophical presuppositions is but another of those comforting illusions that scientists who like to perch in ivory towers employ to rationalize their preferences. Values must be stated even if they cannot be demonstrated to be best beyond a shadow of a doubt." Theories and techniques of psychotherapy are created by one's beliefs, not vice versa. One does not "prove" something about human behavior in a laboratory study and then, as a result of this "objective" finding, form generalized beliefs about human nature. Rather, one holds beliefs, consciously or unconsciously, about the nature of human beings and subsequently develops or chooses theories and techniques congruent with these beliefs.

For instance, if one believes (à la Freud) that human nature is at its core a group of irrational, instinctual urges that must be controlled in order for civilization to continue, then one builds a theory of human personality as consisting of irrational instincts (id) which are controlled by a monitor (superego) which enforces societal laws and a mediator (ego) between the two to provide flexibility and make situationally appropriate decisions. The practice of therapy then becomes directed toward 1) the successful sublimation and repression of destructive instinctual urges into more socially-acceptable and constructive channels, and 2) the strengthening of the ego to allow adequate social functioning. The goal of such therapy is successful adaptation of the individual to societal norms and mores.

If, on the other hand, one conceptualizes human beings as basically benign and as having an innate tendency for growth and creativity (à la Rogers), then one creates a theory of personality as being constantly in a state of growth and evolution ("Being-in-Becoming"). Psychological problems and emotional distress are supposed to be caused by social or intrapsychic impediments to this natural tendency to growth. The function of therapy is thus the creation of conditions that enable the client to express and explore himself without fear of censure; the goal of therapy is personal growth, as defined by the individual.

In this light, one's beliefs may be seen to affect virtually all aspects of treatment, including the definition of mental illness, determination of the need for therapeutic intervention, interpretation of symptoms, selection of goals, and so forth. It is, therefore, a central thesis of this work that people carry their personal philosophy of life (their belief system) with them into their vocational or professional life. When that profession is psychotherapy, one's philosophy of life is translated into a philosophy of treatment. While numerous writers have voiced concern about the role of values in psychotherapy and about moral issues in treatment, none has offered a conceptual framework which would explain how these issues are integrated into the process of therapy. It is my contention that the concept of philosophy of treatment provides this link.

If philosophy is defined as a ". . . critical study of fundamental beliefs and the grounds for them" (Merriam-Webster, 1965, p. 372), then philosophy of treatment becomes the examination of the belief system underlying a given type of therapy, as well as the implications of these beliefs and values for the practice of that therapy. This is as distinguished from *theory,* which is defined as assumptions and evidence about personality dynamics (that is, how people work both intra-psychically and interpersonally); and from *techniques,* which are specific interchanges between therapist and client designed to facilitate reaching therapeutic goals.

■2
Basic Assumptions of Philosophy of Treatment

> Writing about psychotherapy is amazingly like writing about philosophy. It is impossible to define psychotherapy without already implying a point of view about psychotherapy. Any definition immediately contains assumptions and much of what follows after the definition of psychotherapy is already implicit in the definition.
>
> Chessick (1969, p. 13)

Before specifically defining a feminist philosophy of treatment, let us examine what I propose to be four basic assumptions central to the concept of philosophy of treatment:

1. Values are an integral part of psychotherapy. The definition of mental health and mental illness, the determination of the need for therapeutic intervention, the interpretation of symptoms and the determination of therapeutic goals are all based on value judgments. The concept of a value-free psychotherapy and of the therapist as a morally neutral observer is a myth. It is a dangerous myth, insofar as it makes the value judgments upon which therapy is based inaccessible to conscious control.

2. The value system of a school of therapy or of an individual therapist are largely the result of the value orientation of the larger culture from which they are derived. Therapists and therapies there-

10

fore either reflect dominant cultural values or represent a reaction to them.

3. Although modern psychotherapy has arisen from the allied disciplines of psychiatry and psychology, it in fact has its deepest historical roots in philosophy. Because of the value judgments with which it deals and the existential questions that it addresses, psychotherapy is more like philosophy than it is like psychology.

4. Our belief system limits our range of possibilities. In the case of psychotherapy, this means that our philosophy of treatment determines what we see as possible, probable, and desirable for our clients, as well as parameters of change. The belief systems of therapist and client in psychotherapy combine to determine therapeutic process and outcome.

Values and Therapy

> Value-laden psychotherapy is possible because the imprecision of psychiatric theory, especially the ambiguity concerning "normality," permits the psychiatrist's moral preferences to be enunciated "in the disguise of scientific descriptions of fact."
>
> Bart (1971, p. 15)

> Much of the material with which the therapist deals is neither understandable nor usable outside the context of a system of human values.
>
> London (1964, p. 5)

This work is based on the recognition that psychotherapists are human beings, too. This means that we bring with us to the therapy setting our own value systems—beliefs about the essential nature of human beings and varying degrees of optimism or pessimism about their prospects for the "good life"—as well as a body of "scientific" knowledge about human behavior. We hold a variety of attitudes toward people and their behavior and make conscious and unconscious value judgments about what is desirable for them and what is not. London (1964) says, "Perhaps the most general and accurate answer that sensitive and self-conscious therapists could offer to the question of their goals could be put so: 'I want to reshape this person's (the client's) existence so that he will emulate values which I cherish for myself; aspire to what I wish humanity to be, fulfill my need for the best of all possible worlds and human conditions.' "

This is likely to be true. The problem, however, is that for the most part these attitudes and judgments are unconsciously held and thus are implicit, rather than expressed, in the therapy process. Of all the elements of psychotherapy, we are least consciously aware of the values that are the foundation of any sort of therapy and the precursor of both theory and techniques in therapy. We are consciously aware of the theoretical explanations and interpretations that we make of human emotion and behavior in the therapy setting; we consciously make decisions to use one therapy technique rather than another; but we rarely examine, or even admit to, the value judgments that we make in every therapy hour.

For example, Mrs. K. is talking today of feeling like killing herself. The therapist may theorize that this is due to the loss of her youngest child leaving for college last week. S/he may choose to be nondirectively supportive and reflective of her depressed feelings; may actively urge Mrs. K. to develop interests outside the home; or may invite her to engage in a double-chair dialogue that expresses her feelings about the departed child. But rarely, if ever, is the therapist aware of the implicit value judgment s/he has made that suicide is bad; that it is an undesirable and unacceptable way of coping with life stress; that life is worth continuing at all costs. Yet the judgment is there, implicit in both the theoretical interpretations that offer rational explanations for the "irrational" thought of suicide and in the use of techniques to distract the client's attention away from further thoughts of death. Still another value judgment is made if the therapist decides to restrict the focus of inquiry to intrapsychic factors, implying that cultural or developmental factors are not of at least equal importance.

Because we have lacked a concept that would integrate values and value judgments with the theory and practice of therapy, many therapists have seemed tempted, as London (1964) puts it, to "claim the privilege of ignorance." This is confounded by the democratic ideal and the scientific values of objectivity and intellectual comprehension, which cause American therapists to underestimate the persuasive aspects of the therapeutic process. Scientific values of objectivity and intellectual comprehension, as Frank (1975) points out, tend to foster an overemphasis on the cognitive aspects of psychotherapy. As a result, "insight" (the ability to verbalize self-understanding) may be mistaken for genuine attitude change, and the therapist may place undue stress on intellectual interpretations. In addition, the democratic ideal assigns high worth to individual self-fulfillment, and regards behavior that is apparently self-directed as more admirable than behavior directed by external pressures. Since, as Frank comments, members of a democracy do not like to see themselves as exercising power over someone else, scientists like to believe that they only observe (rather than persuade or influence). Consequently, it has been very difficult for American therapists to acknowledge and confront the valuative aspects of therapy. Although there is a growing body of literature on the effects of therapist attitudes and values, it has remained largely a matter of academic discussion, making little impact on the day-to-day practice of psychotherapy. Recently, however, the resurgence of feminism in this country has revived these issues by insisting that we reexamine the sexism and sexist values embedded in traditional forms of psychotherapy.

Rotter (1963) discusses three value concepts that are implicit in the practice of therapy:

1. The *conformity* criterion for adjustment implies that people should accept the values of their culture and that they are maladjusted when they fail to accept the mores, goals, and beliefs of their society. Although few therapists would admit to such a belief themselves, Rotter notes that many may frequently rely on conformity as a criterion for adjustment in the absence of other explicit value concepts.

2. The *self-centered* approach holds that the internal feelings of happiness, well-being, harmony, and freedom from pain and internal conflict are criteria for adjustment. The person who feels more unhappy is more maladjusted; the behavior that results in the feeling of unhappiness or lack of well-being is the maladjusted behavior.

3. The *social-centered* point of view stresses the social contribution of the person and his/her behavior. Does the person contribute to the welfare of others, to society as a whole? Does s/he fulfill some useful function in society? Is the person's behavior, in a broad sense, contributive to the society s/he lives in?

These values are generally applied differentially to men and women. Regardless of the approach that a therapist may take otherwise, virtually all adopt conformity to sex role as a primary criterion for "mental health" or adjustment in women. Our culture is permeated with sexism; therapeutic approaches have not escaped its influence. Whether psychoanalytic, behaviorist, or humanistic, all schools of therapy view successful performance of the female role as part of the definition of a successful woman.

While sex-role criteria may also be a consideration in assessing the adjustment of men, they are not as constrictive nor as stringently applied as they are for women. The male role offers a considerably wider range of acceptable traits and behavior than does the female role. Although many characteristics may be disapproved for men, few are forbidden; for women, the situation is reversed. Even if a man makes choices outside the range of acceptability, he is unlikely to be considered mentally ill strictly because of his nonconformity; he may be considered eccentric or weak, but not "bad" or "crazy," as women often are.

For example, if a man cries, it may be considered "weak" or "inappropriate;" if a woman is angry, it becomes a psychiatric illness (see Rickles, 1971). If a man behaves in a warm, nurturing way, it may be considered a bit out of character (if it is commented upon at all), but if a woman behaves assertively, she is labeled "aggressive," "bitchy," or perhaps even "castrating" if she is assertive with men.

Difficult though it may be to accept, we must recognize that the very nature of the therapeutic interaction is such that communication of some part of the therapist's own moral commitments is inescapable. Psychotherapy is a social, interpersonal action, characterized by an exchange of individual, personal ideas and feelings; values cannot be excluded from this exchange.

Therefore, a major premise of the concept of philosophy of treatment, is that the nature and process of any "helping" endeavor, such as psychotherapy, is significantly shaped by unconsciously held values and beliefs. Obviously, feelings and opinions about women, about their "basic nature," their desired personality attributes, and their place in society will be a part of this exchange.

Culture and Therapy

> It is a truism that the therapist is himself a human being, that he lives in society and that wisely or unknowingly, responsibly or casually, he has made moral commitments to himself and that society.
>
> London (1964, p. 11)

Since values are the product of the dominant culture, it seems reasonable to assume that philosophy of treatment will be strongly influenced by the culture's value orientation; that is, by cultural responses to certain basic human problems.

Value orientation, as defined by Kluckhohn (1956) includes those "value notions" that are general, organized, and that "definitely include existential judgments." The basic assumption here is that there is a limited number of basic human problems for which all peoples at all times and in all places must find solutions. Since psychotherapy confronts human problems directly, it seems appropriate to look at this premise more closely.

Kluckhohn maintains that there are five common human problems:

1. What are the innate predispositions of human beings? That is, what is "basic human nature"?
2. What is the relationship between human beings and nature?
3. What is the significant time dimension of the culture?
4. What modality of activity is to be most valued?
5. What is the dominant modality of people's relations to one another?

In addition, Kluckhohn outlines the ways in which a culture may respond to these questions. The basic "nature of human nature," for instance, can be viewed in one of five ways:

1. As essentially evil, but perfectable.
2. As immutably evil.
3. As a mixture of good and evil (either mutable or immutable).
4. As good and mutable.
5. As good and unalterable.

Similarly, human beings may be seen as subjugated to nature, as living in harmony with nature, or as conquering nature. The valued time dimension, obviously, is either past, present, or future. A culture that has a past orientation looks at the past as something that is the best order to be maintained; Confucian China is a good example of such an orientation. A culture with a future orientation is constantly projecting into the future and values change as a good thing; American society has a primarily futuristic time orientation.

The valued type of activity may also be one of three possibilities:

1. *Being*, defined as spontaneous expression of what is considered to be the innate nature of the personality.
2. *Being-in-Becoming*, which is closely synonymous with self-realization.
3. *Doing*, which emphasizes accomplishment.

People's relation to one another may be *Lineal* (through ancestral descent or hierarchal tribal relations), *Collateral* (in which societal or group goals have primacy over individual ones), or *Individualistic* (which gives preference to individual goals). No society ever emphasizes any one of these principles to the exclusion of the other; rather, it is a matter of emphasis, of value judgment.

This definition of value orientation is readily adaptable to viewing systems of psychotherapy. Traditional psychoanalysis thus views human nature as mutably evil; places greatest emphasis on the formative influence of early childhood (past) experiences; adopts the Being-in-Becoming mode of activity, with its emphasis on self-realization; and sees people primarily in hierarchal relationships with nuclear family members (lineal) while striving to adapt individual libidinal urges to the constraints of civilized goals (collateral). Relation to nature is the same as the culture that gave rise to psychoanalysis: that of conquering nature through scientific knowledge. In this case, psychoanalysis seeks to control human nature through insight into the mechanics of psychodynamics.

The American behaviorists, on the other hand, although they generally ignore issues such as the "nature of human nature" appear, by implication, to view human nature as a mutable mixture of good and evil. They emphasize present activities, value Doing, and seek to conquer nature through extending the principles of behavior modification to apply to human behavior. They work to help individuals extinguish behaviors that are maladaptive within the dominant culture, and thus appear to have a collateral view of people's relations to one another.

Humanistic psychologists and psychotherapists differ from both psychoanalysts and behaviorists by viewing people as mutably good; valuing people who live in harmony with nature; valuing Being, emphasizing growth toward future changes, and indeed expecting change as an integral part of life; and by valuing free and spontaneous expression of the feelings of the moment (Being-in-Becoming). Perl's Gestalt prayer is an explicit statement of the humanist emphasis on individuality in relating to others.

It seems evident that psychotherapies, in their value orientation, may either reflect the dominant cultural orientation or adopt opposing values in reaction against the dominant system. Both psychoanalysis and behaviorism are close reflections of the cultures from which they arose. Humanistic therapies, rising as they did in large part from Eastern philosophies, deviate from the dominant American value system in many respects. They have adopted, for instance, a here-and-now (present) time orientation in contrast to the dominant future orientation of American society and they value people living in harmony with nature rather than attempting to control or dominate it through technology.

And what of the feminist value orientation upon which the present philosophy of treatment is based? Feminists are quick to point out that our culture's value system, like the society itself, is patriarchal and male dominated. Hence, male values predominate and female values are considered trivial or undesirable. Polk (1974, p. 418) makes the following points in comparing male and female value systems:

1. "Just as roles are dichotomized by sex, so are values. 'Masculine' values include competitiveness, aggressiveness, independence, and rationality; 'feminine' values include cooperativeness, passivity, dependence, and emotionality." These values are not inherently male or female but are socially assigned and derived from sex roles.

2. "Masculine values have higher status and constitute the dominant and visible culture of the society." They define the structure of personal, political, and economic relationships and provide the standard for adulthood and normality.

3. Women are oppressed and devalued in part because they embody an alternative culture or value system.

4. "Men are socialized almost exclusively to the masculine value system, but women receive dual socialization because of the dominance of male institutions and because they must comprehend masculine values in order to survive."

5. "Masculine values are largely responsible for the crisis in our society. Competitiveness pits human against human and results in racism, sexism, and the abuse of the natural environment in pursuit of economic power. Aggressiveness leads to war. Exaggerated independence inhibits society's ability to solve common problems by failing to recognize the fundamental interdependence among humans and between humans and the physical environment."

A notable difference between the value orientation of the philosophy of treatment to be presented here and all three of the prevalent schools of psychotherapy in the United States today is that it is consciously based on the female value system rather than the male, and specifically includes women in responding to basic human questions. Hence, women are seen as mutably good; living in harmony with nature is valued over the masculine mode of conquering nature; and self-realization (Being-in-Becoming) is valued for women. The valued mode of relating to others is collateral, which emphasizes cooperation and the interdependence of group and individual goals rather than the individualistic competitiveness valued by men. Future time orientation, with its emphasis on growth and change, is valued, with attention also being paid to present feelings and events.

Philosophy and Therapy

> First in philosophy and literature, then in the emergence of the social sciences, and finally in the advent of a new kind of psychology, Western man addressed himself to the challenge of understanding his own personality, to the questions of his destination and the meaning of his life.
>
> Alexander and Selesnick
> (1966, p. 5)

Psychotherapy may also be seen as an extension of the philosophical revolution of the seventeenth century, in which philosophy moved away from theological concerns to create more secular definitions of man focusing more on his internal life than on his relationship to externals such as the church, the universe, or society. This set the stage for a new curiosity about the world around us (as opposed to the religious world) that would give rise to the scientific revolution and to the kind of search for individual self-knowledge that would eventually result in psychotherapy. Now, almost 300 years later, women also have taken up this search.

While modern psychology may have begun in Wundt's laboratory, the struggle to understand ourselves as human beings has been with us since the beginning of civilization. Questions about the meaning of life and of moral issues of right and wrong, good and bad, as well as the search for self-understanding and personal happiness, have been with us always. In a sense, psychotherapy began the first time that one human being tried to understand and alleviate the emotional distress of another. In ancient times, this job fell to the philosophers who, in their attempts to understand and explain life, offered advice on both physical and psychological illness. With the advent of Christianity, this function was taken over by the church and attention turned from temporal relationships to man's relation to God, and from the quest for happiness and the "good life" on this earth to concern with assuring oneself a spot in heaven. As the power of the church gradually eroded, culminating in the Reformation, people began to turn more of their attention to this life and to the world around them, including all kinds of natural events. Many theological myths were dispelled by the application of the scientific method to examination of both people and animals. Science became the "new religion" and empirical proof the ultimate criterion for belief.

What Freud did, essentially, was to apply the scientific principle of orderly and systematic observation and categorization to the affectual lives of human beings. Although he proceeded to draw some questionable conclusions from the data thus obtained, he nevertheless continued to address the basic issues of human existence: the psychic structure of human beings; what conflicts cause emotional suffering (i.e. neurosis); and the symbolic meaning of human behavior. With the exception of some of the relatively short-term behavioral therapies that aim solely for symptom removal, these existential concerns remain the core of most psychotherapies.

Psychology, on the other hand, grew out of the psychophysiological research of Wundt, Titchener, and others and has remained molecular in its approach to human existence. Psychology examines areas such as cognition, perception, motivation, learning, psychophysiology, and social and individual behaviors. Although a somewhat integrative approach is taken by personality theorists, they, too, tend to deal primarily with questions of how human personality is structured and how it functions. They still skirt the existential questions of meaning, morals, and so forth.

Hence, the bits of data about human personality and behavior produced by psychological research are not very useful in the therapy setting, where the person must be dealt with as a whole entity and not as bits of behavior or cognition. While psychotherapy may draw from psychology for information about human motivation and behavior, it remains an encounter between two complete human beings; as such, it continues to be more concerned with the holistic, existential issues of philosophy than with the molecular issues of psychology.

MacLeod (1975) also has noted that the problems of psychology grow out of the problems posed by philosophy. He maintains that it is difficult to ask a question in psychology or formulate a problem whose foundation is not clearly in one or more of the ancestral philosophical areas. Table 2-1 reproduces in part a chart drawn up by MacLeod showing the questions posed by philosophy and by psychology in five major

TABLE 2-1. Questions Asked by Philosophy, Psychotherapy, and Psychology.

Philosophy	Psychotherapy	Psychology
Metaphysics: What is the nature of ultimate reality? Is a human being different from material substance? Do animals have souls? Dualism *versus* monism	What is considered reality? What is reality for this person (the client)? How does this person distort reality (the assumption being that distress is caused by *unrealistic* fears, worries, anxieties)? What are this person's psychodynamics?	What are the concrete, observable ways in which mental and physical processes are related to one another? What chain of causation leads from physical event (stimulus) to mental response (thought) or action? Or from mental event (like a choice) to consequent change in physical situation?
Epistemology: Can we know the truth?	What is the truth of this person's experience of life? What personal "truths" are revealed through the person's dreams and unconscious processes?	What are the cognitive processes underlying knowing?
Ethics: What is the nature of the good life? What do we mean by good?	What does this person want from life? (That is, what is his definition of the "good life"?)	What are the processes by which behavior is actually initiated, directed, and motivated?

Philosophy	Psychotherapy	Psychology
How are we to distinguish between good and bad?	What is this person's value system? Is it congruent or dissonant from the dominant value system? Are there conflicts between what she values and how she lives? What desires and beliefs motivate this person's behavior?	
Aesthetics: What are the criteria of aesthetic judgment? Issues of objective *versus* subjective judgments	Why are the creative forces in this person blocked? How can this person free up her creativity and ability to enjoy life?	What happens in a person when he apprehends something as beautiful and something else as ugly? What is the nature of the aesthetic response? What are the conditions of artistic creativity?
Politics: What is the nature of the state and what is a person's relation to it? What are the rights and obligations of citizenship?	What are the dynamics of this person's interpersonal relationships? What are the rights and obligations of interpersonal relationships?	What makes a person behave as a social being? Is s/he innately gregarious? Is s/he innately acquisitive?

Adapted from Robert MacLeod, *The Persistent Problems of Psychology.* Pittsburgh, PA: Duquesne University Press, 1975.

21

areas. Between these two categories, I have added questions addressed in the practice of psychotherapy which I believe to be more similar to those of philosophy than to those of psychology.

As we can see from the table, both philosophy and psychotherapy take an introspective, subjective approach to life, while psychology takes an objective, rational approach. Philosophy and psychotherapy deal in subjective judgments and interpretations, while psychology deals with facts. Both philosophy and psychotherapy address, in somewhat different terminology, holistic questions, while psychology addresses molecular ones. Philosophy is introspection on the nature of life as a concept, while psychotherapy is introspection on a single individual life. Psychology, on the other hand, breaks life into components, such as stimulus and response, or cognitive processes, and deals with them separately and concretely without addressing the meaning of the greater whole. Both philosophy and psychotherapy obviously deal with areas that cannot be quantified, that belong to the realm of individual judgments, and thus are not amenable to treatment by the scientific method. One cannot ascertain the definition of reality within the framework of an experimental design, although one may define certain component parts of it, as in perception and social psychological studies. It is impossible to relate these component parts back to the higher concept of "reality" without using individual judgment and subjective speculation, yet it is essential that we do so, since the molecular bits of information produced by psychology are interesting but relatively meaningless without a conceptual system to tie them together.

This is not to say that the basic assumptions of psychotherapy cannot or should not be subjected to systematic scrutiny and either verified or disproved. Rather, it is simply that the scientific method is not the appropriate tool to use. A new approach will have to be devised to deal with the questions posed by psychotherapy (or an existing one from another field adapted, such as Einsteinian physics with its "thought experiments") in order to examine the issues of psychotherapy.

While philosophy and psychotherapy appear willing, as disciplines, to continue to struggle with the "gray areas" of life and with the anxieties of subjective judgments and decisions, psychology, for the most part continues to avoid them. As Rollo May (1967) once remarked, psychology makes molehills out of mountains.

In the case of women, of course, both psychology and psychotherapy have largely ignored the mountain, so to speak. The questions addressed by psychotherapy have been answered by men, out of the male value system, with little regard for whether these answers were valid for women as well. The implicit assumption was that these were universal answers, applicable to all people. If a patriarchal society accorded women less than full human status, then existential questions were not really pertinent for them anyway and any sex differences in response to issues raised by therapy were insignificant.

Now we are beginning to recognize that women's experience of life is very different from men's and that the female value system is different from the male value system. If psychotherapy is to help women, it must begin by understanding the nature of the female experience. Psychotherapists must recognize that although the answers to the questions posed by psychotherapy are often the same for men and women, there are also significant differences shaped by differences in values, in socialization, and in sex-typed life experiences. Women are socialized to one value system (the female) but live largely by another (the male) because it is culturally dominant; thus they are always experiencing some degree of value conflict. Women's experience of life and their definition of reality is different from that of men.

Because these differences have been ignored for so long by psychotherapists, there is now a need for an approach to treatment that is responsive to women's specific needs, to their actual experience of life.

Thus far, I have delineated three assumptions basic to the concept of philosophy of treatment: 1) that values are an integral part of psychotherapy, 2) that the value system that I call philosophy of treatment is largely the product of the culture's response to basic existential questions, and consequently, 3) that psychotherapy is more like philosophy, in the issues it addresses and in its orientation to life, than it is like psychology. Having, I hope, firmly established psychotherapy as related to belief systems and value judgments, it is important now to discuss the limiting nature of belief systems.

Beliefs and Therapy

If the definition of emotional well-being and illness is a function of the value system maintained by the definer, it would follow that the breadth of his system and the ideal of man as it emerges from this system will determine how much or how little he deems pathological. The narrower the ideal, the more one will view as pathology; the wider one's vision of what constitutes humanness, the smaller the area of activities and behavior which can be defined as pathological.

Singer (1970, p. 14)

If, as I have proposed, beliefs create fact and theory and not vice versa, it becomes even more crucial that we realize how beliefs limit our range of conceptualization. Stated very simply, what we believe is what happens. If we cannot conceptualize a certain thing as possible, it won't occur; if our ideal is narrow, much will be construed to be outside the range of human possibility.

The Simontons (1978), for example, have found in their treatment of cancer patients that those who believe that they can control their disease process learn to do so, and through the Simontons' techniques, arrest their cancer indefinitely. Those patients whose belief systems cannot admit the concept of mental control of physiological processes may master the techniques of relaxation and visual imagery but build weak, ineffectual images to use against their cancer and do not get well. They do as much as they believe possible, *and only that much*.

Stated in a more sophisticated way, the limits of our consciousness are determined by our belief system; our assumptions about "reality" act as barriers to understanding and subsequently stand in the way of developing higher-order constructs. Based on our beliefs, we all set somewhat arbitrary limits on our range of possibilities and work within these limits. *This assumptive world is conservative* and, in our culture, the range of possibilities, for women in particular, has been very conservatively defined.

Thomas Kuhn (1970) in his *Structure of Scientific Revolutions*, deals with the limiting nature of the assumptive system in science. He maintains that scientific principles are meaningful and understandable in the context of a paradigm; i.e., of a disciplinary world view that is culturally transmitted and sustained by a set of social institutions. Any community of people, he says, holds in common certain assumptions about reality. In addition, each scientific community (including, I presume, psychologists and psychiatrists) shares a set of implicit assumptions about what is possible, about the boundaries of acceptable inquiry, and about the limiting cases within their disciplines. Within science, such a paradigm allows a stability of knowledge at the price of a "certain insensitivity to new input." The working of these scientific paradigms is similar to the working of an individual's assumptions about reality. Kuhn says, "The development of a successful paradigm, then, enables a scientific community to maintain and share criteria for the selection of problems which might be amenable to solution . . . . But there is a danger here: parochialism. Just as the residents of a certain community may become smug about their town and consider it the 'only' place in the world, so the scientist working under a successful paradigm may begin to lose sight of any possibilities beyond his own particular set of assumptions."

According to Kuhn (1970), scientific revolutions occur when the introduction of new notions (those that cannot be successfully redefined to fit the old paradigm) provoke a crisis that necessitates the creation of a new paradigm. Because belief systems do not invite explanations lying outside their boundaries, however, we go to great lengths to perceive our world in such a way as to make it congruent with what we already believe. It would appear that when something outside our assumptive world (our range of conceptualization) occurs, about 90 percent of the time it is distorted and redefined so that it is congruent with our existing belief system. If nothing else, the novel idea or event can always be redefined as "deviance" from some norm. An example is Scheff's (1966) explanation of mental illness as rule breaking. The remaining 10 percent of the time, the belief system and cognitive set is broken, the nonconforming event is not redefined, and, consequently, a "discovery" or revolution occurs. Subsequently, the paradigm is altered in such a way as to integrate the new information thus discovered.

This is as true in psychology and psychotherapy as it is in the "hard" sciences. According to Lifton (1976), psychological paradigms consist of a set of assumptions about human nature and function, about ways of studying the human psyche, and about ways of healing its patterns of dysfunction. An historical look at the development of human consciousness reveals that, at each stage, certain human potentials were made functionally impossible by the limitations of the existing psychological paradigms about human nature and behavior.

In earliest times, what Jaynes (1978) calls bicameral times, human behavior (including "madness") was assumed to be the result of supernatural forces. People behaved as the gods, or other unnamed cosmic forces, directed them. Within this paradigm, the concept of personal volition or internal motivation was impossible. It would have seemed absurd to the bicameral mind to suggest that people might be able to initiate and direct their actions without the supervision and direction of cosmic forces. Similarly, when human functioning was later conceived of as a rational mechanism, a combination of intellectual and moral free will, operating within the context of biological determinants, the concept of unconscious motivation was impossible. Mental illness was either immorality (for example, witchcraft), to be cured by exhortation and punishment; or an organic anomaly, to be dealt with by a physician.

Freud redefined these assumptions, adding to them the concept of the unconscious and its role in motivating human behavior and emotion. Both he and subsequent analytic theorists, however, confined their inquiries largely to the interior mental life: dreams, thoughts, feelings, and memories. As Kuhn points out, this allowed for a certain stability of knowledge and exchange of ideas within the analytic community, but it also limited the boundaries of understanding and inquiry about human life. For example, psychoanalytic and ego-dynamic therapists continue to assume that concern with social problems or structural deficiencies in society is simply (and solely) a projection of one's inner dynamics. This effectively precludes examination of the way in which sociocultural factors have impinged on or continue to restrict the individual.

The American behaviorists introduced yet another new assumption into the paradigm of introspective psychology: that action—behavior—could be studied, as well as mental processes. This paradigm also had its limitations, in that the scope of inquiry within it became unduly narrowed to processes that were amenable to solution and explanation by behavioral methods. Psychologists began to ignore and even deny the existence of phenomena which did not fit the behavioral paradigm. Sensory and experiential data were considered invalid. The implicit—though erroneous—assumption was that motivation and meaning were irrelevant as long as the maladaptive behavior could be changed. Human motivation was viewed primarily in a mechanistic way and the construct of personal meaning was outside the boundaries of this paradigm. Although the range and focus of acceptable inquiry were different from that of the psychodynamic and psychoanalytic schools, behaviorism was in many ways just as deterministic in its view of the range of human possibilities. In one case, human personality was determined by biology and early childhood experiences; in behaviorism, by biological drives and social learning. Psychoanalysts sought to control libidinal instincts while behaviorists created methods to control behavior. In both cases, the possibility for change was limited and was largely in the hands of the expert psychoanalyst or behavior-modification psychologist. The locus of control was external and the concept of free will alien to both paradigms.

Humanistic psychologists countered this with the assumption that knowledge is experiential as well as cognitive and that personal meaning was the ultimate criterion of validity. Refusing to rely entirely on verbal rationality as a means of gaining knowledge, they introduced the concept of personal experience as a way of knowing. This was used, at times, to the exclusion of intellectual processing. While sometimes taking an almost anti-intellectual stance, humanistic psychology widened the boundaries of the scientific paradigm by introducing new assumptions about human nature, the nature of knowledge, and the range of human possibility. Humanistic psychologists, foremost among them Maslow and Rogers, extended the humanistic image of human beings as innately good and striving towards growth into the field of psychology. They, along with the existentialists, (for example, Rollo May) asserted that people can be in charge of their lives and their destinies to a much greater extent than previously assumed. This implied that change was possible and that it was in large part within control of the individual.

To summarize, then, beliefs are assumptions that we make about our world. When we forget that we have made them and begin to treat them as if they were facts and not assumptions, we greatly reduce the possibility of innovation, flexibility, and further discovery; and greatly increase the possibility of error by beginning to dogmatize whatever errors there are in the assumptive system. In psychotherapy, the assumptive worlds of the therapist and the client combine to determine the goals, the limits of inquiry (what is deemed appropriate material for analysis or discussion), and the range of possible change. Both patient and therapist hold some variation of the cultural value orientation and these assumptions about human nature, about desirable personality characteristics, about people's relation to one another, and so forth, form the boundaries of the psychotherapeutic paradigm and limit our range of conceptualization about therapeutic endeavors.

Implications for Therapy

What has all of this to do with helping women change? The implications for women in therapy seem clear: if a therapist believes that women are "by nature" flighty, irrational, narcissistic, masochistic, or dependent, etc., s/he will do little to help a client become rational, independent, or stable, since such a change is, according to his/her assumptive world, "impossible" for women. Women who display these latter qualities, since they do not fit the commonly held paradigm, are labeled "deviant" (that is, deviating from the "real" nature of women) or "exceptional." "Exceptional" women are tolerated only as long as they are infrequent and individual, since too many women who do not fit the paradigm would threaten its validity. "Deviant" women, of course, are to be dealt with through traditional psychotherapy, which will help them adjust to the paradigm (to their cultural role definition).

Similarly, if it is assumed that women, for whatever reason, appropriately take a secondary role to men, then it will seem logical that their identity be defined by their relationships with the men in their lives. The concept of individual identities for women, then, is outside the paradigm and thus outside the boundaries of inquiry for psychotherapy.

If anatomy is destiny, then an integral part of the definition of womanhood is to be child bearing; childlessness is labeled as deviance, not choice. Other avenues to self-fulfillment for women are outside the assumptive system.

To fully develop and explore the ramifications of this model is beyond the scope of this present work. What is most germane here are the theses that:

1. The therapist's and the client's respective assumptive worlds combine to define and limit the range of possible and desirable change for clients.
2. Specifically, most therapists and their clients have unconsciously held assumptions about the "nature" of women, about women's role in our culture and their place in the world, and hence about women's innate "limitations." Insofar as these beliefs are culturally defined and imposed they are all the more likely to be accepted as "facts" by both therapist and client, rather than viewed as somewhat questionable and unverified assumptions.

Throughout the history of modern psychotherapy, from Freud onward, the error of "innate" female inferiority and the secondary status of women has been almost universally assumed and accepted, gradually becoming psychotherapeutic dogma. As long as feminists were few and far enough between, the psychotherapeutic paradigm could deal with them by a sort of psychological reductionism. Their commitment to an alternative view of women as independent beings could be attributed to personal psychopathology. With the advent of the women's movement, the number of feminists increased so dramatically that there were simply too many to label them all "deviant" and certainly too many for them all to be "exceptional." The paradigm was broken.

Now it is time for a "revolution" within the profession of psychotherapy, in which we reexamine and rebuild our assumptions about the nature of women, about female personality and psychology, and about the range of human possibility for women. In short, we must create a new philosophy of treatment for dealing with women, one that will be congruent with the feminist value orientation that has developed over the past two decades in this country, an orientation that ever-increasing numbers of women are embracing.

■3
The Questions

Having set forth the basic propositions of the belief system that I call philosophy of treatment, let us now examine the specifics of how the therapist's philosophy is translated into a philosophy of treatment. I have stated these as questions which therapists answer for themselves, out of their personal philosophy of life and the philosophy of science underlying their chosen school of psychotherapy. The assumption here is that these questions are germane to any approach to therapy. The broad constructs of feminist therapy are assumed to be the same as those for other forms of therapy; the differences lie in the content of the responses to the questions posed by philosophy of treatment.

What Is the "Nature" of Human Nature?

This is the central question of both philosophy and psychotherapy: what is the innate nature of human beings? Are they basically good or evil? Are they ruled by instinct or reason? Do they have free will? What motivates human behavior? Is it selfishness or altruism; drive reduction or desire for stimulation? Are people best understood as individuals or as members of social groups?

Responses to these questions form the basis for the assumptions and value judgments in other areas of philosophy of treatment; they also imply some ideal constellation of traits and behaviors toward which

30

people should strive. The question of the basic "nature of human nature" reflects most directly psychotherapy's connection with philosophy. The remaining questions that define philosophy of treatment reflect the impact and implications of this philosophical question for a particular area of our culture—psychotherapy.

Within modern philosophy, the extremes of these choices are illustrated in the theories of Hobbes and Rousseau. Hobbes maintained that man in his "natural state" is basically selfish and governed by innate impulses (for example, hunger, thirst, and sex). For Hobbes, the social contract was a compromise made with other individuals in the interest of self-preservation. Freud took much the same view: man was basically evil; the core of his personality consisted of primitive, self-serving instincts that had to be tightly controlled in order for society to be maintained.

Rousseau, on the other hand, believed that the "original nature" of man was good. He maintained that human nature, if allowed to develop and express itself freely, would grow toward a "full and free personality." He also argued that man's inherent nature included not only the primitive individualistic impulses that Hobbes had recognized, but also the capacity for identification with the general interests of the community—with something over and above the will of the individual, but through which the individual could attain maximum self-realization. This is much the same view that American humanistic psychologists have taken. They agree with Rousseau that man's original nature is basically good and that it is largely life pressures which cause neurosis, psychosis, and other psychological distress. In fact, the goal of this type of therapy is to uncover and/or return to one's basic self.

The responses of psychotherapists to this basic question of human nature become crucial for women when we realize that people's beliefs about human nature have behavioral consequences: we act as we think we are and as others think we are (Rosenthal, 1966; Scheff, 1966). If women believe themselves to be passive and intellectually inferior to men, they will behave passively and rely on men for assistance in thinking and problem solving. If they hold an idealized image of women as attractive, charming, pleasing to be with, and married to an attractive, successful man, they will strive to fill this image. It seems obvious that if we would change women, we must first change our image of them; and if psychotherapy is to help women change, it must offer them a more positive image of women than it has done in the past.

What Are the Causes of Psychological Distress?

Based on their view of human nature, psychotherapists develop an explanatory model of psychopathology on the answers to such questions as: Why do people suffer psychological distress? How is psychological distress or "mental illness" identified, and by whom? How can therapy alleviate distress?

Responses to these questions follow logically from one's model of human nature. If people are considered to be basically evil, then they deserve to suffer and suffering is thus an inherent part of the human condition. If, on the other hand, people are basically good, then alternative explanations must be sought in developmental traumas, organic impairments, or environmental influences. If people are seen as essentially selfish and impulse ridden, the definition of suffering or "mental illness" is more likely to be determined by social norms and values and psychotherapy will function as an agent of social control. If, however, people are seen as essentially good, then individual (client) identification of distress will be emphasized and psychotherapy will be viewed as a consumer service and/or an agent of social change.

The position taken on these issues in turn influences what one defines as the appropriate focus of therapeutic interactions. If distress is seen as endogenous or if intrapsychic explanations are utilized, then the primary focus of therapy will be on personality restructuring or on individual change in attitudes and behavior. If situational or interactional models are employed, therapeutic interventions may focus on restructuring interpersonal relationships or on support for active attempts by the individual to change his/her environment.

How Are Symptoms to Be Interpreted?

All models of therapy contain implicit assumptions about how to understand and interpret what has traditionally been termed psychopathology. The interpretation of symptoms of psychological distress helps to form the conceptual framework of therapy.

If people are assumed to be selfishly motivated and driven by instinct, then symptoms may represent varying degrees of failure to control or overcome one's "basic nature." Thus, neurotic symptoms might be interpreted as an inability to reconcile conflicting desires; psychosis as a failure to develop sufficient instinctual control; and characterological problems as an unwillingness to delay or control instinctual gratification. These may be attributed to developmental deficits, intrapsychic conflicts, regression due to current stress or trauma, or a combination of these factors.

If, however, people are seen as more benign, growth oriented, and altruistic, symptoms are seen as the result of trauma or interference with what is assumed to be the innate human urge for growth and self-realization. Symptoms may thus be produced by trauma at any developmental stage or by external environmental constraints. In this case, symptoms of psychological distress are seen as results of interference with the natural growth process and bear no relation to the intrinsic worth of the individual.

What Is the Nature of the Therapeutic Relationship?

If people suffer psychological distress, then we quite naturally wonder what one person can do to alleviate the suffering of another. In therapy, this generates a complex of questions about the nature of the therapeutic relationship. For instance, what is the role of the therapist in the therapeutic process? Is it to serve as an impartial observer who reflects objectively upon the client's feelings and behavior, or is it to be actively involved in an open relationship with the client? Is the therapist an expert/authority or a consultant/facilitator? What are the limitations of the therapist's powers and responsibilities? Who is responsible for (in control of) the direction and progress of therapy? What are the criteria for competence in a therapist? Is competence more related to amount of professional training or to personal qualities?

Answers to these questions are directly shaped by one's view of human nature and of relationships among people. If people are seen as basically evil and hence in need of control, and a hierarchal view of human relationships is adopted (as in psychoanalytic models), the therapist will be seen as an authority/expert who can help others through objective application of his/her greater knowledge of psychodynamics. The therapist will be seen as being in control of and responsible for the course of therapy, and competence will be based on degree of training and experience as well as the extent to which the therapist has successfully controlled his/her instinctual urges.

Conversely, if people are viewed as good, and the collateral mode

of relating among people is valued (as in the humanistic psychotherapies), the therapist's role is defined quite differently. From this viewpoint, the therapist is a consultant/facilitator who becomes actively involved with the client in his/her journey of self-discovery. The direction
and process of therapy is shaped by the client's desires and goals and
therapist and client share equally in responsibility for therapeutic progress. The competence of the therapist may be judged as much by such
personal qualities as warmth, empathy, and skill in relating as by educational standards.

What Is the Goal of Therapy?

The goals of therapy are closely related to the goals of human existence
implied by the various models of human nature. To be considered here
are questions relating to the purpose and desired outcome of therapy:
What are the general goals of therapy? What specific individual and
interpersonal goals are implied by the various schools of therapy? What
is the role of the profession of psychotherapy in society? What are
criteria for successful treatment? How are they assessed? Is change possible? If so, what are the limitations of change within therapy?

Answers to these questions will vary depending upon one's view of
human nature and human relationships. If people are assumed to be
basically bad, then the purpose of therapy is to help the client to reject,
overcome, or restrain his/her natural impulses. The goal of therapy becomes adoption and internalization of essentially alien-but-necessary
controls, as well as remediation of specific problems caused by previously inadequate or inappropriate controls. Insight into one's feelings
and conflicts is assumed to lead to the goal of adjusting the maladaptive
individual to cultural norms, in order to preserve the social contract.
This is implicitly a social control model of therapy in that the therapy is
considered successful if the client is able to accept his/her place in
society and function productively according to the prevalent cultural
value system. Change is limited to individual, mostly intrapsychic,
changes in attitudes, feelings, and intellectual understanding of oneself;
these may be accompanied by some behavioral changes, but behavior
change is not a primary goal.

A quite different view is produced by a model of human beings as
intrinsically good. In this case, the purpose of therapy becomes helping
the client discover, accept, and develop his/her "real" nature. The pri-

mary goal of therapy is the development of autonomy that will maximize individual self-actualization without infringing upon the rights of others. It is assumed that the goal of continual personal growth and development will be obtained through a combination of insight and action that will produce the desired outcome of change in both emotional and behavioral patterns. Because people are seen as innately benevolent, human relationships offer greater opportunity for gratification and hence are given more emphasis. Improvement or development of interpersonal relationships may become a primary goal of treatment. Since the client sets the goals in this model of therapy, this will depend on his/her priorities. This model opens up a much wider range of possible change, including the possibility of significant change in one's environment. Thus, social change may be adopted as an ultimate therapeutic goal.

Summary

Philosophy of treatment is an implicit value system defined by personal and cultural beliefs about the innate nature of human beings, about the causes of psychological distess and interpretation of its symptoms, about the desired relationship between people (in this case between therapist and client), and about the goals of the helping endeavor that we call psychotherapy.

In the chapters that follow, I will briefly trace the development of the social and political forces of the last two decades that gave rise to feminist therapy, I will summarize the feminist value system upon which the therapy is based, and will present a feminist philosophy of treatment by responding to the questions outlined in this chapter.

■two
HISTORICAL BACKGROUND

■4
The Current Feminist Movement

Sometime in the nineteen twenties, feminism died in the United States. It was a premature death. Feminists had only recently obtained their long sought for tool, the vote, with which they had hoped to make an equal place for women in this society. But it seemed like a final one. By the time the granddaughters of the women who had sacrificed so much for suffrage had grown to maturity, not only had social mythology firmly ensconced women in the home, but the very term "feminist" had become an epithet.

Freeman (1971, p. 1)

While achieving a measure of legal emancipation through suffrage for women, the nineteenth century feminist movement left untouched the real social and cultural barriers to full equality for women. Firestone (1970) has detailed the specific ways in which the "myth of emancipation" operated, in each decade of the 50 years between the old feminist movement and the current one, to defuse the frustrations of modern women and to anesthetize their political consciousness. Dixon (1969) and O'Neill (1969) have also explored the conservative trends that operated between 1930 and 1960 to give new ideological support to the patriarchal social order, causing a deterioration in the economic and educational status of American women.

In the last decade, however, three sociocultural factors have com-

39

bined to precipitate the reemergence of American feminism, this time with the emphasis on women obtaining personal liberation, as well as social and political equality. First, because of the wartime need for women factory workers, women composed more than a third of the post-World War II labor force and this figure has been increasing ever since. Second, in the early sixties, women began to be disenchanted with the myth of the happy marriage and the contented suburban housewife. Third, the civil rights movement of the sixties began a process of examining and questioning the American belief system and made protest against inequity fashionable.

Feminist therapy has grown out of the present women's movement, which began in 1963 with the publication of *The Feminine Mystique* by Betty Friedan. In rebellion against the glamorization during the fifties of the "creative homemaker" role—the "feminine mystique"—Friedan gave form to women's vague dissatisfactions by stating that they shared common problems with one another. Calling it the "problem that has no name," she told them that a male-dominated, consumer-oriented society had conned them into producing more children than their mothers had, into giving up career aspirations, into lives deadened by trivia, and finally into a mystified struggle with the emptiness and malaise that came upon them in middle age.

In 1966, the National Organization for Women (NOW) was formed to focus on the legal and economic difficulties faced by women, and women's liberation as a social movement began in earnest. Basically, the movement seeks equality between the sexes, with different groups taking different stances as to emphasis and strategy.

Polk (1972) delineates three types of groups that make up the women's liberation movement: those seeking the expansion of women's rights; those seeking women's liberation; and those seeking a socialist society that includes equality for women. A concise but comprehensive analysis of these three positions may be found in Cox (1976, pp. 436–438).

The first type is represented by liberal feminist groups, such as NOW, that accept the basic structure of society and social relationships but seek to improve the status of women through legal, economic, and political means. To this end, the organization has a hierarchal structure, holds conventions, hires lobbyists, pursues court cases on discrimination against women, participates in orderly demonstrations, and publishes tracts on the legal and economic status of women. Among its major concerns are the end of discrimination against women in employment and salary status, the reform of abortion laws, greater equalization of educational opportunities for women, and adequate childcare facilities.

NOW is composed primarily of middle- and upper-middle-class professional and career women who tend to benefit more from the current economic system and therefore have more invested in its perpetuation. Thus the political objective of these liberal feminists is establishment of women's rights through reform within the present system—full equality for women within this society through changes in ideas, prejudices, habits, and laws, but without change in political or economic institutions.

Liberal feminist philosophy identifies the sources of women's oppression as sexist ideas, habits, prejudices, and laws that are a part of American society. Particularly, liberal feminism focuses on Freudian psychology, functionalist social science, consumerism, and sexist educational theories and practices as being oppressive to women. They acknowledge some "innate" psychological differences between the sexes but believe that men and women will not be as different from each other psychologically with increased flexibility of sex roles. In effect, they seek more of a modernization of women's roles than redefinition. Men are seen as holding most of the power in our society, with women seeking equity with men. Liberal feminists are quick to point out that men would also gain from this equalization of power, as it would relieve pressure on men to compete and achieve.

Polk's second category includes independent women's liberation groups. They usually have no official names but might be characterized by such groups as the Redstockings or Radical Feminists. Most groups of this type consist of 10 to 15 women who come together in consciousness-raising groups for the purpose of developing their own understanding of the condition of women, on the basis of their own experience. Although most such groups are entirely autonomous of one another, it has been noted by Polk that the political analysis that they develop of women's position in American society is remarkably similar. While they agree generally with the need for the reforms pursued by the women's rights groups, they go well beyond them to criticize the basic institutions and power relationships of our society. They agree that male domination of the institutions of society is the cause of women's oppression, and they call for revolution on three levels: sexual, economic, and cultural. They emphasize the common oppression of all women and argue that female oppression is not merely the result of economic oppression but of the internalization of sexist attitudes and beliefs as well.

Philosophically, these groups represent what has been termed "cultural feminism." Cultural feminism defines the cause of women's oppression as being twofold. First, it is psychologically caused by sex roles and any institution that supports a division according to sex roles; second, it is politically caused by any hierarchal structure or institution (Thomas, 1975). This position is represented in the feminist literature by the writings of Firestone (1970) and Koedt, Levine, and Rapone (1973).

Cultural feminists believe that there are no innate psychological sex differences and that sex roles at present are totally artificial bipolarizations of human psychological traits caused by inequalities of power between men and women. They believe that women have personal power that they have been giving to men without acknowledgment or recognition. Women are seen as having emotional/psychological power and men as having material/economic power. Thus far, the cultural feminists maintain, power and success have been defined in male terms; society has defined women's sphere as psychological and trivial and men's sphere as political-economic and important.

Therefore, cultural feminists seek to create a new culture based upon the female mode of consciousness or upon a synthesis of the female and male modes. Feminist consciousness raising has been described (Thomas, 1975) as beginning with personal liberation and expanding to include criticisms of the basic institutions and power relationships in the society as male dominated and therefore oppressive to women. A goal of consciousness raising is change in these institutions and relationships through greater political awareness and personal change.

In addition, cultural feminists stress strategies of sociopolitical action and internal organizational change, to relieve female oppression. To this end, independent women's liberation groups are particularly concerned with being nonelitist, nonhierarchal, and noncompetitive internally. In their groups, they attempt to build within the women's liberation movement new forms of organization and new ways of living that do not import the oppressiveness of traditional male-dominated forms in the society.

Polk's (1972) third type of group in the movement is represented by the women's caucuses of the left-wing political groups, for example, the Socialist Workers' Party and various New Left splinter groups. Although women in these groups typically accept the women's liberation label and concur with many of the views and analyses espoused by independent women's liberation groups, they differ in that they subscribe to a Marxist analysis of society which serves as a framework for their understanding of the oppression of women. It is their fundamental belief that a socialist revolution is a necessary, but not entirely sufficient, precondition for women's liberation. They assert that there is a basic correlation between capitalism and the oppression of women. They are politically radical, believing that women's oppression is related to economic class oppression and, consequently, they call for an overthrow of the present economic system.

These groups view women's oppression as both psychological and economic, but in both cases consider capitalism as the basic source of that oppression. Their strategy and tactics emphasize the connection between class oppression and women's oppression, between economic and psychological oppression of women and capitalism (Thomas, 1975).

Philosophically, this faction represents socialist feminism and has been articulated by Mitchell (1974), Benston (1969), and de Beauvoir (1961). This group believes that psychological differences may result from inequalities in the economic system, but also recognizes the possibility of innate differences as well. The greatest emphasis, however, is on equal respect and value for each person, regardless of sex.

Because of these variations in political, philosophical, and organizational approaches, it is difficult to state a unitary definition of feminism. Cox (1976) summarizes the feminist position by defining feminists as ". . . women who agree that we live in a male-dominated culture in which women remain unacknowledged and invalidated as sources of power" and further describes them as advocating that women and men should have equal political, economic, and social rights. On a more personal level, she points out, feminists are interested in eliminating the negative value placed on women and in disproving the myth that women are secondary; lower in status, worth, or importance; weak; or inferior. Thus, she points out, feminism shares the humanists' goal of promoting and expanding human capacities, since it seeks to remove limitations, imposed by sex roles, that prevent full development of each person's potential. She says:

> Feminism describes the psychology of women and men in terms of the results of power differences between the two groups with regard to real, material conditions. In addition, cultural feminists believe that each person has the potential for all human attributes but that present sex roles separate these attributes artificially into two distinct categories. It is thus possible,

they assert, that changing the social and material conditions that result in power differences and eliminating sexism—which both results from and produces and maintains the inequalities of material conditions—will allow greater opportunity for each person to become fully human. (p. 4)

Freeman (1971) suggests that, even among the diverse groups that make up the women's movement, there is agreement on two theoretical issues: 1) the feminist critique of society, and 2) the idea of oppression of women. Thomas (1975) describes the feminist critique as rejecting the traditional view of biological determinism, which holds that women differ biologically from men and that because of this they should serve different social functions and engage in different social roles. Instead, feminism believes that men and women are constitutionally equal and that differing roles and functions are the result of social conditioning and an institutionalized sexual caste system.

Feminists stress the importance of sociocultural factors over biological factors in the creation of sex roles. Following closely from this is the idea that social conditioning and institutionalized sexual roles (particularly as played out in marriage and the nuclear family), while oppressing both women and men, have oppressed women in particular by: 1) preventing them from functioning and contributing according to their potentials, and 2) relegating them to and enforcing their status as second-class citizens in society. Thus, the movement seeks an end to the myth that men are superior to women and an end to those practices and institutions of the society perpetuating that myth. It is unfortunate that psychotherapy has been one such institution.

In looking at the movement that gave birth to feminist therapy, we should also consider its goals. Eastman (1973, pp. 164–165) has summarized the goals of the women's movement as follows:

1. Promotion of mutual trust, pride, and cooperation among women, rather than following the "feminine mystique," copying men as models, or competing for male approval.

2. Individual and collective decisions by women to take control of their lives in creating support for one another in alternative ways of living.

3. Increasing personal understanding in women of the ways in which women have been programmed and oppressed and of the social institutions that create the context of this oppression.

4. Changing the external reality of women's situations through an

economic revolution that will end a system that exploits most people for the good of a few.

5. Creation of a cultural revolution that will undermine the centuries of social programming that women have undergone; that is, realization that the quality of women's lives is not determined by accident or biology, but by our social system.

6. Freeing women from the tyranny of their reproductive biology by giving them control of their reproductive functions.

7. Full self-determination, including economic independence, of both women and children and integration of them into all aspects of the larger society.

8. Freedom for women to choose their own forms of sexual expression.

9. Examination and questioning of the nuclear family, with a view toward seeking alternatives and/or building greater flexibility within it.

10. Permission for and encouragement of expressions of anger and frustration in women.

These points represent both political/social and personal goals, many of which are reflected in feminist therapy.

Developmentally, feminist therapy has closely paralleled the divisions of the larger women's movement, with all three types of groups and philosophical viewpoints being represented among feminist therapists. Thus, the liberal feminist position has been taken by Elizabeth Friar Williams (1976). The opposite extreme, socialist feminism, is represented by Miriam Greenspan (1976) and members of the IRT Collective, represented by Hogie Wyckoff (1970; 1973a,b; 1975). The majority of feminist therapists, however, seem to fall in the middle, adopting a cultural feminist approach. This conclusion is supported by Thomas' (1975) finding that for the feminist therapists she interviewed, cultural or personal feminism was more important in their therapy than was political feminism.

What all three types of groups within the women's movement have in common is the use of consciousness raising as a vehicle for personal liberation. Perhaps the crucial differences between the current feminist movement and the nineteenth-century feminist movement are: 1) the recognition of the psychological oppression of women through internalized attitudes and prejudices that denigrate women as inferior to men, and 2) recognition of the external oppression evidenced in political, vocational, and educational discrimination. As a result, in addition to focusing on equal opportunity for women in the political, educational, and job arenas, the current movement utilizes consciousness-raising groups as a means of changing the prejudicial attitudes that devalue women and discount the existence or importance of their oppression.

As mentioned earlier, consciousness-raising groups were fundamental in the genesis of the independent women's liberation groups. They have also been utilized with a more political orientation by the socialist feminists and, in recent years, have been adopted and institutionalized as a part of NOW's programs (Bonetti et al., 1974; Perl and Abarbanell, 1976). Eastman (1973) describes consciousness-raising groups as small, leaderless groups of women designed to promote feelings of sisterhood and solidarity, heighten self-esteem, and develop a political perspective on women's personal problems. The purpose of consciousness-raising groups seems to be threefold: 1) development of a group consciousness among women, 2) personal awareness of oppression, and 3) generation of political action.

Martin (1976) traces the origin of consciousness raising to the late 1940s when, after Mao Tse-tung's Revolutionary Army had purged the villages of North China of enemy control, political workers called the townswomen to the village square to testify to the crimes that had been committed against them. The women told of their oppression: of being sold as concubines by their fathers, of being raped by landlords, of being beaten by their husbands and fathers-in-law. Martin concludes that the process of venting anger became personally liberating and out of these "Speak Bitterness" meetings, as they came to be called, women found the strength and support they needed to confront their oppressors and demand equality.

Dreifus (1973) calls the Speak Bitterness meetings "the first consciousness-raising groups, the first known attempt to convert womankind's private laments into political acts. . . . Through public recitations, women discovered their situations were not isolated. They developed self-confidence. From self-confidence grew action." (Martin, 1976, p. 160). This is what seems to be the heart of consciousness raising: that women share common problems, that these problems are caused by the oppression of a sexist society, and that women must work together to forge common solutions to their problems.

Note the similarity between Dreifus's description of the Speak Bitterness meetings and Freeman's (1971) description of consciousness-raising groups:

> From this public sharing of experiences comes the realization that what we thought to be individual is in fact common; that what was thought to be a personal problem has a social cause and probably a political solution. Women learn to see how social structures and attitudes have molded them from birth and limited their opportunities. They ascertain the extent to which women have been denigrated in this society and how they have developed prejudices against themselves and other women. (p. 5)

Thus feelings and politics become intertwined; as the oft-quoted slogan of the movement goes, "The personal is political." Morgan (1970) notes, "Women's Liberation is the first radical movement to base its politics, in fact, create its politics out of concrete personal experiences. We've learned that those experiences are not our private hang-ups. They are shared by every woman and are therefore political." In their handbook on consciousness raising, Perl and Abarbanell (1976) stress the importance of making this concept explicit in consciousness-raising groups. They insist that until women see the connections between what happens to them as individual women and what happens to all women in a sexist society, they have not experienced real feminist consciousness raising. Polk (1972) maintains that the purpose of these consciousness-raising groups is to develop both an analysis of society and an appropriate politics based on the experience of being female. Like Morgan (1970) and Perl and Abarbanell (1976), she stresses that the personal becomes political through the process of women sharing their experiences. They find that personal problems related to being a woman in our society cannot be solved without an understanding of the society and, often, without an attempt to implement changes within it as well. Out of their own experience, women begin to establish priorities, invent their own approaches to problem solving, forge a feminist ideology, and take action. This is another concept crucial to consciousness raising: that out of the political analysis of society based on one's experiences of being female must come political action directed at solutions to women's common problems.

On a more personal level, consciousness-raising groups serve to help a woman assess the reality of her oppression, to help her recognize how she is participating in her oppression by believing in her own and other women's inferiority, and to encourage her in continuing to seek equal treatment in the face of negative sanctions. In this process, women become less isolated, learn to recognize and interpret their feelings, begin to value friendships with other women, and learn to utilize women as a reference group and to rely less heavily on the approval of men. In short, consciousness raising becomes a resocialization experience for women, in which group members' views of themselves and their social world are restructured.

Although participation in consciousness-raising groups may be therapeutic, feminists are quick to point out that they do not regard consciousness raising as therapy (Eastman, 1973). Therapy, they say, assumes that the "patient" (usually a woman) is "sick" and consequently that the solution to her problem is individual to her. Perl and Abarbanell (1976) state:

> . . . therapy by its inherent nature . . . implies that someone—the woman patient—needs to be made well and that someone else—the therapist, more often than not a male—has the know-how to effect the cure. . . . consciousness raising on the other hand, presupposes that the *woman* is not sick but her *society* is; what the woman sees as her own deficiencies [are] more likely to be the flagrant abuses and shortcomings of a male-dominated society. Society is sick; society needs changing. The woman is made sick by society; society has conditioned her to be a supporter of the system which oppresses her. This concept is fundamental to feminist consciousness raising and cannot be emphasized too much: society, not the individual woman, is sick. (p. 1)

For this reason, feminists contend that solutions to individual women's problems will come from group efforts, not from the individual solutions offered by psychotherapy.

Consciousness-raising groups have become the heart and core of the women's movement, and the ideology of consciousness-raising groups has heavily influenced the conceptual development of a feminist therapy.

5
The Women's Movement and Freud

The Women's Movement and Freud

[Psychoanalysis is] a dynamic psychological process involving two people, a patient and a psychoanalyst, during which the patient insists that the analyst be one-up while desperately trying to place [her] one-down and the analyst insists that the patient remain one-down in order to help [her] learn to become one-up. The goal . . . is the amicable separation of analyst and patient.

Jay Haley (Quoted in Tennov, 1975, p. 8)

Life was a long disease to be cured by psychoanalysis. You might not cure it, but eventually you'd die anyway. The base of the couch would rise around you and become a coffin and six black-suited analysts would carry you off (and throw jargon on your grave).

Jong (1973, p. 134)

The political analysis of consciousness-raising groups, with its emphasis on sociocultural factors as the basis of women's problems, added fuel to criticism by the women's movement of the mental health establishment. Initially, criticism focused on Freudian theory, with its obviously fallacious distinction between clitoral or "immature" and vaginal or "mature"

49

orgasms in women; its dogmatic insistence that anatomy is destiny and that penis envy exists in all women; and its blatantly prejudicial view of the inherent nature of women as passive, narcissistic, and masochistic. This criticism, while contributive to the development of feminist therapy, is tangential to my primary purpose of constructing a new approach to treatment. Therefore, only a brief synopsis of this material is given, and the reader is referred to the excellent critiques of Freudian theory by Millett (1969), Sherman (1971; 1975), and Schafer (1974) for more detailed analysis of this topic.

Thomas (1975) points out that much of the feminist literature argues against Freudian ideas, charging that they have served to crystallize the feminine mystique, justify male chauvinism, heighten the split between mind and body, perpetuate unwarranted myths about female sexuality, and reinforce the authoritarian hierarchy of the nuclear family. As she points out, however, it is not so much that Freud was a male chauvinist—history and psychology have produced others before and since—rather, what concerns feminists is the extent to which his theories have permeated our culture and become dogma.

As a biological determinist, Freud assumed that women's sexual organs (or lack of them) were of primary importance in the formation of female personality. He assumed that women's conflicts stem from the fact that they are not like men physically and that they therefore feel inferior and either struggle constantly to prove their equality or are consumed with envy and discontented with their lot. The theory he spun from this assumption lacked recognition of the social reality that in addition to having different anatomy from men, women also had a different, and lesser, social status and less personal power than men. Sherman (1975, pp. 10–11) says "Freud knew that there was something about being female that is impossible to cure. It is not penis envy; it is being female. . . . Freud mistook discontent with sexual caste for discontent with sexual anatomy." Thus, feminists firmly reject the notion of penis envy, stating that it is not men's penises that women envy, but their greater social, economic, and personal power. Surveying the literature in this area, Thomas (1975) concludes that, rather than understanding women's dissatisfaction as arising from the Victorian social milieu that was in fact self-limiting, anger inducing, inferiority invoking, and sexually repressive to women, Freud substituted the symptom for the cause.

This forms the basis for what is perhaps the most frequent feminist criticism of Freudian theory: its insistence on intrapsychic causation and its failure to recognize the impact of sociocultural variables on personality development. Generally, Freud's observations are not at issue; rather, it is the interpretations and prescriptions for feminine personality he drew from those observations. Millett (1969, p. 179) says, "Through his clinical work, Freud was able to observe women suffering from two causes: sexual inhibition . . . and a great discontentment with their social circumstances. In general, his tendency was to believe the second over-dependent upon the first and to recommend in female sexual fulfillment a panacea for what were substantial symptoms of social unrest within an oppressive culture."

Similarly, Thomas (1975, p. 26) states, "Freud began with descriptions of the women around him, descriptions often based on observations of accuracy and sensitivity. However, what he did was to declare that what he saw was inevitable, and in so doing, his descriptions became prescriptions, forcing women to adjust to an inherently unhealthy position, to accept a subordinate role, and to submit to an inferior fate." As one critic (Krakauer, 1972) has put it, Freud was a good observer, but a lousy theorist.

In addition to criticizing the three basic constructs of Freudian personality theory on women—penis envy, the Oedipal complex, and the transfer of the focus of female sexuality from the clitoris to the vagina—feminists criticize Freud's sexist bias in using male standards as normative for all human behavior. Freud, they charge, did not see the "normal" woman as different from man in any positive sense because she was already by definition abnormal when compared to the male standard of normality; she was inferior when compared to men's superiority. Thus, femininity was, for Freud, the absence of masculinity; but since masculine traits were the valued traits, the presence of femininity was always ultimately negative. As Thomas (1975) points out, Freud described women as passive, masochistic, narcissistic, jealous, suffering from self-contempt, opposed to civilization, less intelligent, less ethical, less judicious, psychologically rigid, often sexually frigid, and tending toward hysteria. Until recently, this view of women has persisted, unrecognized and largely unquestioned throughout most subsequent developments in the history of psychotherapy. Notable exceptions are neo-analysts Karen Horney (1963) and Clara Thompson (1963), who attempted to integrate the social realities of being a woman into female psychology. Unfortunately, little importance was attached to their work by the analytic community and hence their contributions have had minimal impact on theory or training in psychoanalysis or psychotherapy.

When subjected to close scrutiny, Freudian theory on the personality of women does not fare very well. Sherman (1971) examined the empirical evidence relating to psychoanalytic constructs and found little to support Freud's theories about women. Schafer (1974, p. 483) examined the logic and internal consistency of Freud's ideas and found them to be significantly flawed by the influence of traditional patriarchal and evolutionary values and by "questionable presuppositions; logical errors; and inconsistencies and suspensions of intensive inquiry, underemphasis on certain developmental variables, and confusions between observations, definitions, and value preferences."

Proponents of psychoanalytic theory will undoubtedly protest at this point that Freud never intended his ideas about the psychology of women to be viewed as a comprehensive or systematic treatment of the area and that, in fact, he at several points indicated his own dissatisfaction with his theories in this direction and clearly saw them as incompletely developed and unfinished. While this is true in fact, it is not so in practice. Analysts using Freudian theory do not stop to tease out cultural myths about women from the larger body of Freudian theory. In fact, as Levine, Kamin, and Levine (1974, p. 329) have noted, "The psychoanalytic practice of ascribing biological certainty to cultural conjecture continues unabated." Although some feminists, notably Mitchell (1974) and Firestone (1970) have attempted to reinterpret Freud within a feminist context and thus reunite Freudian theory and feminism, these attempts have been largely unsuccessful.

Sherman (1975) has detailed specific ways in which psychoanalysis has been used destructively with women. She categorizes these as: 1) the authoritative relationship that analysts have with patients, which promotes dependency and mystification; 2) the analytic practice of locating the problem and the blame within the woman—"victimizing the victim"; 3) providing a negative view of women; 4) providing so distorted a view of women as to engender iatrogenic disease; and 5) providing handy rationales for the oppression of women. While she is critical of Freudian theory, she is also critical of the ways in which that theory is put into practice with women.

The APA Task Force on Sex Bias and Sex Role Stereotyping in Psychotherapeutic Practice (1975) also lists the sexist use of psychoanalytic concepts as one of the ways in which sexist bias and sex-role stereotyping are carried out in therapy settings. Specifically, they cite therapists who insist on the use of Freudian interpretations while ignoring reality factors (for example, how the patient reports feeling about the therapist or about a given incident). They also cite therapists who maintain that vaginal orgasm is a prerequisite for emotional maturity, thus making it a goal of therapy, and therapists who label assertiveness and ambition with the Freudian label of "penis envy."

Thus we see that Freud's impact, ultimately, was to legitimize sex-role stereotypes by embodying them in a "scientific" theory. His theories sanctified the oppression of women because, within his system, all alternatives for women were labeled "neurotic." Observing how Freudian theory is applied, as well as how it is structured, we can only conclude with Walstedt (1971) that our culture is "cancerous" with psychoanalytic mythology passing as human traits. Unfortunately for women, the majority of American psychotherapists continue to adhere to a psychoanalytic orientation to therapy, according to Sundland and Barker (1962).

To summarize, feminists argue against both Freudian theory and practice. They argue that anatomy is not destiny; that female envy of males is not of their genital apparatus but of the greater power and status that our society affords them as men; and that the passivity and narcissism observed by Freud in the female patients he saw are not universal female tendencies but socially and culturally prescribed behaviors for the women of his time. Whether other parts of Freudian theory (e.g., unconscious motivation, psychodynamic theory) may yet prove compatible with feminist ideology has not been addressed by feminist therapists. Rather, at this point there seems to be a sense of urgency to identify and ameliorate the destructive effects of abuses of Freudian theory with female psychotherapy patients.

In addition to the theoretical content, feminists also find the process and practice of psychoanalysis to be oppressive to women. This psychoanalytic style of therapy, consisting of a hierarchal (and usually patriarchal) relationship between therapist and patient, personal aloofness of the therapist, and control of the therapy process by the therapist has been perpetuated by many, if not all, subsequent schools of psychotherapy regardless of theoretical orientation (Sundland and Barker, 1962). As we shall see, feminist criticism of this style of relating between therapist and patient has had significant impact on the development of feminist therapy.

6
The Feminist Critique of Psychotherapy

> Psychotherapy is an unproven and expensive tyranny of one individual over another, supposedly in an effort to "help" but often to the detriment of the recipient. It is an intransitive and hierarchal relationship in which the therapist is defined as a person able to understand the patient, but not the reverse.
>
> Tennov (1973, p. 107)

> Women and psychotherapy have had a strange symbiotic relationship. It may be that the field of psychotherapy could not have developed and flourished if it were not for the pervasive and chronic unhappiness of many women who no longer somaticized their pain through physical ailments and vapors. As therapists, it is easy to see all human experience as universal and to overlook women's disadvantaged position . . . .
>
> Hare-Mustin (1976, p. 5)

Feminist criticism of psychoanalysis spread quickly to include all of psychotherapy as a profession. It came first from ex-patients who, as consumers of mental health services, began to complain about sexist bias in their treatment. They charged that psychiatric theory and practice is based on oppressive definitions of women and that, "When women step out of line and refuse to submit, psychiatrists quickly apply some mean-

ingless 'descriptive' label to their behavior and often send them to punitive institutions all in the name of mental health." (Anthony, 1970, p. 1.)

Mental health professionals first criticized the sexist bias of psychology in general (Weisstein, 1972) but soon they, too, joined the growing
criticism of the way that sexist beliefs and attitudes were being perpetuated in psychotherapy (Fields, 1972; Gardner, 1971).

Chesler's (1972) book, *Women and Madness*, was the first intensive
look at exactly what effects this sexism has had on the women who
continue to make up the majority of psychotherapy patients; the criticism by mental health professionals of sexism in psychotherapeutic practice has been growing ever since.

Major works that criticize psychotherapy from a feminist viewpoint
include *Psychotherapy: The hazardous cure*, by Dorothy Tennov (1975)
and *Women Look at Psychiatry*, by Smith and David (1975). These
critiques provide numerous examples of the impact on psychotherapy of
culture-specific assumptions about human nature—in this case, about
women.

The Double Standard of Mental Health

Feminist criticism of psychotherapy centers around two main areas. One
is the failure of psychotherapy to acknowledge the effects of sociocultural
factors on women. This will be discussed later in this chapter. First, let
us turn to the feminists' charge that the androcentrism of the psychological theories underlying psychotherapy has resulted in a double standard
of mental health that is characterized in the attitudes and practices of
psychotherapists.

Broverman et al.'s (1970) now-classic study was the first to docu-
ment the sexist attitudes of psychotherapists. This study found that "mature, healthy, socially competent" women, as seen by both male and
female clinicians from psychiatry, psychology, and the social work professions, were expected to be more submissive, less independent, less
adventurous, more easily influenced, less aggressive, less competitive,
more excitable in minor crises, more emotional, more conceited about
their appearance, less objective, and to have their feelings hurt more
easily than mature adult men. They also found that while there was no
significant difference between adult (sex unspecified) and masculine concepts of mental health, there was a difference between the adult and
female concepts.

This came to be defined as the double standard of mental health because of the double bind in which it places women: they can either be healthy, mature adults, or healthy mature women, but not both. This is further complicated by the fact that, in actuality, only men are expected to be able to fill the description of a mature adult and if a women strives toward being the sort of person that therapists value—independent, rational, and realistic—she then runs the risk of losing societal support and may even, according to Chesler (1972) run the risk of persecution. Broverman et al. (1970) affirm this in their conclusions about their findings. They state:

> These results, then, confirm the hypothesis that a double standard of health exists for men and women; that is, the general standard of health is actually applied only to men, while healthy women are perceived as significantly less healthy by adult standards. . . . Thus, for a woman to be healthy . . . she must adjust to and accept the behavioral norms for her sex, even though these behaviors are generally less socially desirable and considered to be less healthy for the generalized competent, mature adult. . . . [This] then places women in the conflictual position of having to decide whether to exhibit those positive characteristics considered desirable for men and adults, and thus have their "femininity" questioned, that is, be devalued in terms of being a woman; or to behave in the prescribed feminine manner, accept second-class adult status, and possibly to live a lie to boot. (pp. 5–6)

The Broverman study was replicated by Nowacki and Poe (1973) and by Fabrikant (1974), with similar results. Their allegations also have been supported by Abramowitz and Abramowitz (1973), who found that nonliberal counselors imputed greater maladjustment to leftist-oriented politically active females than to an identically described male client. In addition, Schlossberg and Pietrofesa (1973) reviewed several studies on counselor bias and found that counselors rate traditionally feminine (conforming) career goals as more appropriate for female clients than traditionally masculine (nonconforming) career goals. The counselors in these studies also believed female clients with deviant goals to be more in need of counseling than those with conforming goals.

More recent studies have obtained results somewhat at variance with these, some of which are reviewed by Stricker (1977), who believes that conclusions regarding a double standard of mental health and negative evaluations of women are premature in light of this conflicting data.

Nevertheless, the Broverman-type studies served to alert the professional community to the possibility that the sexist bias of the larger society may be carried over into therapists' expectations for their therapy clients. If it is the case that clinicians, as well as their patients, adhere to a masculine standard of mental health, women may be viewed as psychiatrically impaired regardless of whether they accept or reject the female role, simply because they are women. Although many clinicians are quick to label themselves exceptions to this supposition, it is unlikely that such is the case. Bernardez-Bonesatti (1975b) outlines ways in which therapists' behavior with women may betray their unconsciously held biases against women, even when the therapist consciously believes that such beliefs and attitudes are anachronistic and not conducive to psychological growth.

These factors are much more subtle than professed attitudes, and have not been adequately researched. Certainly, this group of studies strongly suggests that the criticism of psychology as using male characteristics as normative also extends into the practice of psychotherapy.

Further evidence on the prevalence of sexist attitudes among psychotherapists comes from the Roche Report on "Women's Liberation" (1971) and from the Report of the APA Task Force on Sex Bias and Sex Role Stereotyping in Psychotherapeutic Practice (1975). The Roche Report found that 53.1 percent of the psychiatrists they polled believed that maintaining clearly defined sex roles was more likely to be beneficial than not; 70.8 percent agreed that physiological differences between women and men produce to some degree a "natural" division of roles; and 73.9 percent agreed that psychiatrists have a stereotype of the "normal healthy male" role and "normal healthy female" role. In addition to the sexist use of psychoanalytic concepts, the APA Task Force found three areas of sex bias and sex-role stereotyping identified by the therapists they surveyed:

1. *Fostering traditional sex roles.* This was manifested in the therapists' assumption that self-actualization and resolution of problems for women will come from fulfillment of the traditional female sex role of wife and mother and in the use of female clients' attitudes towards childbearing and childrearing as an index of their emotional maturity. Concurrently, therapists were seen as discounting the importance of female clients' career and vocational aspirations and activities. They also were felt to be deferential to the husband's needs in the conduct of the wife's treatment, often to the detriment of the woman's needs. This

supports Weisstein's (1969) charge that male clinicians tend to define women in terms of their ability to attract men and in fact see no alternative definitions for women. There seem to be two erroneous assumptions that underlie these attitudes. One is that a woman who is unhappy with the female sex role, or who rejects that role, wants to be a man or is acting "like a man" and therefore is exhibiting pathology. The other is that women who develop their rational, logical thinking abilities and problem-solving skills automatically give up their more traditional "feminine" qualities, such as warmth, intuition, and nurturance.

In addition, in family therapy or treatment of children, therapists seemed to support the traditional notion that childrearing—and thus the child's problems—are solely the responsibility of the mother. This is what Seiden (1976) has termed the "blame the mother" tradition in clinical psychopathology. She notes that there is considerably greater and earlier literature on allegedly schizophrenogenic mothers than on fathers, "despite the lack of clear evidence that either is specifically responsible for the more serious disorders of their children" (p. 1116). Similarly, Kellerman (1973), in a survey of the psychological literature concerning attribution of parental blame for children's psychological disturbances found that it was usually the mother who was held responsible for psychopathology in the child.

2. *Bias in expectations for and devaluation of women*. Specifically, the Task Force found that sexist jokes and offhand comments by the therapist as well as the use of inaccurate and demeaning labels (such as seductive, hysterical, manipulative) in describing women, had the effect of belittling and demeaning women.

These are what Tennov (1975) has labeled "patriarchy-serving, woman-derogating themes": discussions of "castrating" women and "dominating mothers," and professional articles on the "angry woman syndrome" (Rickles, 1971) and the "intractable female patient" (Houck, 1972). She concludes that:

> The "castrating woman," the "angry woman," and the "intractable woman"—none of whom is usually or necessarily considered seriously mentally ill, and all of whom are troublesome with respect to fulfilling the normal, passive, feminine role—may in fact represent the emotional reactions of the (male) psychotherapists to their patients' behaviors. (p. 218)

The APA Task Force (1975) also charges that therapists are biased in that they persist in seeing passivity and dependence as desirable female traits, thus denying the adaptive and self-actualizing potential of assertiveness in women. They also note the dangerous practice of therapist use of theoretical constructs (for example, masochism) as a means for ignoring or condoning violence toward and victimization of women. Thus, therapists tend, knowingly or unknowingly, to collude in the victimization of women who are rape victims or battered wives (see Martin, 1976; Tennov, 1975).

3. *Responding to women as sex objects.* This includes the seduction of female clients. Specifically, the Task Force lists the double standard for male and female sexual activities used by many therapists and the way in which therapists stress physical appearance of female patients in selecting patients or in setting therapeutic goals. Fabrikant's (1974) findings support the allegation that therapists do indeed have a double standard for male and female sexual activities; many feminists, including Chesler (1972) have criticized the practice of using conformity to or deviancy from traditional standards of physical beauty (for example, wearing makeup) as an index of mental health in women.

Even more seriously, the Task Force discusses the seduction of female clients by male therapists under the guise of therapy. As one of their respondents noted: "This is the ultimate of sex-role bias: the rationalization of the therapist that his exploitation of the doctor-patient relationship for his gratification could be construed as therapeutic 'for a woman' " (p. 1173).

Seiden (1976) asserts that sexual abuse of the therapeutic relationship is more common and often more devastating than has previously been recognized. Despite some clinicians' assertions that such behavior may generate iatrogenic psychiatric illness (Robertiello, 1975), the practice continues, apparently with a remarkable lack of concern on the part of male practitioners as to its unethical nature and destructive consequences (Fields, 1972). Some have even gone so far as to publish books and articles giving "therapeutic" rationales for sexual contact between therapist and patient (McCartney, 1966; Shepard, 1971).

Contrary to this the APA Task Force (1975) reports a study by Belote of 25 women who had sexual relations with their therapists and who reported that they were nonorgasmic, both before and after therapy, with all men, including their therapists. The Task Force concluded that, thus far, the literature has failed to reveal even anecdotal cases in which sex with the therapist was reported as beneficial. The physicians surveyed by Kardener, Fuller, and Mensh (1976) who did not have sexual contact with their patients support this conclusion, being unanimous in stating that, at the very least, erotic contact was never beneficial. In somewhat stronger terms, Marmor (1972) warns of the possible harmful effects of sexual contact between therapist and patient: "I have yet to see a woman who became involved in an erotic relationship with a therapist who did not subsequently end up resenting him and feeling betrayed by him. Some of these patients were actually precipitated into psychotic decompensation by these experiences" (p. 6).

Psychotherapy and Social Control

In addition to the double standard of mental health, feminists criticize the theories upon which psychotherapy is based for their failure to acknowledge the effects of sociocultural factors (such as sex-role demands, cultural expectations, and discrimination) in the etiology of women's emotional problems. They charge that psychotherapy thus functions covertly as a means of social control. Pointing to the data from social learning research, they draw the analogy between women and other oppressed minorities and find the adjustment model of mental health to be sexist and parochial, and therapists' insistence upon intrapsychic causation of all emotional problems to be archaic.

Tennov (1975), in her excellent critique of the psychotherapy profession, says:

> Women, whose problems emanate from the sex discrimination and prejudices of the society they live in, are additionally damaged by psychotherapists who find the roots of the difficulties in the women's own behaviors, attitudes and feelings. The principle of individual causation is the very cornerstone on which the edifice of individual psychodynamic insight therapy has been erected. Both in principle and practice, such therapy ignores the role of the societal environment. (p. 199)

Simon (1970) puts forth the thesis that the way in which one conceptualizes human problems has a significant political component and that it is possible to view some of the past and present activities of clinical psychologists as expressive of an implicitly political point of view. He maintains that the typical way in which clinicians conceptualize problems represents an avoidance of their social sources and charges that psychological interpretations are frequently used to divert attention for the possibilities of social causation. Heide (1969, p. 1) points out that, prior to the 1960s civil rights movement and subsequent black militance, society accepted the stereotyped docile, unambitious, child-like Negro as a mentally healthy adult because he was "adjusted" to his environment. She draws an analogy between this viewpoint and the way in which mental health practice has adopted a comparable pseudoscientific rationale and adjustment orientation to standards and therapy in relation to women.

This conclusion is supported by data from the Roche Report (1971), which cites 65.5 percent of the psychiatrists they polled as agreeing that psychiatrists consciously or unconsciously attempt to influence their patients to "adjust" to the psychiatrist's own sex-role stereotypes. This report concludes: "Although psychiatrists, and especially analysts, profess that they do not try to pass their standards on to their patients, it is actually unavoidable. Patients are made to believe that unless they change—which implies conforming to social standards—their rejection of these standards is perpetuation of infantile conflicts" (p. 11).

Miller and Mothner (1971) also maintain that psychiatry is too limiting in its application to women's present situations—that therapists have an obligation to understand that women's condition of social and sexual inequality is real and that the striving for liberation is valid. They, too, call for recognition of the political roots of much of what is now labeled "mental illness" in women:

> When more than half the nation (women) is fighting to establish its sense of self-value and the other half (men) is defending, with untruths, its irrational dominance, and all of this is going on in disguised and confused ways, there would seem to be a basis for much of what we now consider "functional psychological disturbance." (p. 773)

Yet, within the adjustment model of mental health, therapists continue to label role conflict as psychopathological and to interpret it solely in intrapsychic terms. Rather than being viewed as manifestations of a "slave psychology of the oppressed" (Szasz, 1961), women's symptoms of depression, inferiority, and low self-esteem are seen as signs of neurosis, hysteria, or personality disorder—as indicators that something is wrong with women's basic personality structures. Accordingly, feminists charge that the adjustment model of mental health is really a tool to keep women "in their place." As Firestone (1970) has pointed out, asking women to adjust to the cultural definition of mental health for women is asking them to adjust to the sexism that has limited their potential from the beginning.

In addition, feminists argue that psychotherapy not only encourages adjustment to an unhealthy society, but defuses women's collective energy into futile attempts to find individual solutions (Thomas, 1975). The women's movement has come to distrust psychology's association with the "personal solution"—that is, with the belief that things can be improved by changing individual people rather than by changing social, economic, and political structures. They complain that therapy is merely an individual solution that cannot affect the larger social structure, and point out that no matter what individual changes a woman in therapy may make, she still returns to a sexist society that imposes a very limited role upon women (Thomas, 1975). Yet, as Tennov (1975) points out, the general commitment of psychiatry to locating pathology within the patient inhibits any true comprehension of women's situations. Hurvitz (1973) comments:

> The practice of psychotherapy personalizes the client's perspective and fosters an individualistic instead of a social effort to change the causes of the client's psychological problems. Aspects of psychodynamic theory with regard to women create their problems; and the practices based on these theories exacerbate their problems. (p. 237)

The political aspects of this insistence upon dealing only with intrapsychic causation are discussed by Simon (1970). He states:

> Freud's work with Dora may be viewed as an attempt to deal with the effects of the exploitation of women that characterized the Victorian period without even an admission of its existence. We may conclude that Freud's failure with Dora was a function of his inappropriate level of conceptualization and intervention. He saw that she was suffering, but instead of attempting to deal with the conditions of her life he chose—because he shared in her exploitation—to work within the confines of her psyche. (p. 339)

Thus, feminists conclude with Simon (1970), Halleck (1971), Hurvitz (1973), and others that the latent purpose of psychotherapy is social control. From an historical viewpoint, Simon notes that

> What emerges so clearly is that approaches to the diagnosis and treatment of the "mentally ill" that were once regarded as enlightened and empiri-

cally justified can, at a later date, be seen as gross translations of the prevailing social ideology into "mental health" practices, and these practices, in turn, as little more than efforts to maintain social control. (p. 336)

In recent years, this concept has been increasingly discussed both in professional and counterculture literature. The issue has been stated concisely by Hurvitz (1973), who says,

> Psychotherapy serves as a means of social control because it is based on and fosters an ideology that accepts the status quo and proposes that changing individuals will improve society. This ideology, which is fostered by intellectuals who identify with the existing order, . . . psychologizes, personalizes, and depoliticalizes social issues [and] . . . fosters a concept of adjustment which often implies submission. (p. 235)

The purpose of this is the protection of the status quo against those who would change it (e.g., feminists); to this end, Hurvitz charges, the psychodynamic ideology makes personal problems of political problems.

Psychotherapy also functions as social control in that the therapist has the power to define the nature of reality vis-à-vis his or her patients.

The very process of defining a person as a patient or as mentally ill constitutes control of information consistent with general societal norms about what kinds of social relationships and behaviors are appropriate and normal. That is, the diagnostic process itself is in the service of the status quo. This power to label a person as "normal" or "mentally ill" has particular political implications for women, in that most therapists are male and most "patients" are female. If psychiatric treatment is in fact an effective means of social control, used when people depart from the traditional roles assigned to them by society, then insofar as these roles have been formulated by men, women in therapy are at a distinct disadvantage.

Specific ways in which the social control function of psychotherapy is carried out are discussed by Tennov (1975). She studied female psychotherapy patients who expressed "wholly or partially negative reactions" to their psychotherapy and found that they identified various therapist attitudes and behaviors as responsible for their adverse reactions to therapy. This study documents examples of therapists encouraging guilt feelings in patients in order to motivate them to remain in treatment; of therapists blaming the patient for failing to improve; of allowing women to continue in therapy for many years without improvement; and of keeping women in therapy through the use of threats, such as telling them that they are "too sick" to quit therapy, etc. Tennov (1975) cites instances in which therapists failed to refer women elsewhere, did not end treatment, or change methods, despite lack of improvement or even deterioration in the patient. She specifically condemns the use of the medical model: participants in her study who, in retrospect, saw themselves as confronted with environmental pressures and realistic problems, were at the time labeled neurotic and their "inner pathology" emphasized. In addition, Tennov discusses cases in which the therapist allowed or encouraged emotional dependency on the part of the patient; failed to respect confidences; directed or interfered with major life decisions by the patient; or were "cold, impersonal, and nonsupportive," leaving the woman feeling that she could do nothing right. Her subjects also felt that their therapists had held and expressed patriarchal values; tended to see more pathology in women than in men, to the extent of overlooking or even excusing deviant behavior on the part of males; and held baises with respect to material presented by their female patients, accusing them of inventing, fantasizing, or lying about things that ran counter to the therapist's theories and values. The therapists of these women had often shown more interest in sexual fantasies, dreams, and childhood events than in current problems and sexual seduction, attempted seduction, or accusations that the client was trying to seduce the therapist were cited as contributive factors in the negative outcome of therapy for them. Most importantly, however, Tennov reports that with only two exceptions the therapists focused almost entirely on the intrapsychic makeup of the woman herself, and failed to recognize societal and environmental pressures as important sources of difficulty.

Social control functions are also reflected in the hierarchal nature of the therapy situation itself, in which the "expert" therapist advises and guides the "patient" back into compliance with social norms. Feminists charge that the usual situation, in which a male therapist is in a position of authority and control and an unhappy woman comes to him seeking advice, help, and guidance, simply replicates the patriarchal structure of our sexist society and carries out the traditional dominant/subordinate roles of male and female. Chesler (1972) has likened the therapy relationship to marriage and maintains that both are tools of the oppression of women:

> For most women, . . . psychotherapeutic encounter is just one more instance of an unequal relationship, just one more opportunity to be rewarded for expressing distress and to be "helped" by being "expertly" dominated. Both psychotherapy and marriage isolate women from each other; both emphasize individual rather than collective solutions to women's unhappiness; both are based on a woman's helplessness and dependence on a stronger male authority figure . . . . (p. 108)

In addition, research evidence on nonverbal communication (Henley, 1970; Jourard and Laskow, 1958; Jourard and Rubin, 1968) supports the contention that subtle, nonverbal signals in the therapy situation may also function to perpetuate women's one-down status. These researchers' findings indicate that self-disclosure, personal space, touch, and body postures may be "status reminders" and, as such, are forms of informal social control and reinforcers of interpersonal control. Henley's (1970) work is particularly important in its discovery of direct analogies between the dominance-submission signals used by primates and the nonverbal and paralingual signals used by women and men.

This leads Silveria (1972) to comment that " . . . if the goal of therapy is to bring the patient to the point where she can manage her own life happily and successfully, where she has power over her own life, it seems strange to me that this is attempted in an environment which constantly communicates to her that she is powerless" (p. 12).

Summary

In summary, feminists allege that therapy is bad for women because it is a male enterprise designed to assure that men's needs continue to be met at the expense of women's self-fulfillment; therefore, it contributes to women's oppression rather than alleviating it. Hurvitz (1973) summarizes this viewpoint as follows:

> Psychodynamic psychotherapy . . . has fostered a view of women as appendages to men, as less developed human beings and as "natural" or "instinctive" mothers and homemakers, fostering conditions and attitudes

that create problems for many women. Psychotherapy thus presumes to help these women overcome their problems by inducing them to accept the very conditions that give rise to their complaints. (p. 235)

Feminists maintain that, instead of helping women, therapy functions primarily as a mechanism of social control, preserving the status quo and protecting the patriarchal structure of our society by perpetuating sex-role stereotypes in both its theoretical stance and practical application. Thus it is geared to "adjusting" women to fit existing sex roles rather than helping them to reexamine the appropriateness of the roles themselves. Because of this orientation, psychotherapists typically view role unhappiness in women as pathological rather than as appropriate or growth-producing.

■7
The Emergence of
Feminist Therapy

. . . we badly need a psychology of the oppressed and the oppressor. We need guidelines of mental health for a person whose environment is totally opposed to her personal fulfillment because she is a member of a class.

For women in particular, we need a psychology which understands the results of being trained from the day you are born to live intimately with your oppressor, to have no home away from him, and to seek your total personal fulfillment through him.

Silveria (1972, p. 15)

The women's movement needs to form counter structures—therapy forms which incorporate some of the skills and knowledge of the existing structures, but which gear them toward helping women find their own values and needs rather than molding them into prefabricated roles.

Lindsey (1974, p. 2)

With the growing distrust of psychotherapy, feminists began to search for alternatives for dealing with women's problems. Feminist therapy arose partly in revolt against the oppression of male-dominated psychotherapy; but primarily in response to the demands of women who, as primary consumers of mental health services, were demanding a therapy that would really meet their needs. In the early 1970s, women's centers began appearing around the country. These centers, designed to serve a variety of needs for women, also often served as therapeutic communities for the women who came to them.

Some feminists suggested consciousness raising as an alternative to therapy for women. Others, criticizing consciousness-raising groups for their lack of concrete action to implement social change, combined consciousness raising with therapy. Still others (notably Tennov, 1974; 1975), rejecting the profession of psychotherapy, developed self-help counseling projects based on a cocounseling model in which roles of interviewer and interviewee were interchangeable and equal in status. "Self-help" and personal growth books for women began to appear.

The great majority of women seeking help with problems, however, continued to look to professional therapists for assistance, so feminists also began to advise women who were seeking therapy to be selective in their choice of a therapist. Articles appeared in both the popular and alternative press that made explicit the role of values in therapy, demystified therapy, and advised women to trust their own judgment in choosing a therapist based on their response to the therapist in an initial session. Stressing the fact that a therapist's theoretical orientation and personal politics affect the way s/he approaches therapy, they urged women to ask questions of their prospective therapist about values, theoretical orientation, and politics and to look for candor, nondefensiveness, and unpretentiousness in the therapist's responses.

They took the view that therapy was a mental health service and that, as consumers of that service, women had a right to know what they were buying and to get what they needed. They stressed that the final decision as to whether or not to buy that service from a particular therapist was ultimately up to the woman herself; they made the heretical assumption that women were competent to make this judgment themselves and gave this kind of advice:

> Even where women's therapy referral services exist, a woman will ultimately have to decide for herself whether a given therapy has something she can use, whether a potential therapist would be an ally in her liberation. . . . Ask whatever questions you want, and see how you feel about the answers. Finally, arm yourself with a healthy irreverence and the understanding that, regardless of politics, a therapist who implies that you should be a certain way (whether that way is "normality" or that therapist's particular notion of acceptable "deviance") might make it harder to explore who you are.
>
> Krakauer (1972, p. 34)

While stressing that therapists do not have magical powers, feminists seemed to realize that asking one's friends and family to act as therapist was an unrealistic expectation. They recognized that often, more skill, commitment, and detachment are required of therapists than can legitimately be expected of friends and consciousness-raising group members. Feminists also began to realize that, whatever the benefits of consciousness-raising for women, it was not a panacea. Lindsey (1974) says, "The knowledge that most personal hangups are rooted in the training we received under the patriarchal structure is important, but not enough: the process of unlearning that training and retraining ourselves is a complex one, and it is more than many of us can handle alone" (p. 2).

Thus it was that feminists began to call for a *feminist* therapy, a "radical therapy of equals [in which] . . . the process would be democratized, the perspective would be on the "pathological" forces in the culture that uniquely damage women, and the therapeutic goals would go beyond internal psychic changes to creating new sensibilities, ambiances, and social contexts" (Walstedt, 1971, p. 10). Stressing the need to develop a "special therapeutic psychology of women," Walstedt reasoned that, in order to negate internalized negative sex roles, women must obtain a "psychic distance" from the culture that formed them. This would seem to indicate the need for a therapy based on the female value system rather than a male-dominated system.

Calling for the formation of new forms of therapy to counter the patriarchal structure of psychotherapy, Lindsey (1974) says:

> What is required for women, then, is the development of a specifically feminist therapy geared to resolving this paradox within women—to help women overcome the training of their culture. Such a therapy aims not at "adjustment" in the conventional sense of accepting the legitimacy of social norms, but at the strengthening of a woman's capacity to resist those norms when they have succeeded in stunting her. (p. 2)

The response to this call came first from women who already identified themselves as feminists. Some of them had been professionally trained as therapists, but most had not. They began to form therapy collectives around the country in order to explore new ways of working with women in therapy and to develop a feminist approach to therapy. These centers appeared in such diverse places as Tulsa, Oklahoma; Fayetteville, Arkansas; and Iowa City, Iowa; as well as on the always-innovative west coast.

Some collectives were formed around one or two women professionals who, although traditionally trained, were now identifying themselves as feminists and what they did as feminist therapy. The Feminist Counseling Collective in Washington, D.C., and the Feminist Therapy Collective in Philadelphia are examples of collectives that combine professional and paraprofessional therapists. The IRT Collective in Berkeley, which publishes *Issues in Radical Therapy*, includes several feminist therapists, the most prolific of which is Hogie Wyckoff. Although she identifies herself primarily as a radical therapist, she is also a feminist and her writings have influenced the political analysis of many feminist therapists. In still other places, female professionals who identified themselves as feminists formed group practices to create counseling services specifically to meet women's needs.

Concurrently with these developments, certain articles began to appear in the professional literature. While never using the term "feminist therapy," they clearly advocated the aims of the women's movement and recognized and discussed the special needs of women in therapy. Echoing many of the feminist criticisms of traditional psychotherapy, such articles marked the beginning of the "legitimization" of a feminist approach to therapy with women.

One group of articles centered around the "discovery" of sexism in the practice of psychotherapy. Its stance is well summarized by Barrett, Berg, Eaton, and Pomeroy (1974) who state: "Behavioral scientists' and clinicians' affirmation of the secondary status of women, whether explicitly stated or tacitly implied, has strengthened the myth of the inferiority of women and has directly oppressed them" (p. 11).

This group of articles presents, in the professional literature, the feminist critique of psychotherapy. It criticizes Freudian theory as being both sexist and oppressive to women in the double bind it creates for them; points out the power aspects of the predominance of male therapists treating female patients; and discusses the psychological effects sex roles have on women and how to deal with this in therapy. It also points out the intrinsic conflict between a woman's need for intellectual and vocational achievement and a society that defines a woman's worth in terms of "affiliation achievement . . . not what [they have] accomplished, not how far [they have] come, but rather from whom [they have] gained affection" (Levine, Kamin, and Levine, 1974). These authors point out that "The adult woman is *not* inferior on a biological basis, nor must she live an intellectually restricted, experientially constricted, dependent, obsequious existence; yet society demands this of most women." These and similar articles call for increased sensitivity to these issues on the part of therapists working with female clients, but do not propose new treatment models.

They also stress the importance of recognizing that therapy is value laden and that a therapist's attitudes and values are communicated both directly and indirectly to his/her clients:

> The therapist's underlying attitude toward his female patient is communicated in subtle and uncontrollable ways. If he sees her as a passive and dependent being . . . he will communicate this attitude no matter how hard he attempts to be neutral. This attitude will permeate his whole stance—the areas in which he seems most interested, and on which he chooses to focus, his demeanor, tone of voice, posture, and most minute facial expressions. . . . How therapists feel about themselves, how they relate to others, what kind of behavior makes them uncomfortable or they approve of are readily seen by patients. . . . Thus, unless a therapist can truly empathize with a woman's need to assert herself socially and intellectually—as well as physically and emotionally—he cannot help her to develop her human potential.
>
> Insofar as a therapist accepts society's role prescription for women, he is implicitly accepting the value judgment that underlies it: that women are basically inferior to men. . . . Thus even when no specific role conflicts are at issue in therapy . . . the therapist's unconscious attitude toward his patient is to some extent anti-therapeutic.
>
> Stevens (1971, p. 14)

Articles continue to appear on the special needs of women in therapy, the impact of sex-role stereotypes on women in therapy and on the therapists and counselors who treat them, and on developing new models of service delivery.

Although these writers rarely identify themselves as feminists and only imply what "feminist therapy" might be, they have had the effect of fostering interest among mental health professionals in examining the female sex role and its consequences, and of stimulating discussion among professionals on how to best fill women's needs in therapy. Thus, the last five or six years have seen special issues of professional journals which focused on women and on sexism in therapy, as well as the development of new journals dealing with the psychology of women, sex roles, and other related issues. The Association for Women in Psychology has emerged and expanded and the American Psychological Association has formed a new division on the Psychology of Women (Division 35).

All of these factors seem to indicate a growing receptivity on the part of the professional community to innovative ideas in the treatment of women and suggest that the time is ripe for a well-articulated model of feminist therapy.

Summary

We have seen that feminist therapy has grown out of the following factors:

1. The reemergence of American feminism, with its recognition that traditional sex roles have been a tool of oppression of women and, thus, that psychological liberation must accompany economic and political liberation for women.
2. The development of consciousness-raising groups as a vehicle for personal liberation, with their recognition of the feminist adage that "the personal is political"—that women's personal problems arise from the patriarchal structure of our society.
3. The feminist critique of Freudian and analytic theory as legitimizing sex-role stereotypes by embedding them in a "scientific" theory of human behavior that has been used against women in psychoanalytic treatment.
4. The feminist criticism of psychotherapy as a male-dominated enterprise that holds a double standard of mental health for men and women. It thus effectively functions as a means of social control to protect the status quo because it is geared to "adjusting" women to fit existing sex roles. Thus it contributes to women's oppression rather than alleviating it.
5. The emergence of a "grassroots" feminist therapy movement in response to the call by feminists for a new kind of therapy for women.
6. The gradual recognition by professionals of the sexist bias inherent in the theory and practice of psychotherapy, and subsequent discussion in the professional literature of how to correct this and better meet women's needs in therapy.

■three

A FEMINIST PHILOSOPHY OF TREATMENT

■ 8
The Value System of Feminist Therapy

We believe in the capacity for humans to develop and change and that women have the ability to transcend traditional sex-role stereotyping. We believe in the need for both men and women to develop a special understanding of women within all environments and that such knowledge can increase the ability for humans to understand and help themselves. We affirm the validity of personal and group experience and value the female system perspective. We appreciate the contributions of existing psychologies while recognizing their limitations and biases. We will incorporate the learnings from humanistic, transpersonal, eastern, and western systems in synthesizing new models and building positive alternatives.

> Statement of philosophy of the
> Women's Institute of
> Alternative Psychotherapy
> (1976, p. 1)

It is now clear that what began five or six years ago as a grassroots movement is rapidly developing into a new school of therapy characterized by the conscious integration of feminist ideology into conceptualization of the nature and process of therapy. Cursory examination of a few articles on feminist therapy might leave one with the impression that it is only a loosely defined ideology held by some female therapists. A complete survey of the literature, however, makes it clear that this attitude is held by more than a few therapists, and that, increasingly, professionally trained women are becoming committed to the development of feminist therapy as a treatment modality.

In 1975, a conference on feminist therapy was held in Boston to explore ways to integrate feminism into the therapeutic process. The organizers of the conference posed the following questions for examination by conference participants:

> (We) wanted to know what other women think feminist therapy is—a philosophy, a practical theory, a definable skill? . . . Where does therapy stop and consciousness-raising begin? While there is no such thing as value-free therapy, and we believe in the value of feminism for women, at what point is a client making her own choices, at what point reacting to her social condition—or her therapist's politics?
>
> Edwards, Cohen, and Zarrow (1975, p. 18)

Such questions are being responded to in professional journals as well. What stands out most clearly in reviewing the literature is that feminist therapy is, more than anything, a system of values and attitudes, as well as beliefs about how these values should be implemented in the therapy setting. Feminist therapy is not a clear-cut theoretical stance, nor does it have a group of specific techniques. Rather, it is a value system—the feminist value system—around which some female therapists have begun to build new conceptualizations about therapy with women. The degree of congruency among feminist therapists as to what constitutes this value system is all the more remarkable for the fact that feminist therapy has no "name" leader, no professional journal, and few training seminars.

It is this clear commitment to feminist values as a basis for conceptualizing therapy that differentiates feminist therapy from nonsexist therapy. Feminist therapists, while echoing many of the same concerns voiced in articles on "women and therapy," make it clear that they are struggling to build a new treatment modality—feminist therapy—rather than simply trying to modify existing approaches. It is not enough, they say, simply to be nonsexist, to attempt to keep one's prejudices out of therapy. More than that, one must be aware of the role that sociocultural factors play in generating emotional distress in women and must develop special expertise in dealing with women's issues and problems.

Based on her survey of 104 feminist therapists, Thomas (1975) described two major parts of the feminist belief system held by feminist therapists: *Feminist Consciousness* (the belief that women differ from men because of social conditioning on the basis of sex-role stereotypes and the belief that this socialization has been destructive and oppressive for women); and *Feminist Humanism*—a "highly positive belief in the ultimate capacity of each woman for self-actualization based not on sex-role stereotypes but on her own self-knowledge and human potential" (p. 264).

Feminist ideology is clearly reflected in feminist therapy's rejection of the constrictive traditional female role as a viable model for women. Indeed, Seiden (1976) lists as one of the major trends in feminist therapy a "hearty laugh" at the idea that a healthy woman is characterized by passivity. Instead, feminist therapists view women as competent adults, capable of controlling their own lives and destinies. They believe that women are potentially competent and independent human beings; to this end they seek to foster the development of self-definition, self-nurturance, and autonomy in their female clients. They urge women to care for themselves as well as they have traditionally cared for others. They emphasize the need for women to define themselves as individuals rather than in terms of their affiliative relationships.

Mundy (1974), for instance, says:

> I see a parallel between what is happening in the women's movement and what I am doing as a feminist therapist. Women in the movement used to define themselves according to their relationships with other people. . . . These women are now moving toward defining themselves as individuals. . . . As a feminist therapist, I believe that a woman should be self-defined rather than being defined by the person she is relating to sexually. If a woman does define herself solely in terms of her relationships, she lives like a prisoner, always in fear of abandonment. (p. 154)

Lindsey (1974) breaks down the process of helping a woman to assume responsibility for her own life into three steps: (1) helping the client learn what her feelings are, (2) helping her learn to recognize the process of these feelings and how to control their expression, and (3) accepting responsibility for her own actions.

The feminist belief that, in theory, all roles are open to all people regardless of sex implies that the concept of androgyny is a part of the philosophy of feminist therapy. Martin (1976) comments on this: "Basic to the notion of feminist counseling is the integration of what were previously known as 'masculine' and 'feminine' qualities and the recognition that they are really 'human' traits possessed by every individual to greater or lesser degrees and at various times" (p. 158).

This assumption is confirmed by Aslin (1977), who, in a comparative study of feminist therapists and community mental health center therapists, found feminist therapists to have an androgynous orientation characterized by both "masculine" and "feminine" traits in describing mentally healthy adults, females, wives, and mothers. Both feminist therapists and female community mental health center therapists were found to maintain this single standard of mental health, while male community mental health center therapists' perception of mentally healthy adults differed significantly from their perceptions of mental health for female, wife, and mother, with the adult characteristics in more male-valued terms.

A logical extension of feminist therapists' emphasis on women defining themselves is the belief that women must also redefine female sexuality from the viewpoint of their own experience and desires, rather than in order to please men. This includes tacit acceptance of lesbianism as an alternative lifestyle and an implicit belief in the basic bisexuality of human beings. Leidig (1976) summarizes the feminist perspective on this area well.

> . . . female sexuality and the handling of critical issues in this area, I feel, are best done from a feminist perspective. This perspective takes into account the years of medical oppression (false information and patriarchal doctors), [woman's] need to "please" her man, and the objectification of women's bodies by a sexist society. A feminist perspective also includes fresh and clear new ideas about the prospect of lesbianism and bisexuality. This perspective says that we must *question* a great proportion of what we have been trained to accept as theories about homosexuality. (p. 9)

Feminist ideology is also reflected in the assumption by feminist therapists (see, for example, Brodsky, 1975) that the female sex role itself will generate emotional conflict, with the subsequent realization that women's emotional problems occur on two levels: the internal (psychological) and the external (sociocultural). Earnhart (1976) summarizes the problem this way:

The first is the level of personal discomfort, the level at which therapy has traditionally felt most comfortable in intervening. But there is a second level of impact, and that is the political or sociocultural. Women have personal problems because they live in a society that encourages and produces the circumstances that allow this personal discomfort to exist. It is this process of sorting out the personal from the political and most importantly encouraging the realisation of the political implications of the personal problems of women that is a major hallmark of feminist therapy. (pp. 8–9)

This represents the incorporation into therapy of the feminist adage that the "personal is political"—that women's individual problems have social as well as personal causes. The importance of helping women clients to differentiate between external, relatively uncontrollable socio-cultural conditions (such as prejudice in the job market) and internal feelings and reactions to these conditions (which are changeable), is emphasized in all of the more comprehensive papers on feminist therapy (Brodsky, 1975; Earnhart, 1976; Leidig, 1976; Lerman, 1974).

Within this context, women's anger is viewed not as a sign of personal pathology, but as a legitimate response to both internal and external oppression. Lerman points out that women often experience a great deal of anger as they begin to realize what they have allowed others to do to them without protest. This is treated as an important therapeutic issue for women. Since anger is perhaps the single most prohibited emotion for women, learning to experience and appropriately express anger is seen as essential to the growth process in women. Mueller and Leidig (1976) have devoted an entire paper to the subject of women and anger, in which they outline their goals for clients as being: (1) recognition of anger, (2) realization that there are valid external reasons for this anger, (3) identification of the source(s) of her anger and what specifically about that thing angers her, (4) validation of her expressions of anger and encouragement of her attempts to gain power over some of the areas of her life about which she feels angry, and, finally, (5) "mellowing out" after she has faced her rage.

Rather than viewing anger as a destructive emotion to be repressed or sublimated, feminist therapists view women's anger as a potential source of constructive energy for change. Owning their anger is seen as an important step towards personal power for women.

The feminist emphasis on the sociocultural roots of women's emotional distress has resulted in feminist therapists adopting a commitment to social learning theory as a theoretical model for explaining women's psychological problems. In comparison with a group of therapists who had a master's degree in social work, Poverny (1976) found that significantly more feminist therapists agreed with the statement: "As a therapist, I focus on the biopsychosocial interplay between the individual and society" (p. 2). The result is that environmental interpretations of the etiology of psychological distress are given relative priority over intrapsychic ones. Consequently, feminist therapists have adopted a growth/development model of therapy rather than the illness/remediation model utilized by traditional therapies. Within such a model, change, social as well as personal, becomes the primary goal of therapy, instead of adjustment. Because of this, political action is seen as an integral part of feminist therapy.

Although feminist therapy is not consciousness raising, it has clearly adopted several values from it, including the importance of women attaining some degree of solidarity with one another if they are to effect either social or individual change. Consequently, most feminist therapists prefer group over individual therapy. They believe that a group setting will facilitate recognition of the commonality of women's problems, through seeing their life experiences mirrored in other women's. The feminist therapy group thus becomes a forum for the discussion of distinctly female issues—the psychological experiences that are "unique to women and ignored by men and not mentioned by women around men" (Lerman, 1974, p. 9). These include menstruation, pregnancy and childbirth, rape, seduction, issues of physical power, and psychological molestation. Through this experience, feminist therapists hope to replace the androcentric bias that is a part of both male and female socialization with the realization that women are essential to one another's lives, not peripheral.

Feminist criticism of the abuse of power by psychotherapists and the social control functions of psychotherapy have significantly affected feminist therapists' attitudes about the nature and process of therapy, especially the relationship of therapist to client. The Association for Women in Psychology statement (Liss-Levinson, 1976) defining feminist therapy deals almost exclusively with these issues. They list as characteristics of feminist therapy: discretionary and appropriate use of self-disclosure by the therapist, viewing the client as a consumer who is expected to take an active part in setting treatment goals and evaluating treatment outcome, making values explicit, formation of an egalitarian therapist/client relationship, providing a realistic role model, emphasizing the client's strengths and assets, and understanding the social context of personal oppression. Almost all of these attitudes are reflected in the written statement given to clients by three Arizona feminist therapists who comprise Alternatives for Women:

> We are here to help you get what you want and need for yourself . . . whatever your lifestyle and cultural background. We believe that we should each have control over our own life, so we urge you to take an active, critical part in your own counseling. We trust that each of you will make sure that what goes on during your work with us is in your best interest—and you are the only one who can decide that. . . . We know that we have to work on changing the social structures which keep us from knowing or realizing our own power . . . from taking control of our lives and creating alternatives based on equal, loving, cooperative energy. As feminists, we believe that these alternatives, whatever they may be, should be based on honest, empowering, nonhierarchal relationships between people.
>
> Kay (1974, p. 1–D)

These factors are reflected in the literature of feminist therapy through an emphasis on the importance of making values explicit. Feminist therapists assume that the best way of handling the possibility of subtle coercion of the client to adopt the therapist's values is for the therapist to make her values explicit so that the client has the power to accept or reject them (Dejanikus and Pollner, 1974).

The importance of de-mystifying the therapist and forming an egalitarian relationship with the client is also stressed in feminist therapy. Women in Transition (1975), for instance, point out that a therapist "should be willing to share her skills with her clients, rather than impress with them" (p. 463). Feminist therapy is very much a consumer product in which the client's goals are served, not the therapist's. Poverny (1976) found that feminist therapists also have a more egalitarian and more positive assessment of their female clients than did the traditional practitioners. They tended to discourage dependency on therapy, to believe that their clients knew more about their problems and the effects than did the practitioner, and to believe that women can be responsible for themselves and their lives.

While feminist therapists recognize the necessity for the therapist to have greater therapeutic competence, they insist that therapist and client are absolutely equal in personal worth. Because of this, feminist therapists do not assume the role of "expert" vis-à-vis their clients, or presume to tell the client about herself. Rather, they assume that the client is the "expert" on her own feelings and experiences and so they work toward assisting the client to become more autonomous by validating her own experiences and perceptions. By setting such an expectation of competence and personal power from each client, the feminist therapist immediately begins a reversal of the usual socialization process in which women are taught to be passive, dependent, and incompetent. Brodsky (1975) comments, "The more the relationship separates the therapist from the client in a power or authoritarian dichotomy, the less likely that the product of therapy will be an independent person able to act upon convictions" (p. 6).

Seidler-Feller (1976) lists specific "power-sharing strategies" through which power may be redistributed in the therapeutic relationship. These include fee negotiation, the use of therapy contracts, encouraging client feedback to the therapist on his/her style and effectiveness, suggesting alternatives to or adjuncts to therapy when they seem appropriate, and refusing to participate in therapeutic encounters where social control elements predominate (for example, prison, court, or mental hospital work). Using French and Raven's (1959) categorization of social power bases, Seidler-Feller concludes that only informational power and referent power (based on identification and similarity between the "influencee" and "influencer") should predominate in feminist therapy. She finds the use of coercive, expert, and legitimate powers inimical to feminist therapy. (Expert power is based upon the credentials, special knowledge and training of the influencer while legitimate power derives from socially defined, hierarchal role relationships between persons.) She concludes that one cannot employ these means of influence and maintain a commitment to power redistribution, social equality, and the autonomy of women at the same time.

The feminist model of therapy also stresses the function of the therapist in serving as a role model for female clients. Lerman (1974) says, "The therapist, by being who she is, can serve as a model for the kind of woman who knows herself and her psychological boundaries, who relates in a human female way and can express her own gentleness along with her own definiteness" (p. 8).

It is crucial for the therapist to have integrated feminist values into her own life and behavior. Partly because of this, most feminist therapists agree that feminist therapy can be done only by women. Earnhart

(1976) points out that, since men have been the major oppressors of women, it is more difficult for men to be aware of their oppressive biases against women. She cites as reasons why male therapists are likely to be inappropriate for female clients that men: [are less likely to reject the "expert" role; are more likely to be patronizing and label women as seductive or dependent; are more likely to see strong or forceful women as sick; are more likely to try to "help" a woman or try to show her that "all men aren't bad" and that there is one man—the therapist—who can care.] Such situations simply perpetuate the traditional relationship of a man in a position of authority and a woman subordinate to him.

hmm

Similarly, Leidig (1976) maintains that, although some men can be sensitive to women's issues, they cannot be feminists and therefore not feminist therapists. She points out that male therapists who are sensitive men and are committed to combatting sexism can be most effective by working with male clients and providing them with a role model of a nonsexist man.

Johnson's (1976) research confirms the importance of these therapist factors to therapy outcome in feminist therapy. She discusses data from the Feminist Therapy Collective of Philadelphia's ongoing research project that indicate that one of the factors that contributes to successful outcomes in feminist therapy is the fact that feminist therapists are viewed by clients as desirable and powerful role models. Specifically, three of the ten factors that Collective clients found most helpful in therapy were "feminist" items, two of which had to do with the therapist herself: seeing the therapist as a competent woman; knowing that, as a woman, the therapist has shared the female experience; and discovering that other women are central to their lives and helpful to them.

In summary, we see that feminist ideology is reflected in the value system of feminist therapy in the following ways:

1. The feminist critique of American society has resulted in the rejection by feminist therapists of the traditional female sex role as a viable model for women; in fact, feminist therapists assume that the stereotypic female role will itself generate conflict in women. Instead of the dependence and passivity prescribed by the traditional role, feminist therapists make the assumption that women are potentially competent and independent people, capable of autonomy and self-direction. To these ends, feminist therapy emphasizes the importance of self-nurturance and self-definition in women in all spheres of their lives.

2. The philosophy and practice of consciousness-raising groups is reflected in the integration of political analysis into feminist therapy and the consequent assumption of dual causality of emotional and psychological problems in women. As a result, relative priority is given to environmental interpretations of psychopathology, as opposed to intrapsychic explanations. Like consciousness-raising groups, feminist therapists believe in the importance of validating the reality of women's oppression and their subsequent feelings about it, particularly their anger. They stress the commonality of women's problems and experiences and believe that women must develop a sense of community in order to effect the individual and social change that are goals of feminist therapy. Because of this, feminist therapists generally prefer group therapy over individual sessions.

3. Feminist criticism of the theory and practice of traditional psychotherapy has resulted in the adoption by feminist therapists of a growth/development model of therapy rather than the illness/remediation/adjustment model; a belief in the necessity of action as well as introspection; a concern for social system change as well as personal, individual change; and orientation of therapy around the client's goals rather than around the therapist's. Feminist therapists believe in having an egalitarian relationship with their clients and emphasize the importance of the therapist serving as role model for female clients. Because of previous abuses of power by traditional psychotherapists, feminist therapists strongly emphasize the necessity of making values explicit during the therapy process.

If we translate these values into Kluckhohn's (1956) scheme, we have a value orientation which views people, including women, as mutably good; values people living in harmony with nature and with one another without strong emphasis on issues of control and dominance; and focuses primarily on the present time dimension, while planning for the future. A collateral style of relating between people is valued (for example, the stress on egalitarian therapist/client relationships) and the valued personality type is that of Being-in-Becoming as reflected by the emphasis of feminist therapy on change and growth for women. This value orientation forms the basis for a feminist philosophy of treatment and carries within it feminist therapy's answers to the questions of philosophy of treatment.

■9
The Nature of Woman

excellent!

. . . one observes constant change of the models of [woman] which various theorists propose. But interest in [woman's] betterment and resultant changes in conceptual schemes . . . cannot take place unless there exists a particular essential psychological precondition in innovators. This psychological foundation is the inner freedom to be dissatisfied with the status quo and a self-image that includes a strong sense of independence. So long as [woman] thought of [herself] as an essentially helpless creature dominated by forces outside [her] control, precise understanding of [herself] and [her] universe was precluded. Conversely, only when [woman] experienced [herself] as capable of mastery and control could [she] address [herself] to the task of greater exploration and understanding; only then could [she] actually conceive of [herself] as capable of understanding and modifying what is.

Singer (1970, p. 5)

This quotation, in which the gender of the nouns has been changed for emphasis, places the development of feminist therapy in historical perspective. The author was speaking here of the Age of Enlightenment, which historically occurred for men 200 years ago. For women, however, the conditions described by Singer as necessary for changing our image of women and our assumptions about female nature did not exist until the advent of the current women's movement.

A society must be relatively affluent, with the basic necessities of

85

life assured, before women or men can experience the "freedom to be dissatisfied" that Singer describes. Fighting for survival, economic or physical, takes precedence over self-understanding. Even now, there are many working class women and welfare mothers who cannot be drawn into participation in the women's movement because their energies are totally absorbed by the struggle of day to day living. There are, however, enough middle-class women who have experienced some of the mastery and control Singer mentions through working or higher education and who have begun to reflect on who they are and on what kind of human beings women are. In addition, until women could control their reproductive biology, they were indeed controlled by outside forces. With control of their biology and some economic security, large numbers of women are now ready to analyze their lives and begin to define themselves.

Implicit in all approaches to psychotherapy are beliefs about the basic nature of human beings: their innate disposition, their capabilities and limitations, their purpose in life. Until the present, the term "nature of man" has been used as a generic phrase to describe the nature of human beings, with women being either ignored or defined by contrast to a male norm. In psychology, this is seen most clearly in personality theories, which are then carried into the therapy setting as part of the professional belief system of the therapist.

This has extended into psychotherapy in the prevalent, if largely unfounded, assumption that women can be understood by first making men the standard and then comparing or contrasting women to this standard. This would seem to imply that men and women are essentially similar in nature. The sexist bias in psychotherapy, however, reveals a differential view of male and female nature in which female differences are judged inferior or less desirable (see McKee and Sherriffs, 1957). From this, one would conclude that the nature of women does not warrant separate examination except to comment on female deficiencies in comparison to the "nature of man."

The true nature of human nature will, of course, never be known, since all of our perceptions and beliefs are colored by current social and cultural prescriptions and expectations about what people are like. Feminist therapy has adopted a view of people, including women, that is supported by cross-cultural research. This view holds that people are malleable—having potential for both good and evil—and that they exhibit those qualities expected of them and valued by their culture. The purpose here is not to state some absolute "truth" about human nature, but to describe one view—the feminist view—of the nature of women as part of the larger belief system labeled "philosophy of treatment."

Polanyi (1974) maintains that knowledge is political, not scientific. He asserts that it is not what the facts say, but what the majority of people in a field believe that determines what "truth" is. As we have seen, until very recently, the "truth" about women and their mental health (or illness) has been defined by what male psychologists believed to be true about women. These beliefs have been determined primarily by studying men and then comparing women to a male-defined standard. If we assume that the core of "personality" (or human nature) is experience plus conceptual interpretation of that experience, then we realize that women have been alienated from their experience of life by a conceptual system that: 1) defines much of their experience as too trivial to address directly, and 2) tells them that they are incapable of interpreting for themselves, accurately or meaningfully, their experience of life.

Feminist therapy seeks to establish a philosophy of treatment that incorporates the female value system in defining human nature and which establishes women rather than men as the criterion reference group for defining mental health in women. Feminist therapy represents the first attempt within the psychotherapy profession to create a model of the nature of women as defined by women themselves and to be based on an assumption of female competence and autonomy. Within this system, the nature of women is presumed to include beliefs about women's basic nature, beliefs about what represents optimal realization of women's potentials, and beliefs about desirable directions for further human development.

As we have seen, feminist therapy has its roots in the feminist ideology of the current women's movement and in the humanistic psychology of the last decade. Lasky (1974), Lerman (1974), and others imply that feminist therapists basically concur with the humanist perspective on the nature of human nature. In this model, human beings are seen as active, complex, ever-changing individuals who have the capacity to choose, to assign meaning to their lives, and to be autonomous. Yet, as Kasten (1972) points out, humanistic theory, like others, has been contaminated by unexamined sex-role stereotypes. She notes, for instance, that for Maslow, masculinity and femininity were innate characteristics and also dichotomous. She goes on to discuss specific ways in which, even within the humanistic framework, women are accorded a secondary status, not expected to become "self-actualizing" and labeled "exceptional" or "unusual" if they do so. Therefore, what feminist therapy does, in part, is to explicitly extend the humanistic view of human nature to include women as well as men.

The Humanistic View of Human Nature

For purposes of defining this viewpoint, I will summarize the constructs developed by Saleebey (1975) to describe the view of human nature underlying humanistic psychology. Following from this definition, the basic assumptions of this view are that:

1. Human beings are animals to an extent, but the human powers of conceptual thought, the ability to symbolize, and, thus, the powers of propositional language and abstraction set humans off as distinctly different and superior to animals.
2. Because of this, the ethics of treatment of human beings is more complex and problematic than that governing the treatment of animals. Because of their conceptual and symbolic powers, human beings have ethical responsibilities centering on the problems and consequences of choice.
3. Human beings have consciousness of themselves and their being and thus have the potential to be in the world both objectively and subjectively. Saleebey says, "The self is always a tentative construction manufactured out of the cognitive structuring of transactions with the world. It determines transactions in the world and is the locus for choice and decision. Action flows from the self and the consequences of action may lead to continual cognitive restructuring of the self" (pp. 469–470).
4. Each man has the capacity for autonomy. He has an internal life that is uniquely his and which may or may not influence his behavior at any given moment. The uniqueness of each individual lies in this ever-changing inner self, which is, however, never completely synonymous with social imperatives or observed behavior.
5. Man is a functioning whole and cannot be understood except as a whole.

Against this background, feminist therapy has developed <u>a feminist</u> <u>humanism</u> based on two factors: ① an extension of the humanistic view of human nature to clearly include women, and ② a positive reevaluation of the female value system so that some attributes and qualities traditionally assigned to women, and thus devalued as trivial, unimportant, or undesirable for "human beings," become valuable and valued traits.

While feminists agree with the humanistic view of human potential, they also recognize that extending this view to include women has specific implications for women that have not been acknowledged or dealt with by humanistic psychologists. For instance, human beings are presumed to be superior to animals, but why are men presumed to be superior to women? If human beings have ethical responsibilities, why have these been assumed to be primarily male concerns, with women being presumed too shallow or too stupid to understand them? If human beings have the capacity for autonomy, why have women been discouraged and even forbidden to develop this ability? It is the recognition and discussion of these implications that differentiates feminist therapy from humanistic psychotherapy. Basic to feminist humanism is an implied image of Woman as potentially competent and independent and as intellectually and morally equal to men; in other words, as autonomous and fully human.

The Feminist Image of Woman

> I have pointed out that characteristics and inferiority feelings which Freud considered to be specifically female and biologically determined can be explained as developments arising in and growing out of Western women's historic situation of underprivilege, restriction of development, insincere attitude toward the sexual nature and social and economic dependence. The basic nature of woman is still unknown.
>
> Thompson (1963, p. 84)

> Only when women escape from being who they are not can they themselves begin to define who they are.
>
> Kaschak (1976, p. 62)

The image of Woman underlying feminist therapy is understandably nebulous. Here, as elsewhere, the struggle is first to expose the myths about women for what they are, in order to clear the way for creation of new and more accurate images. In this case, we must reject the prevailing negative images of women in both psychology and in the larger culture in order to build a more positive image. Hunter (1976), in a historical survey of social attitudes toward women, found three images of women dominant throughout history: Woman as inferior, woman as evil, and woman as the love object (in which, from the tradition of courtly love, women were confined to an essentially passive role). Similarly, Whitbeck (1976) outlines three views of women in Western culture: Woman as partial man, the feminine as the second of two opposing principles, and woman as defined in terms of man's needs. These views of women are reflected in theories of psychotherapy as well as in philosophy.

Freud, for instance, clearly saw women as "partial men," with "missing equipment" both physically (in lacking a penis) and psychically (in their faulty superego development). With his phallocentric view of human development, he could only compare women to a male-defined standard of normalcy and declare any differences between the two to be "deficiencies," whether in superego development, ego development, or amount of libido. This position largely corresponds with the image of women as inferior.

Jungian theory most clearly illustrates the integration of the second view of women into the realm of therapy. Jung saw feminine nature as one pole of a masculine/feminine polarity in which abstract and analytic thinking and objective judgment are considered to be "masculine" and relatedness and interest in the personal and emotional side of life are judged to be feminine. Jung did not, however, clearly distinguish between what he held to be true of the "feminine nature" and what he held to be true of women as a group, so that the "nature of Woman" came to be synonymous with "feminine nature." The result was that women were judged deficient in areas generally considered to be governed by the male principle, or logos. Whitbeck (1976) cites, for instance, Jungians who maintain that women's ego is "less consciously defined than the male's and less firm" (p. 65), and who describe women as living unreflectively and being largely unaware of their own personalities. Part of this, however, is due to the fact that Jung, like other theorists, devoted his primary efforts toward constructing a model of Man's psyche, a model that would be adequate to men's experience of life. He and his followers then attempted to derive from this a model of Woman's psyche; it has proved, however, to be ill-suited to women's actual experiences.

The third view of women defines criteria for successful womanhood in terms of men's needs. Of this position, Whitbeck says:

> The definition of women in terms of men's needs admits of variations. In particular it varies depending on whether it is the adult male or the male child's perspective that is regarded as primary. In the first case, it is the role of assistant/wife that is considered as definitive for femininity and for "fulfilllment" as a woman; in the second case, it is the role of mother that is definitive for femininity and womanhood. (p. 61)

This has been the "phallacy" of humanistic psychology: that women self-actualize because of, or in the service of, their relationship with a man and/or family. Bettelheim's (1965) now-notorious quote regarding the desire of women to be "first and foremost good wives and mothers" and Erikson's (1973) virtual identification of female identity with motherhood are two examples of this viewpoint.

This view of women contains a potential double bind for women: since the qualities of the assistant/wife are different from those of mother, success as an assistant/wife runs the danger of making a woman a bad mother and the perfect mother is at risk for being a bad assistant/wife. What both have in common, however, is their emphasis on the special competence required of a "good woman," though not to an extent that might put her in competition with her man/son. Therapists who adopt this view of women often see themselves as "liberated," since they do in fact offer women a more positive identity and greater opportunity for competence. However, it is still a narrowly defined view and one that values women according to men's estimation of them.

What all of these images of women have in common is that they were created by men. De Beauvoir (1961) says, "Representation of the world, like the world itself, is the work of men; they describe it from their own point of view, which they confuse with absolute truth" (p. 133). Men have created images of women as other than what they (men) are, according to what they needed them to be, and then have mistaken these images for reality. Thus, if men conceive of themselves as superior, then women being defined as different, as "other," must be inferior; if men debase themselves as evil, then women, by virtue of their biological difference (and hence attractiveness) must be evil seductresses; if men are rational and logical, then women must be illogical, irrational; if men are active, women must be passive or reactive, etc. When men created the reality that they needed in order to define themselves, a concept of femininity was imposed upon women that was based more on what men needed women to be than on what they actually were. The end result is that the image of women was (and still is) that of less than fully human. They have been two dimensional; whether exalted or defiled, they have been more a creation of men's needs and imagination than of their own reality. Vivian Gornick (1972) in "Woman As Outsider" gives voice to this problem.

> I am not real to my civilization. I am not real to the culture that has spawned me and made use of me. I am only a collection of myths. I am an existential stand-in. The *idea* of me is real—the temptress, the goddess, the child, the mother—but *I* am not real. The mythic proportions of woman are real; it is only the human dimensions that are patently false and will be denied to the death, our death. James Baldwin once wrote: "The white man can deal with the Negro as a symbol or as a victim, but never as a human being." It was given to the black in the second great wave of black civil rights to understand that he lives as symbolic surrogate, as a deliberate and necessary outsider, as an existential offering in his own civilization. Now, in the second great wave of feminism, the same understanding is being granted to women. (p. 144)

In response to these externally imposed male definitions of women, feminist therapy creates an image of the "Woman-defined Woman." It is an image of women as self-defined rather than male-defined, as oriented toward women rather than toward men, and as gaining strength from women rather than being drained by men.

In recent historical times, the image of women, as Hunter (1976) points out, has been largely that of an inferior, an image necessary to maintain male dominance and superiority in our society. Feminist therapy, however, conceives of women as equal to men, being not substantially different in their intellect and moral stature. Feminist therapy thus places a highly positive value on women, as opposed to previous cultural trends that devalued women. Women are seen as having great human potency based on their unrecognized strengths, their endurance, and their willingness to take interpersonal risks in becoming emotionally involved with others.

Rejecting the myth of female inferiority also means ascribing positive value to many of the traditionally "female" traits that have been discounted in comparison with traditional "male" traits. This means that, while rejecting some of the male-defined images of Woman, feminist therapy accepts others as accurate but changes their valence so that they are seen as strengths rather than as weaknesses. Within this framework, cooperation as an interpersonal mode is valued over the competitiveness that characterizes most men in our society. Similarly, traditionally female traits such as nurturance, willingness to compromise, and interpersonal sensitivity become primary, valued human traits, instead of being secondary (and hence devalued) traits used for contrast in defining the primary (masculine) traits of instrumentality, coercion, and egocentricism.

Our male-dominated culture places high value on the principle of rationality, which holds that reality can be adequately examined and understood by viewing it as totally material; hence, nonrational ways of knowing have become devalued. Feminist therapy, however, views this position as incomplete and attaches equal importance to the intuitive, nonrational, and spiritual modes of being, which are usually characterized as particularly female. Both rational and intuitive modes of awareness are seen as necessary parts of all human nature. If we accept the humanist assertion that personal experience is a valid means of knowing the world, then intuition, a traditionally female trait, should also be a valued human characteristic.

Feminist therapy rejects the image of Woman as the incarnation of "sex and carnality," in favor of an image of Woman as a freely sexual, sensuous being who attaches a positive value to her sexuality. In the past, men have viewed female sexuality as both exciting, and therefore desirable, but also as evil and destructive. De Beauvoir (1961) discusses this in terms of women being the projection of men's "carnal contingence"; that men's conception of female sexuality depends upon their feelings about their own carnality. Thus, says de Beauvoir, in times of cultural romanticism, female fertility and fecundity are seen as the root of the cosmos; during periods of classical rationality, they are seen as disgusting evidence of men's own sexuality and become taboo. Either image is artificial and two-dimensional. Feminist therapy views female sexuality as an integral and positive part of female nature and as a rich source of female power and energy.

The male-defined image of women also views female nature as being determined by biology, believing that women are passive because their genital apparatus is "receptive" rather than "active." This assumption of a causal relationship between biology and female nature may represent, more than anything else, an overemphasis on the importance of physical equipment in men's psychosexual development (Tooley, 1977). As a result, intellectual, cognitive, and affectual similarities between women and men are obscured. In view of the now very obvious fact that women can control their reproductive functions, feminist therapy rejects biology as a primary influence on female nature.

Biological determinism also serves as the basis for an image of women as incomplete and as needing a man to complete them—hence, as defined primarily by their relationships with men. This is a belief that, more than any other, women have accepted and internalized. Barbara Harrison (1974) notes that "In between love affairs, we waited, like Frankenstein's monsters in mothballs, for a new creator to tell us who we were and what we lived for. . . . We *became* our lovers and we shed successive selves" (p. 40).

Hence, de Beauvoir (1961) reflects: "Women do not set themselves up as Subject and hence have erected no virile myth in which their projects are reflected; they have no religion or poetry of their own: they still dream through the dreams of men" (p. 132). Feminist therapy, on the other hand, creates an image of women as "free and independent existents," of women as whole human beings, complete in and of themselves, and capable of self-definition. In other words, feminist therapy assumes that women must begin to create themselves as subjects rather than as objects and that, instead of being reactive to events around them, spectators to the adventures of men, women can and will become active creators of their own lives.

Therefore, the image of Woman underlying feminist therapy is that of Woman as Subject; of women not as collateral to men, defined by their biology or their relationships with others, but as complete and independent human beings who possess the rich internal life and diversity of consciousness that we call "human." Just as humanists seem to assume that people are intrinsically good and to trust in what liberated human powers will produce, so specifically feminist therapy trusts that full realization of women's potentials in defining themselves will produce good, both for individual women and for society.

Self-Actualization

> (I'm) living my own life, not some man's life I'm helping him out with.
>
> Ellen Burstyn in an interview
> with Richard Schickel (1975)

If women are to be accorded full status as human beings, then the humanist ideal of self-actualization must be extended to them, as well as to men. Feminist therapy makes the assumption that women, as well as men, have a basic tendency toward psychological growth and self-actualization; it values women, as well as men, becoming fully human and realizing as much of their potential as possible within the reality of their situation. This means taking responsibility for developing as fully as possible their intellectual, emotional, and physical potentials.

Feminist therapy assumes that full realization of one's intellectual potential means having consciousness of one's self as an individual being; having the ability to create meaning in one's life; and becoming autonomous. Within the traditional female role of serving others, so much of women's identity has depended on their relationships with others that they have had little consciousness of themselves as individuals. The current women's movement marks the reawakening of this individual self-consciousness in women, the urge to experience oneself. This is reflected not only in writings about the women's movement itself, but in the tremendous upsurge of female literary figures, such as Erica Jong, Lois Gould, Lisa Alther, and Jane Howard, writing of their search for their "selves."

This self-consciousness is a necessary precondition for assigning meaning to one's life, for, without awareness of the self, there is no one to assign meaning and little to assign meaning to. It is a basic assumption of humanistic psychology, as well as of feminist therapy, that human beings strive to create meaning. Indeed, much of the feminist complaint against the "feminine mystique" is its meaninglessness. Usually, however, we create meaning not by creating our own meanings, but by subscribing to meanings provided by others. The conviction for these meanings comes from aligning oneself with a sustaining source of authority. For women, this has traditionally meant accepting and subscribing to meanings and values created by men about what women should be like. Women have attempted to create meaning in their lives by trying to adapt themselves to men's theories about women—by living up (or down) to men's images of what women are like. Karen Horney says:

"Women have adapted themselves to the wishes of men and felt as if their adaptations were their true nature. That is, they see or saw themselves in the way that their men's wishes demanded of them: unconsciously they yielded to the suggestions of masculine thought" (Cox, 1976, p. 134).

While men have long been defined as subject, not as object, as actor, not as audience, it is only now that we have begun to consider that women may have the same abilities. Subjects define themselves through their own activities, while objects are defined by the activities of subjects; subjects modify, while objects are modified.

Feminist therapy assumes that, in order to become self-actualized, women must create meaning from their *own* experiences, thoughts, feelings, and perceptions, using other women as a reference group for validation, rather than looking to men for approval. It is, perhaps, unique in this emphasis on the role of the gender group in creating meaning, for within feminist therapy, as in consciousness raising, women come to understand their experiences not only as personal events but as part of the female experience. By using other women as a reference group, women can assign both personal, individual meaning to their lives and social meaning as well; they can understand the psychology of their feelings and behavior as well as the politics.

This process is all a part of women learning to define themselves. Singer (1970) states that the "essence of man" is the ability to define himself. If this is true, then we must ask ourselves: Do women also have this ability? How are women's definitions of themselves, and of human beings in general, different from those of men?

As we have noted, women traditionally have been defined primarily by their relationships with others—they are someone's daughter, someone's wife, someone's mother. Consciousness of one's self as a unique individual and the assignment of meaning to one's experiences implies the existence of an independent identity and, indeed, feminist therapy makes just this assumption: that women do have independent identities, separate and apart from their relationships with others. It assumes that women have the freedom and the ability to define themselves, and to determine their own needs, values, actions, and thoughts, although in the past they have often abdicated this ability to others. One woman, writing about this process in her own life, put it this way: " 'I'm the woman in charge around here,' I would think to myself. And I set about learning who that woman was and feeling that I was responsible for her life" (Kwitney, 1975, p. 71). In addition, women are assumed to be potentially competent and independent, to be capable of actively directing their lives rather than being reactive to the situation or to the wishes of others, and to be capable of taking charge of their lives and setting goals. In short, they are assumed to be capable of autonomy.

While autonomy has long been a desirable goal for men, it has been subtly withheld from women. Women who were autonomous were considered "exceptions" and experienced subtle social sanctions that accentuated their difference from other women, functioning to isolate them from both men and other women. Consequently, women have usually assumed that the answer to their problems was in better role-playing, rather than in discarding roles altogether.

Although women are assumed to be capable of exercising free will, feminist therapy recognizes that social and economic oppression have severely limited women's choices and, in fact, have prevented them from learning to exercise this ability. The latter factor represents an internal psychological barrier to autonomy and self-actualization. McKeachie (1976) points out that freedom is not only a matter of external circumstance but of internal beliefs as well. He says,". . . if I assume that I have no choice, I do not attempt to exercise the choices I have, and I do not strive to increase the arena of choice" (p. 830). Many women currently are at a stage of failing to recognize their widened choices because of internalized beliefs, which were accurate in the past, that they have no such choices. Feminist therapy assumes that, once internal barriers to doing so are removed, women will begin to recognize and insist upon a wider arena of choices for themselves.

One such arena of choice is women's emotional life. Actualization of women's emotional potentials consists of two things: 1) recognition and appreciation of the emotional responsiveness and intuitive perception that has always been prescribed as "feminine," and 2) development of a full range of emotional expressiveness. Although women traditionally have been stereotyped as being "emotional," this quality, whether it meant sensitivity to others' feelings, offering nurturance, or crying spells, has not been highly valued in our culture. Feminist therapy assumes that the emotional responsiveness that most women attain through traditional socialization represents a valuable asset; it encourages women to value their intuitions and feelings and to trust them as accurate perceptions of their experience.

While women have always been encouraged or allowed to be emotionally involved with other people's lives, to care about what is happening to them, and to express their involvement in overt ways, what has not been allowed is for women to be this involved and caring with themselves and their own lives. This was labeled "selfishness." For women, then, realization of their full emotional potential means redirecting toward themselves some of this sensitivity to emotional needs. It means becoming as sensitive and assigning as much importance to one's own feelings and emotional needs as to those of others, and learning to nurture oneself as well as women have traditionally nurtured others.

In doing this, women must learn to accept all of their feelings, not just those prescribed by the female role, and must allow themselves the full range of appropriate expression of all emotions if they are to have a sense of control over their own lives and respect for themselves. Since anger is perhaps the most rigidly proscribed feeling for women, feminist therapy emphasizes allowing women to experience anger and to develop effective ways of expressing it. In other words, it is assumed that women cannot fully actualize their potential for emotional experiencing and expression if they curtail the range of feelings they allow themselves.

Finally, full actualization of women's potentials means developing the physical aspects of their being: their physical strength and well-being and their sexuality. Kerr (1972) states, ". . . to not believe in her physical power causes a woman to feel vulnerable and powerless in her soul, too. . . . Both sexual and physical passivity result in women handing power over to men out of debilitating habit and ignorance." Feminist therapy believes that women must learn to value their physical health and to extend their range of physical development and expression through exercise, sports, and bodywork, in order to increase their sense of personal power.

As for sexuality, Koedt (1976) has pointed out that, until recently, a woman wasn't seen as an individual wanting to share equally in the sex act, "any more than she was seen as a person with independent desires when she did anything else in society" (p. 288). In fact, until recent research proved otherwise, women believed their sexuality to be inferior to the male sex drive and to be dependent on male stimulation for arousal. In addition, female socialization has given women conflicting messages about their bodies: female bodies are seen as both pretty and dirty. This results in a confusing dual body image for women and in confusion and ambivalence about their sensuality and sexuality.

Kerr (1972) discusses Reich's assertion that sexual repression creates the kind of personality that is incapable of rebelling against authoritarian (father-dominated) oppression. From this, she concludes that breaking down sexual inhibitions is the first step for women in claiming power with respect to men and thence to the world as a whole. She maintains that a woman's ability to have orgasms and her personal sense of power are inseparably related.

Therefore, feminist therapy assumes that, as part of the actualization of their full human potential, women must redefine their sexuality in their own terms, according to their own needs and desires. It assumes that women have equal rights to initiate and engage in sexual relations, to achieve physical pleasure from them, and to refuse or withhold sexual favors. It is assumed that female sexuality is active rather than reactive; that women can and should be in charge of their own sexuality; that they need not depend on men to initiate sexual contact or to "give" them orgasms; and that their sexuality is something they can enjoy with or without a partner. Cox (1976) says,

". . . women must no longer become sexually whatever pleases men—be it remaining virgins until marriage, participating in 'free love,' having babies for the revolution, having monogamous or nonmonogamous relationships, or even being bisexual and multiply orgasmic—simply because it pleases men. Women must have full self-determination for sexual expression, however each individual woman defines it for herself." (p. 263)

One description of self-determined female sexuality has been offered by Childs, Sachnoff, and Stocker (1976) who list as characteristics: 1) a woman being able to enjoy her own body apart from others (that is, having a "primary sexual relationship to herself"), 2) being able to have sexual experiences for her own reasons, 3) being able to experiment with and experience different sexual relationships, and 4) having her own standards and using herself as a measure of her own experience.

Feminist therapy also considers the possibility that, without social conditioning arising from present sex roles, bisexuality might be the norm. Hence, bisexuality or lesbianism are seen not as deviance from the established heterosexual norm, but simply as alternative lifestyles based on individual preference or politics. Variations on this position range from the radical feminist therapists who vow that unless a woman is bisexual she does not truly value women as highly as men, to the "liberal" feminist therapists who take a less rigid stance but who nonetheless accept lesbianism and bisexuality as alternative styles of sexual relating that are not necessarily psychopathological.

The feminist model of self-actualization values who a human being is more than what she can accomplish. This corresponds to what Kluckhohn (1956) has termed "Being-in-Becoming" and described as a valued personality type. This means that the qualities that are culturally valued in individual persons are a combination of doing and being, in which the emphasis is on continual exploration and realization of all human potentials. In describing this concept, Kluckhohn refers to Fromm's conception of the spontaneous activity of the totally integrated personality, which he described as the ability to operate in one's emotional, intellectual, and sensuous experiences and in one's will as well. Such integration can only be achieved, Fromm implies, through acceptance of the total personality and the elimination of the artificial split between "reason" and "nature," between intellect and the emotions. Within feminist therapy, this is articulated as the ideal of the androgynous person; for, in order to achieve the "wholeness" that both humanistic psychology and feminist therapy value, people must become androgynous.

Androgyny

> Men have forgotten how to love
> Women have forgotten how not to.
> We must risk unlearning
> what has kept us alive.
>
> Morgan (1970)

At the base of feminist therapy's view of women and their potentials is the implication that the personality structure of human beings is basically androgynous; that is, that all human beings have the capacity for what our society has classified as "feminine" and "masculine" characteristics. Feminist therapy appears to be based on the assumption that all human beings are essentially the same in their emotional and intellectual capacities. In principle, all roles should be open to all people. Feminists recognize, however, that the distinctive social and historical experiences of women have produced fundamental, if artificial, differences in their personality structure and the expression of their abilities. While the distinctive experiences of women in our society and the resulting differences between men and women must be taken into account in doing therapy with women, we must not forget that these differences are not innate but are the product of social conditioning and an institutionalized sexual class system. Therefore, psychological sex roles are seen as totally artificial bipolarizations of human psychological traits that are due to our artificial sex roles and the inequalities of power between women and men.

It is thus assumed that sex roles are more a function of social and cultural expectations and proscriptions than of innate differences in abilities between men and women. Cox (1976) has pointed out that until the "crucial experiment"—one in which social expectations for men and women are the same—can be performed, we do not know what, if any, innate psychological sex differences exist. Thus, until such time as this kind of experiment can be done, feminists assume that there are few, if any, innate psychological sex differences and that any differences in personality makeup between women and men are due to cultural influences and social conditioning.

This position is supported by the cross-cultural research of Margaret Mead (1968), who says:

> If these temperamental atttitudes which we have traditionally regarded as feminine—such as passivity, responsiveness, and a willingness to cherish children—can so easily be set up as the masculine pattern in one tribe and in another to be outlawed for the majority of men, we no longer have any basis for regarding such aspects of culture as sex-linked. (pp. 76–77)

Therefore, it is assumed that there is no way a woman can be "feminine" or a man "masculine" and also be fully human, because both sex roles are constricting and incomplete. The assumption is that, if given the opportunity to realize all aspects of their human potential, role differences between men and women could largely disappear, resulting in an androgynous personality that would integrate and balance the best aspects of each role. Personality traits considered desirable for one sex would be considered equally desirable for the other. The implicit assumption is that androgynous persons are able to function more effectively and thus to realize more of their human potentials than stereotypically masculine or feminine persons.

This assumption is supported by research surveyed by Rawlings and Carter (1977) indicating that androgyny is related to maturity in moral judgment (Block, 1973); higher levels of ego maturity (Block, 1973); optimal cognitive functioning (Maccoby, 1966); and greater creativity

(Hammer, 1964; Helson, 1966). In addition, Bem (1975) cites her findings that psychologically androgynous individuals (those possessing both stereotypically feminine and stereotypically masculine traits) have greater sex-role adaptability which allows them to engage in situationally effective behavior without regard for its stereotype of being more appropriate for one sex than for the other. She found that androgynous subjects (as measured by the Bem Sex-Role Inventory) of both sexes displayed "masculine" independence under pressure to conform, and "feminine" playfulness when given the opportunity to interact with a kitten. In contrast, all of the nonandrogynous subjects were found to display behavioral deficits of one sort or another. This research supports the assumption of feminist therapy that androgynous persons are able to function more effectively and achieve greater self-actualization.

Within an androgynous model, dimensions of human personality are assumed to be on a continuum, rather than being bipolar dichotomies. Kaplan (1976) outlines points along such a continuum as follows:

1. *Pre-androgyny:* Current sex-role polarities where qualities and behaviors deemed appropriate for one sex are largely prohibited or negatively sanctioned in the other.
2. *Beginning androgyny:* Equal presence of masculine and feminine traits in an individual, which are expressed as appropriate to the situation, as in Bem's (1975) experiment. Thus, a woman might be assertive at times and a man nurturing at times, according to the situation.
3. *Hybrid characteristics:* The integration of stereotypically masculine and feminine traits to produce new traits or behaviors, such as "assertive warmth" (Sedney, 1976).
4. *Sex-role transcendence:* New hybrid characteristics and behaviors become divorced from the stereotypic roots from which they developed and are accepted as appropriate and as a "natural" part of the personality makeup of both males and females.

This last concept has been discussed by Rebecca, Hefner, and Oleshansky (1976), who describe their concept of sex-role transcendence as follows:

> In this stage, the individual can move freely from situation to situation and behave/feel appropriately and adaptively. Choice of behavior and emotional expression is not determined by rigid adherence to "appropriate" sex-

related characteristics. Individuals feel free to express their human qualities without fear of retribution for violating sex-role norms. There has been
a transcending of the stereotypes. . . . Assigned gender is irrelevant for
decision-making for a transcendent person. (p. 204)

Thus, feminist therapy stresses the integration of emotion and intellect and of feelings and intuition with thinking and problem solving,
giving both equal status and equal importance for the androgynous person. As a result of socialization, women have overdeveloped such attributes as warmth, compassion, tenderness, intuitiveness, nurturance,
and flexibility at the expense of certain others equally important for
effective human functioning, e.g., assertiveness, endurance, initiative,
industry, risk-taking, self-confidence, rationality, and self-reliance. Feminist therapy assumes that, for most women, androgyny will likely begin
with recognition and appreciation of many of these traditionally female
qualities that have been assigned less social desirability by our male-
dominated culture. Women may then move toward expanding their
self-concepts to include some of the qualities and behaviors that have
previously been assigned to males. Hybrid characteristics, for the most
part, have yet to be invented, although Kaplan (1976) and Sedney (1976)
suggest what some of them might be like; transcendence, realistically, is
still far in the future.

Clearly, however, feminist therapy values the struggle toward androgyny as a useful and valuable one for both the therapists and their
clients. Ultimately, of course, what feminist therapy seeks is equal respect and value for each person, regardless of sex, and androgyny represents a step toward that goal.

Thus far, I have discussed the image of woman implicit in feminist
therapy, what is seen as possible for women (androgyny) and what is
considered desirable (self-actualization). In most treatment modalities,
these concepts are expressed indirectly in some kind of description of
"mental health." Since feminist therapy is based on a growth model of
human nature, rather than an illness model, and since human functioning (and ultimately personality) is understood to be integrally related to
situation and social context, it seems logically inconsistent to talk about a
definition of "mental health" for women. Although some feminist therapists (Bernardez-Bonesatti, 1974; Lasky, 1974; Perlstein, 1976) continue to use this term, I think its use is idiomatic rather than descrip-

tive. In practice, feminist therapists make it clear (Lasky, 1974) that there can be no single definition of "mental health," since a single standard always implies that deviation from it is less than good; this is not the position of feminist therapy.

Summary

The view of human nature presented here represents a feminist interpretation of humanistic psychology's views. It specifically addresses the question of the nature of Woman and consequently expands the range of women's human potential and attributes to them a wider variety of personality characteristics than either the traditional or the humanistic model, including many of the socially desirable traits previously described as exclusively male. It also marks the first time an androgynous model of human nature has been advocated in a treatment modality. (Although Jung recognized the existence of both "masculine" and "feminine" traits in all human beings, he persisted in labeling this artificial division of human qualities according to sex.) This view of the nature of Woman defines what androgynous self-actualization might mean for women but also recognizes that women face unique problems in attaining this state, not the least of which is the fact that society does not expect women to be self-actualized and that the female sex role actually limits women to realization of only a small part of their potentials.

■ 10
The Etiology of Psychological Distress in Women

> [A general conceptual framework for psychotherapy] should be able to relate a person's inner life to his interactions with other persons and to his group allegiances. It should suggest how certain kinds of distress might arise from and contribute to disturbed relationships with others, and how particular types of interpersonal experience might help to ameliorate both.
>
> Frank (1975, p. 24)

The conceptual framework of a treatment modality is assumed to begin with beliefs and assumptions about the etiology of emotional distress. From this grow interpretations about the meaning of symptoms of emotional distress as well as assumptions about what focus therapeutic interventions should take and how these interventions facilitate change.

A fairly consistent element of philosophy of treatment or discussion of conceptual frameworks of psychotherapy is some speculation about what causes less than optimal functioning and, thereby, "mental illness." Historically, mental illness has been attributed to one of three causes: 1) biological events, such as genetic damage or drug toxicity, 2) individual experiential events, such as childhood traumas, or 3) metaphysical causes, such as loss of soul, possession, or the like. "Possession" as an explanation for strange or unusual behavior is precluded in our society by Western scientism and, while feminist therapy recognizes the influence of past individual traumas, these are interpreted primarily as the result of socialization experiences, either within the family or outside it. Therefore, assuming the absence of organic impairment, feminist therapy views "mental illness" in women primarily as logical, if dysfunctional, results of the female sex role, female socialization, and women's minority-group status.

Feminist therapy assumes that women are prevented from full realization of their human potentials by the very nature of the female sex role. In fact, it assumes that the female sex role not only hinders optimal functioning in women but it actually engenders psychological disturbance. This assumption is based on the feminist allegation that society makes women "sick," that the female sex role drives them "crazy." It is supported by recent research on the psychological results of sex roles and on sex role and incidence of mental illness in women. I will focus here on how the female sex role affects women's "mental health," as well as on female socialization as a process of enforcing women's minority-group status. The ways in which these factors interfere with women's realization of their full potentials as adult human beings will also be examined as part of feminist therapy's belief that the female sex role is the root of much of women's emotional distress.

The Female Sex Role Defined

For purposes of definition, Suzanne Keller's (1974) description of the "core elements" of the female sex role will be used. They are:

1. "A concentration on marriage, home, and children as the primary focus of feminine concern."
2. "A reliance on a male provider for sustenance and status"; this is "symbolized by the woman taking her husband's name and sharing her husband's income."
3. "An expectation that women will emphasize nurturance and life-preserving activities . . . Preeminent qualities of character stressed for women include sympathy, care, love, and compassion, seemingly best realized in the roles of mother, teacher, and nurse."
4. "An injunction that women live through and for others rather than for the self. Ideally, a woman is enjoined to lead a vicari-

ous existence, feeling pride or dismay about her husband's achievements and failures or about her children's competitive standing."

5. "A stress on beauty, personal adornment, and eroticism, which, though a general feature of the female role, is most marked for the glamor girl."

6. "A ban on the expression of direct assertion, aggression, and power strivings, except in areas clearly marked women's domain (as in defense of hearth and home). There is a similar ban on women taking the direct (but not indirect) sexual initiative."

This description makes it obvious that women's self-actualization has been artifically constricted by a sex role which prescribes overdevelopment of some qualities (for example, affection, emotional sensitivity, and an affiliative mode of relating) while prohibiting the development of others (such as rationality, independence, and assertiveness). While sex-role definitions and behavioral options for men are broadened by the socialization process, the options for women are narrowed. While women may modify their role somewhat, they must abide by its two principle tenets: economic dependence on males and a heterosexual orientation. "Once in place," Keller (1974) notes, "sex roles become firmly locked into the psychic system, forming a permanent screen through which to perceive and experience the world" (p. 412).

Emotional Results of the Female Sex Role: Frustration, Ambivalence, and Discontinuity

It appears that the primary result of the female sex role is the exchange of autonomy for (supposed) economic security. In addition, the description given above precludes development of many of the aspects of optimal human functioning previously outlined. This description clearly prevents or hampers development of personal or economic autonomy; restricts the woman's sphere of interest and influence to the home and family, making it unlikely that she will develop a sense of connectedness with other women; and encourages an overdependence on others for definition of her identity and importance.

David (1975a) has explored the psychological results of women having been defined primarily by their relationships with significant others (usually husband and children). She maintains that many of the problems women experience are by-products of being other-directed instead of self-directed:

> Since the support services women perform are taken for granted and not fully acknowledged by the recipients of those services, women are frequently unaware of the extent to which they subordinate their own needs to those of others. Since society sanctions such self-sacrifice, many of the women who are aware of it come to experience it as virtuous rather than oppressive. (p. 176)

Adams (1971) maintains that this manipulation of women's psychological resources is exploitation as blatant as the economic exploitation which keeps them out of high-salaried jobs and pays them less than men at all levels.

In addition, David (1975a) maintains that this "other-directedness" generates self-doubt. She says, "A woman in a dependent relationship with a person who is highly critical of her may come to believe the negatively assigned characteristics" (p. 177). Other-directedness also fosters a strong need for approval from others; holding oneself entirely responsible for the success or failure of relationships; and the creation of artificial dependencies. She points out that, if self-esteem is based on the successful support and nurturance of others, it becomes necessary to be needed and depended upon. This creates a double bind: if a woman's children and husband succeed, they become less dependent on her; if they do not succeed, she fails.

By investing most of one's identity in others, one also gives them the power to define reality. This leaves women open, as David points out, to having behaviors that are inconvenient for friends and family labeled as negative; for instance, self-confidence, assertiveness, autonomy, and independence might be labeled as arrogance, aggressiveness, selfishness, and indifference by disapproving friends or families. Finally, David points out that, to the extent that women are preoccupied with their appearance, they are distracted from learning the skills necessary for independent living, such as assertion, problem-solving, and decision-making.

Gove and Tudor (1973), in an excellent survey of relevant literature, summarize five factors that they conclude are "ample grounds for assuming that women find their position in society to be more frustrating and less rewarding than do men" (p. 54):

1. While most men in our society occupy two roles (household head and worker), most women are restricted to a single major societal role—that of housewife. While a man thus has two potential sources of personal gratification, if a woman finds her family role unsatisfactory, she typically has no major alternative source for gratification.

2. Many women find their major instrumental activities—raising children and keeping house—frustrating, unchallenging, and repetitious.

3. The role of housewife is relatively unstructured and invisible. This makes it more likely that her activities will be noticed more when she does not do them than when she does, inviting more opportunity for negative reinforcement than for positive rewards for role performance.

4. Even when a married woman works, she is typically in a less satisfactory position than the married male because of job discrimination. Gove and Tudor cite data showing that women are discriminated against in the job market, that they frequently hold positions that under-utilize their educational backgrounds, and that there has been a persistent decline in the relative status of women in business since 1940 as measured by occupation, income, and education.

5. They cite numerous papers and studies that indicate that the expectations confronting women are unclear and diffuse, thus creating confusion for women. They note that the feminine role is characterized by constant adjusting to and preparing for unknown contingencies, due to the emphasis on pleasing others and the auxiliary role that women take with regard to their husbands. Thus, women may experience a good deal of frustration about their lack of control over their own lives and uncertainty about their future.

This confusion and frustration is exacerbated by the fact that behavior that is valued and rewarded in one situation is not rewarded in later life stages. An example is the reinforcement of intelligence and academic achievement given to a schoolgirl, which is later devalued in the roles of wife and mother. Such serious discontinuities in female socialization between childhood expectations and adult realities add further to women's conflict. Keller (1974) points, for instance, to women's lack of preparation for earning their own living or being able to cope with life, "if Prince Charming does not chance by." She says, "Expecting to find a nest with a built-in male provider may set up false hopes and virtually guarantee later disappointments" (p. 432). Where women do seriously pursue vocational ambitions, she continues, they soon come up against quotas and exclusion devices of which they had been unaware. Frequently, any success they do have is discounted by attributing it to good luck rather than ability, so that repeated success is not expected.

Keller (1974) also mentions the discontinuity of erotic focus for women; unlike men, women must shift their primary emotional attachment from mother to men. All of these factors, Keller concludes, represent reasons why women may be expected to suffer certain role-determined symptoms and maladjustments, for which there are few avenues of expression.

Rossi (1972) maintains that the female sex role generates constant ambivalence that women are not allowed to express openly. She maintains that, although there is no social role toward which there is no ambivalence, ambivalence can be admitted most readily toward those roles that are optional. The more critical the role is for the maintenance and survival of a society, she says, the greater the likelihood that the negative side of ambivalence will be repressed and negative sanctions applied to their expression. Since the maternal role is essential to the survival of society, negative ambivalence toward it is strongly repressed, causing women to displace their ambivalence onto other targets, without resolution.

Psychological Effects of the Female Sex Role

These conclusions are supported by recent research on the psychological effects of sex role on women. Gump (1972) found ego strength to be negatively related to adoption of the traditional female sex role; Bem (1975) cites studies finding high traditional femininity to be associated with high anxiety, low self-esteem, low social acceptance, lower overall intelligence, and lower creativity; and Rose (1975) discusses the reduction of autonomy in women who follow the female sex role as well as the negative effects of social reinforcement for being passive and dependent. After reviewing the research, Block (1973) concludes that the achievement of higher levels of ego functioning is more difficult for women because individuation for them involves conflict with prevailing cultural norms. And, Weissman and Klerman (in press) report that there is convincing evidence that social role plays an important part in the vulnerability of women to depression.

Baruch and Barnett (1975) review research studies on conflicts associated with femininity, including low self-evaluations in areas such as academic ability and athletic performance; devaluation of other women's professional competence compared with men (even when no difference in competence exists) and lower IQ in girls who accept the traditional female role. They also cite studies in which a high degree of sex-role socialization in girls was found to be negatively related to autonomy and self-esteem. They go on to discuss the double bind that women face due to the fact that competence and self-esteem are not valued parts of the female role, so that if a woman increases her feelings of self-esteem and competence, she decreases her feelings of femininity, and vice versa.

Similarly, Maccoby (1963), in her survey on sex roles, discusses the anxiety and conflict created in women who value and strive for intellectual achievement. Since intellectual achievement is not a part of the traditional female role, these women are caught in the same kind of double bind described by Baruch and Barnett (1975): if they achieve intellectually they run the risk of feeling or being labeled "unfeminine." Maccoby (1963) concludes that this creates such great anxiety that it does, in fact, impair women's intellectual functioning, particularly in areas requiring creative thinking. She says, "It would appear that even when a woman is suitably endowed intellectually and develops the right temperament and habits of thought to make use of her endowment, she must be fleet of foot indeed to scale the hurdles society has erected for her and to remain a whole and happy person while continuing to follow her intellectual bent" (p. 37).

In addition, many feminists allege that the institution of marriage is particularly bad for women. Rose (1975) reports research indicating that women who married and became homemakers immediately after high school generally regressed in both "intellectual disposition" and autonomy, while college women in the same age group increased in autonomy. Bernard (1976b) asserts that marriage has a depressive effect on women and Maracek (1976) cites statistics from the New York Narcotic Addiction Control Commission (1971) indicating that the institution of marriage increases the risk of psychiatric disorder for women, but offers protection for men. She asserts that married women who are not employed are at the highest risk for psychological disorder, that they have the highest rates of entry into psychiatric treatment of any occupational group, and that they request and receive the greatest quantity of prescribed mood-modifying drugs. This is supported by the work of Gove (1972), who found that married women had a higher rate of mental illness than married men. In fact, of all groups studied (single, married, widowed, and divorced, of both sexes), married women had the highest incidence of mental illness.

Conversely, among single people, Gove found single men to have a slightly higher chance of mental illness than single women.

These theoretical observations and research data lead feminist therapists to the assumption that women are at a higher risk than men for role-determined symptoms of psychological disturbance. In addition, Bem (1975) cites evidence that the highly sex-typed person becomes motivated, during the course of sex-role socialization, to keep his or her behavior consistent with an internalized role standard. Thus, feminist therapy assumes that the psychological distress of individual women may be understood in terms of oppression of the self through internalized attitudes, values, feelings, and self-images, as well as the resultant behaviors that are necessary to fulfill the female sex role but which are oppressive to personal growth. The fact that women labor long and hard at acquiring these attitudes and behaviors only makes them the more resistant to change, despite the insufficient rewards received for them.

Psychological Effects of Minority-Group Status of Women

Not only are women at higher risk than men for role-induced symptoms, they are also at risk for psychiatric disturbance because of their relative powerlessness over their lives, which is presumed to be caused by their lesser, unequal status in our society. This thesis has been developed by Polk (1974, pp. 420–422), whose excellent analysis of male power forms a feminist view of female socialization as well as a background for feminist therapy's views of female personality and behavior. According to this analysis, men have greater normative, institutional, and psychological power, and power of expertise. In addition, men control options through reward power and also have greater physical power than women: The following is an adaptation of Polk's definitions of these types of power differentials between men and women:

1. *Normative power.* Because "of their sex and their control of traditional sex-role definitions, men are able to manipulate women's behavior by ignoring, misrepresenting, devaluing, and discrediting women or their accomplishments, especially when women deviate from traditional roles." Excellent examples are the omission of women's contributions from history texts and the attribution of women's scientific discoveries to men.

2. *Institutional power.* Males have differential amounts of and

access to money, education, and positions of influence and "they use this control to limit life options for women and to extend life options for men." Males use public socialization institutions to inculcate traditional role and value systems in both females and males, thereby reducing the probability that females will aspire to or succeed in moving beyond traditional roles. When women do attempt to change or broaden their roles, they are blocked by male dominance of the economic institutions. In addition, male dominance of law and politics supports their control through other institutional means.

3. *Control of options through reward power.*"Men use their institutional and normative power to control women's life choices, not only through restricting their options but also through reinforcing choices within them. Since women do receive some rewards for 'appropriate' behavior, those who rebel risk losing real rewards."

4. *The power of expertise.* In all areas, the experts are male. "For a woman, this means that when she wants information or advice in any field, she must rely for the most part on men whose expertise may serve the interest of male supremacy or male values, rather than her own interests."

5. *Psychological power.*"Males, having suppressed feminine culture, have access to institutional power partly because they 'fit' the value structure of the institutions better than do women. The confidence of being 'right,' of fitting, gives even incompetent men an important source of psychological power over women, who have not been so wholly socialized into the masculine value structure."

6. *Brute force.*"Not only are most men stronger than most women, but they are trained to develop their physical strength. Men physically dominate women by beating them and by rape and threat of rape." Within this context, rape is seen as a form of social control that serves to restrict women's autonomy and mobility.

This greater relative power of men over women results in a dominant/subordinate relationship between the sexes which, as Miller and Mothner (1971) point out, has characteristics that lead to profound psychological results. They describe various aspects of the relationship between a dominant group (for example, whites or males) to a subordinate group (for example, blacks or females) as including the following characteristics:

1. Both parties are tied to each other in many ways and, indeed, they need each other.

2. Actions of the dominant group tend to be destructive to the less powerful group.

3. The dominant group usually puts down the less powerful group, labeling it defective in varying ways ("blacks are less intelligent than whites" or "women are ruled by emotion").

4. The dominant group usually acts to halt any movement toward equality by the subordinate group. It also militates strongly against stirrings of rationality or greater humanity in any of its own members.

5. The dominant group obscures the true nature of the relationship; that is, the very fact of the existence of inequality itself. It rationalizes the situation by other, always false explanations, such as racial or sexual inferiority.

6. By proffering one or more "acceptable" roles, the dominants attempt to deny other areas of development to the less powerful. These acceptable roles usually provide a "service" that the dominant group does not choose to, or cannot, do for itself. The ability of subordinates to perform other roles is usually manifest only in emergency situations, such as wartime, when inexperienced and untrained blacks and "incompetent" women suddenly "man" the factories with great skill.

7. Since the dominants determine society's philosophy and morality, they legitimize the unequal relationship and incorporate it into all of society's guiding cultural concepts.

8. The dominant group is the model for "normal human relationships." Thus, it may be "normal" to treat others destructively and derogate them, obscure the truth of what you are doing, create false explanations for it, and oppose actions toward equality.

9. The dominant group, then, is bound to suppress disruption of these relationships and to avoid open conflict that might bring into question the validity of the established situation.

The result of this relationship is that the subordinate group is primarily concerned with its survival, and consequently avoids direct, honest reactions to being treated destructively. For women in our society, this kind of reaction might mean economic hardships, social ostracism, psychological isolation, or even the diagnosis of personality disorder by some psychotherapists.

women learn to be dishonest, indirect

Miller and Mothner (1971) point out that the less powerful group may absorb some of the untruths created by the dominants, so that there are blacks who feel inferior and women who believe they are less important then men. This forms a powerful psychological mechanism for internal maintenance of sex roles. Hacker (1976) says, "Since a person's conception of himself is based on the defining gestures of others, it is unlikely that members of a minority group can wholly escape personality distortion. Constant reiteration of one's inferiority must often lead to its acceptance as a fact" (p. 158). Thus it is that much of the lower self-esteem, greater self-effacement, and lack of self-confidence that characterize women in the literature on sex roles may be a direct result of their lesser status with respect to men.

Similarly, Miller and Mothner (1971) interpret the psychological mechanism called "identification with the aggressor" as a tendency for some members within each subordinate group to imitate the dominants and to treat their fellow subordinates just as destructively. One has only two choices in this situation: (1) to identify oneself as a member of the subordinate group and, therefore, as inferior (generating symptoms of loss of self-esteem, lower self-confidence and lack of autonomy), or (2) to form an identification with the dominant group that is maintained in part by adoption of the attitudes of the dominant group toward the subordinate group (frequently termed by therapists as "sex-role identification problems" or "aggressive woman").

Members of the subordinate group also have experiences and perceptions that more accurately reflect the truth about themselves and the irrationality of their positions. These more truthful conceptions are bound to come into opposition with the mythology they have absorbed from the dominant group. Miller and Mothner (1971) conclude that an inner tension between these two sets of concepts and their derivatives is almost inevitable, thus generating psychological conflict and distress.

Carter (1977) summarizes these factors and others in a table ("Types of Ego Defenses among Victims of Discrimination") that demonstrates correspondence between ego defenses observed in minority groups, as described by Allport (1954), and ego defenses exhibited by women. From this, traditional (as opposed to feminist) women who are intropunitive are seen to turn their anger about their subordinate position inward, utilizing defenses of withdrawal and self-hatred, denial of members in their own group, "clowning," in-group aggression, sympathy for all victims, symbolic status-striving, and neuroticism. Traditional women who are extropunitive turn their anger outward but still express it indirectly through slyness and cunning, competitiveness, and neuroticism.

This, again, demonstrates the thesis that psychological disturbance in women is a result of the conflict and tension generated by the female sex role and by women's socialization to their unequal status in our society. Within this framework, the psychological pain and distress that motivate women to seek therapy are seen as reasonable, almost inevitable responses to their sex-role socialization and social position. Thus, sex-role norms are believed to play as important a part in symptom formation as they do in everyday social behavior. For instance, Maracek (1976) notes that, due to their sex role, women are at heightened risk for disorders marked by symptoms of low self-esteem, of self-punishment, passivity, guilt, depression, and social withdrawal, all of which reflect the passivity and intropunitive orientation characteristic of the female role. Men, on the other hand, tend to externalize conflict in a more active orientation; their disorders involve antisocial behavior, aggression and violence, criminal acts, impulsiveness, and psychopathy.

Feminist therapy assumes that, until the impact of the female sex role and female socialization can be "factored out," it is impossible to accurately assess how much, if any, of women's emotional distress is generated solely by intrapsychic factors. Therefore, the concept of internally generated psychopathology is largely rejected by feminist therapists. This is in contradistinction to most contemporary theories of mental illness which locate the "neurotic system" within the individual. Such theories view external situations in which the individual is involved as only a source of "triggers" for a fully developed internal neurotic conflict within the individual, and thus view symptoms of psychological disturbance as internally generated. Feminist therapy, however, rejects this conceptualization in favor of a more integrated and existential viewpoint in which women are seen as social as well as intrapsychic beings and in which the etiology of psychological distress is related to social factors as well as internal conflict.

■ 11
Interpretation of
Symptoms

> . . . how [do] therapists determine the meaning of symptoms, always contextual, if they do not know the standards of normality and conventionality governing their patients' conduct? How, furthermore, do they distinguish between conformity and emotional illness? And when do therapists decide that a problem is individual rather than cultural and, if cultural, how much can individual therapy help?
>
> Keller (1974, p. 413)

Symptoms do not become "symptoms" until they are so labeled by someone. They are merely feelings, attitudes or behaviors that take on the meaning assigned to them by the observer according to his/her value system. What is seen as a symptom of psychological disturbance in one culture is called "possession" in another and in a third may be taken as a sign of religious stature.

Therapists generally understand symptoms as expressions of conflicts. They hold (implicitly) the conviction that human beings will inevitably express their inner states symbolically—that this is a human universal. The work of the therapist rests on the belief that human beings are capable of understanding the symbolizations employed by other people. If symptoms are viewed as symbolic representations of inner states, there are within the mental health profession widely divergent views regarding the nature and meaning of these symbols.

Psychoanalysts view symbolization as an archaic function and assume that it appears in states where archaic ego functions dominate—hiding unacceptable thoughts, fatigue, sleep, psychosis, and early childhood. Hence, they view symptoms as symbolic distortions of inner states, designed to obscure or repress unacceptable wishes or impulses. Singer (1965) says, "So long as the image of man was a vision of him as both inherently regressive in nature and simultaneously eager to hide this tendency, symbols had to be understood as methods of dissembling rather than tools in expression" (p. 81).

Humanistically-oriented therapists, on the other hand, posit a human need for meaning and hence for symbolization. As a result, they view symbols as expressive, not repressive. Singer (1970) cites the research of Spitz (1945, 1946, 1957) and Harlow (1958) as indicative of a basic human need to communicate. If this is so, then communication becomes a hallmark of emotional well-being: human beings are psychologically healthy when their activities are intelligible and accurate symbols of their inner experiences and are pathological when their activities disrupt adequate communication. Within such a framework, it is assumed that all activity is communicative and is either adequate or inadequate expression of inner states. Even obscure symbolizations, such as symptoms, are also expressive (albeit paradoxically) and therefore communicative.

Singer (1965) continues, "An individual's symbolic expressions become unintelligible when he feels that active attention to himself (as a separate entity) and the activity implied in emotional and intellectual living are frowned upon and he therefore experiences them as dangerous" (p. 80). These conditions are remarkably close to the constraints of the female role: women are defined by their relationships with others, not as "separate entities," and are required to be passive by a society that makes it dangerous for them to be otherwise. If symptoms are thus understood as obscure symbolic communications, then what they say is that the person is afraid of knowing him/herself. Women, so long defined as adjuncts to men, have known themselves primarily as reflections in the mirror of others' lives, and it thus seems logical that they would be afraid of knowing themselves in any other way. Their attempts to do so generate anxiety that is often labeled neurotic by therapists.

Psychoanalysts view neurotic symptoms as symbolizing both an impulse and an effort to oppose it. (For women, this may be understood as an impulse to grow and an effort to oppose this growth in order to fill the female role.) For humanistic therapists, however, symptoms represent a compromise between a desire to survive and to progress, and outside forces, which eventually are internalized (as in the case of sex roles), that oppose survival and progress.

What I offer here are specific interpretations of symptoms as the result of sociocultural forces that oppose women's growth. This feminist interpretation links the symbolic communication of symptoms not only to individual past events but to the wider societal events experienced by all women. While feminist therapy recognizes as signals of distress many of the same symptoms called "psychopathology" by traditional psychotherapists, (such as depression, anxiety, and lack of self-confidence), it interprets them in very different ways, making different assumptions about their etiology. Thus, symptoms of psychological disturbance in women are interpreted by feminist therapy in five ways:

1. As being the direct result of the female role.
2. As representing role conflict.
3. As being the result of female socialization.
4. As being "survival tactics."
5. As representing societal labeling of role deviancy.

These five areas will be the focus of this chapter.

Symptoms and the Female Role

Within the context of feminist therapy, many of the personality traits and character structures designated by traditional psychotherapies as being individual psychopathology are interpreted as the direct result of the female sex role. These traits either may be concomitants of the devalued female role or may result from an exaggeration of this role.

For instance, Keller's (1974) description of the female sex role overlaps considerably with factors hypothesized by Horney (1963) to lead to the development of masochism. Horney suggested that any culture that contained one or more of the following factors would predispose the appearance of masochism in women:

1. Blocking of outlets in women for expansiveness and sexuality.
2. Restriction in the number of children, especially when children are the measure of a woman's social and personal contribution.

3. An estimation of women as inferior to men.
4. Economic dependence of women on men or on family.
5. Restriction of women to spheres of life built chiefly upon emotional bonds, such as family life, religion, or charity work.
6. A surplus of marriageable women, particularly when marriage offers the principal opportunity for sexual gratification, children, security, and social recognition (cited by Rawlings & Carter, 1977).

Horney concludes that, when some or all of these six factors appear in a culture, certain fixed ideologies concerning the "nature" of women appear. The psychoanalytic belief that women are by nature masochistic is one such belief. Yet Horney's description clearly suggests that women's passivity in the face of abusive or derogatory treatment may represent resignation to a severly constricted role rather than an inherent "need for punishment."

Similarly, Thompson (1963) maintains that women's alleged narcissism (generally defined as a hallmark of the hysterical personality) and greater need to be loved may be accounted for by economic necessity. She points out that, if women's primary security and social position come from establishing a permanent love relationship with a man, then love, in essence, becomes women's "profession." She says, " . . . the character trait of having no strong beliefs or convictions is not found universally in women and it also occurs frequently in men in this culture. . . . It is an attitude typical of people whose security depends on the approval of some powerful person or group" (p. 77). Since the female role places women in exactly this position, it is not surprising that they often become preoccupied with their appearance and with obtaining admiration and approval from others; in short, that they develop narcissistic personality characteristics.

In addition, feminist therapy views the hysterical personality structure as an exaggeration of the female role, which, in fact, is difficult at times to distinguish from the "normal" female personality. The psychodynamics of the hysteric are often "uncomfortably close" to the dynamics of the idealized feminine personality. Indeed, the designation of "hysterical personality" seems to represent what Rubins (1975) has described as an exaggeration of cultural values and norms into an "irrational idealized self-image," in which women carry to an extreme the characteristics assigned them by their social role. This thesis is supported by Belote (1976), who cites extensive research indicating that women are accepted and rewarded for exhibiting passivity and dependence in their behavior, affect, and cognitive styles, thereby illustrating that every American woman is conditioned to develop an hysterical character in nonpathological, or acceptable, form. Yet, to the extent that women attempt assimilation into our male-dominated culture, they have little choice other than to perform the role proffered them by society. When they find that this role is not personally rewarding for them, they may exaggerate their role performance, rather than reexamine the role itself.

Symptoms as Role Conflict

Symptoms of emotional distress may also be viewed as the result of conflict generated by the double bind created by incongruity between female role demands and women's postulated tendency to self-actualization. In addition to generating the symptomatic personality characteristics and structures already discussed, it is assumed that the female role causes considerable internal conflict for women.

Feminist therapy interprets much of what has traditionally been called neurotic symptomatology as role conflict. Brodsky (1975), for instance, asserts that role conflict is inherent in sex-role stereotypes and, indeed, many of the "painful symptoms" described by Mahrer (1967) may be understood as the result of the constrictions of the female role. These include "feelings of being limited, anxious, and angry, with strong feelings of personal and social inferiority"; the pain of an "inability to determine things for oneself, being unable to set one's own goals"; distancing of oneself from one's own needs and feelings (engendered by women's orientation to pleasing others); and the "pain and hurt" of arrested development and of being blocked in the growth process (p. 278).

Rubins (1975) supports this position in his discussion of how cultural factors influence the "form and flavor" of "pathological" processes. He hypothesizes that cultural reinforcement of "compulsive intrapsychic attitudes" occurs when the adult is either so outer directed or alienated from his own inner experiences that his attitudes are determined mainly by external factors. As we have seen, this is the usual situation for women and minorities, who have been demonstrated to be necessarily outer directed in order to ensure their survival; consequently, they are alienated from their inner experiences, and are prone to anxiety and other neurotic symptoms.

A comparison of the female sex role and our description of self-actualization shows them to be logically inconsistent, if not mutually exclusive. Since it appears to be impossible for women to successfully fulfill the female role and also to achieve self-actualization, they experience great internal conflict.

If neurosis is defined as a "compulsive" drive to satisy contradictory needs or attitudes, then neurosis is inevitable for women who seek self-actualization outside the traditional female role. Thus, anxiety and/or neurotic conflicts in women may be interpreted as being due to conflict between social pressures to fill the stereotyped female role and their own natural tendency toward realization of their full human potential. Mannes (1964) comments:

> What I call destructive anxieties are not the growth of women's minds and powers, but quite the contrary: the pressures of society and the mass media to make women conform to the classic and traditional image in men's eyes. They must be not only the perfect wife, mother, and homemaker, but the ever-young, ever-slim, ever-alluring object of their desires. Every woman is deluged daily with urges to attain this impossible state. . . . The legitimate anxiety—am I being true to myself as a human being?—is submerged in trivia and self-deception.(p. 412)

In order for a woman to develop her potentials outside the female role without incurring negative social sanctions, she must do so *in addition to* filling the traditional role. Mannes further comments, "Nobody objects to a woman's being a good writer or sculptor or geneticist if at the same time she manages to be a good wife, a good mother, good looking, good tempered, well dressed, well groomed, and unaggressive" (1963, p. 123).

Feminist therapy assumes that the conflict of trying to become a superwoman in order to attain some degree of self-actualization can only generate anxiety, tension, and conflict. By labeling these feelings in women as neurotic, traditional psychotherapy implies that they are somehow inappropriate or out of proportion to the stimulus situation. When understood within the context of role conflict, however, they are seen as the logical and appropriate result of the conflicting demands placed upon women in our society.

Symptoms and Female Socialization

Feminist therapy also views symptoms as the result of women's socialization to powerlessness and helplessness. Because female socialization
reinforces powerlessness and helplessness in women, some psychological disturbances, particularly depression, may be viewed as a manifesta-
tion of female socialization, rather than solely as individual personality
structure. If, as many theorists suggest, passivity is the core of psychopathology, we must consider the results of female socialization to helplessness to be catastrophic; it produces not only depression, but a kind
of psychological "failure to thrive" syndrome, observable in many
women as they slowly cease to grow as people.

Maracek (1976) discusses three types of powerlessness: 1) chronic
powerlessness produced by social inequities, 2) temporary loss of power
resulting from stressful life events, and 3) helplessness induced in the
behaviorist's laboratory. All three lines of evidence, she says, support the
conclusion that powerlessness has negative consequences for the individual's psychological health. (Chronic powerlessness due to social inequities
has been discussed in the previous section as an etiological factor in
psychological disturbance in women. In intropunitive women, the primary result of this socialization to powerlessness seems to be depression.)

Bernard (1976a) maintains that sex role is a major factor in depression
in women, due to the emotional dependence on men inherent in the role,
as well as isolation from other women. Bart (1975) goes further, suggesting that the traditional female role is "depressenogenic" and that Seligman's (1975) helplessness model explains the relationship between powerlessness and depression. Learned helplessness, as defined by Seligman
in his animal experiments, is created by placing the animals in a situation
in which their actions and responses have no effect on environmental
events (in this case electric shock). After a period of time, the animals simply gave up trying to effect an impact on the environment, having learned
that their actions produced no predictable or observable responses. Thus,
they learned to be "helpless." This learned helplessness appears to be an
experimental analogue for the powerlessness or loss of control over the
environment that characterizes women's position in society.

Radloff (in press) has done extensive work relating sex role with
vulnerability of women to depression, maintaining that elements of the
female role, either through learned or real helplessness, may contribute
to depression. Depression continues to represent the most frequent

complaint presented by women coming to therapy, as well as the pre-
dominant diagnostic category of women in psychiatric hospitals (Chesler,
1972). The argument, Radloff says, is that, if women in our society have
more helplessness than men, and if helplessness contributes to depression, then a sex difference in helplessness could explain the excess depression in women as compared to men. She cites research evidence
showing that women are typically described or portrayed as not active,
not independent, not competent, not successful, not able to take care of
themselves, and in need of help and protection. This description held
true whether portrayed by parents, teachers, children, TV programs,
TV cartoons, TV commercials, children's literature, textbooks, advertis-
ing, or psychotherapists. This, plus evidence from developmental
studies, leads her to conclude that there is a sex difference in "helplessness training": the actions of girls are less likely to have consequences
than are the actions of boys. She also cites research which indicates that
women talk less than men in group discussions; demand and are given
less personal space; and have less influence in problem-solving groups.
She also asserts that, in the groups she observed, any attempt on the
part of women to influence the group was seen as "pushy" and did not
increase ratings of their competence as it did for men.

Clearly, then, there are correlations among women's unequal status
in our society; the resulting powerlessness that women experience; and
depression, the primary psychiatric symptom exhibited by women.
Hopelessness, helplessness and low self-esteem are thus no longer
viewed merely as symptoms that diminish as the underlying source of
the depression is resolved; they are considered to be the source of the
depression itself. These feelings are presumed to be natural consequences of women's socialization to helplessness.

Therefore, it seems that the theories and data presented here all
point to this conclusion: if it is correct that powerlessness has negative
psychological consequences, then being a woman should raise one's risk
of psychological disorder in general, and of depression in particular.

Symptoms as Survival Tactics

Women's minority-group status forms the basis for feminist therapy's
interpretation of some symptoms of psychological disturbance in women
as survival tactics: behavior and attitudes developed in order to exercise
power indirectly and to express anger covertly.

Since both the female sex role and women's subordinate status preclude the exercise of direct power to obtain needed emotional and intellectual gratification from the environment, women often resort to indirect ways of meeting their needs and to covert expression of resentment about their status. Miller and Mothner (1971) point out that denied access to direct sources of economic, political and personal power, underpowered groups resort to various disguised reactions in order to express their dissatisfaction while appearing to please dominant-group members. The covert conflict and psychological sabotage that women often use as means to get what they want from men or to indirectly express their frustration and resentment about their lesser status may thus be seen as adaptations to their minority-group status.

Within this context, psychological disturbances characterized by manipulativeness, angry affect, passive-aggressiveness, "hysterical" personality structure, and psychophysiological symptoms are understood to be the result of women's lack of direct power, rather than as individual psychopathology. These results may take the form of an exercise of the indirect forms of power allowed women, or indirect expressions of rebellion.

Keller (1974) discusses two types of indirect "personal" power that women exercise; in the family as wives and mothers, and through their erotic power. She says that, "Both as wives and mothers, women may derive a sense of power from organizing households, dominating kinship networks, disposing of family budgets, making demands on husbands, and supervising their children's lives" (p. 425). It should be noted, however, that this kind of exercise of power "behind the facade of male supremacy" often becomes "dominance" and is labeled as psychopathology. In addition, "dominant mothers" are blamed by traditional psychotherapists as the cause of all kinds of later psychological disturbance in children. Similarly, the erotic power discussed by Keller as the power to "arouse, withhold, or gratify sexual desires and emotional longings in men" is labeled "hysterical" if carried out too blatantly.

El Sendiony (1975) discusses the relationship between the low status of Egyptian women and the types of psychological conflicts seen in female patients, the "defense mechanisms" chosen, and the ways in which women react to anxiety. This author discusses conversion reactions and psychophysiological reactions as nonverbal expressions of Egyptian women's disgust, fear, and rebellion against their tightly restricted cultural role. For instance, the frequent incidence among Egyptian women of nausea and vomiting during the sexual act is interpreted as indirect rebellion against the Egyptian custom of arranged marriages, as well as disgust at the husbands that they are thus forced to couple with against their will.

Although such dramatic conversions are relatively rare in Western societies, there is other evidence of more subtle psychophysiological reactions to oppression among Western women. Greer and Morris (1975), for instance, have found evidence linking breast cancer in women to suppressed anger.

Further support for the theory of "psychopathology" in women as a protest against their subordinate status comes unwittingly from Wolowitz (1972). He comments on a "sense of personal injustice" that he maintains is central to "all types of neurotic involvement." He defines this "sense of personal injustice" as having two principles. First, he says the experience of being unjustly treated "in the pursuit of character aims and gratifications" at the hands of socializing agents (who are themselves responsible for the character adaptations required of a child) leads to the covert wish to seek self-defeating forms of involvement, in order to retaliate against them. Secondly, he states that different forms of psychopathology are a consequence in part of both different types of experienced injustices and of the depth of the perceived injustice.

Wolowitz (1972) applies these principles only to experiences in the nuclear family (although he is correct in labeling the family a "socializing agent"). A feminist analysis, however, suggests that this experience of personal injustice is central to the socialization experience of women in our society. Thus, feminist therapy concludes that the syndrome commonly called "hysterical personality," in addition to being engendered by the female role, may also be understood as a logical response not just to a "sense" of injustice, but to the *fact* of injustice to women in our society.

Symptoms as Role Deviancy

It is by now very obvious that feminist therapy relies more on sociological analyses of women's status than on psychological theories of intrapsychic causation to explain psychiatric "symptoms" in women. It is congruent with this position to adapt from sociology the theory of symptoms as societal labeling of role deviancy.

Thomas Scheff's (1966) theory of mental illness is one such analysis that has particular significance for women who become psychiatrically hospitalized and perhaps go on to adopt the "career" of mental patient. Scheff maintains that rule breaking in society—transgressing rules of social conduct and attitudes—is highly prevalent among ostensibly "normal" people; that the usual societal reaction to rule breaking is denial that it has occurred; and that, in such cases, rule breaking is usually transitory. He points out, however, that under some conditions (here assumed to be transgression of sex roles) the societal reaction to rule breaking is to seek out signs of abnormality in the deviant's history to show that s/he was always essentially a deviant. Scheff asserts that this labeling process is a crucial contingency for most people who adopt the role of a chronic mental patient. He says, " . . . [rule breaking] may be stabilized if it is defined to be evidence of mental illness and/or the rule breaker is placed in a deviant status and begins to play the role of the mentally ill" (p. 54). He further states that when a rule breaker organizes his or her behavior within the framework of mental disorder and when this organization is validated by others, particularly "prestigeful others" such as physicians, s/he is "hooked" and will proceed on a career of chronic deviance (i.e., "mental illness").

This theory seems to have particular significance for female schizophrenics when coupled with research studies discussed by Chesler (1972). She cites three researchers who have done studies on sex roles and schizophrenia; Angrist et al. (1961, 1968), Cheek (1964), and McClelland and Watt (1968), all of whom found evidence to support the theory that female schizophrenics reject the female role to a large extent.

In comparing female ex-mental patients who were returned to the hospital with those who were not, Angrist et al. (1961) found the principal difference to be that the returned women had refused to function "domestically" in terms of cleaning, cooking, child care, and shopping; they were no different from their nonreturned counterparts in other areas such as willingness to socialize in various ways. Angrist also notes that the husbands of the returned women seemed to have very low expectations for their wives' overall human functioning, being willing to tolerate extremely childlike and dependent behavior in them as long as their domestic duties were carried out. According to Chesler (1972), however, they expressed great alarm and disapproval about their wives' "swearing, cursing and . . . temper tantrums" (p. 50).

Angrist et al. (1968) also compared returned female mental patients with "normal" housewife controls and found that both returned and nonreturned female ex-mental patients performed more poorly domestically than did "normal" housewives. Chesler (1972), in reporting on the Angrist study, also notes that, "Ex-patients, whether they were rehospitalized or not, swore more often, attempted aggressive acts more frequently, got drunk, did not want to 'see' people, and 'misbehaved sexually'—behaviors considered more 'masculine' than 'feminine.' "

Cheek (1964) found that female schizophrenics were more dominant and aggressive with their parents than were either female or male normals or male schizophrenics. The male schizophrenics, on the other hand, presented a more "feminine" pattern of passivity; more so than schizophrenic females and normal males. In discussing this study, Chesler refers to an earlier study by Letailleur (1958), in which he suggests that "the overactive dominating female and the underactive passive male are cultural anomalies and are, therefore, hospitalized," concluding that this "role reversal" is a function of the disease process. Chesler, however, in congruence with Scheff (1966) concludes that the role "reversal" or "rejection" *is* what is labeled "crazy" or is partly what the "disease" of schizophrenia is about.

McClelland and Watt (1968) refer to this phenomenon as sex-role alienation. In a study that measured conscious attitudes and preferences for abstract geometric figures, McClelland and Watt found a general pattern of more "masculine" test behavior among female schizophrenics and more "feminine" test behavior among male schizophrenics. For example, female schizophrenics significantly preferred the "intruding" and "penetrating" abstract geometric forms usually preferred by the normal males in the study; they were significantly less "nurturant" and "affiliative" than normal female controls; etc.

Taken together, results of these studies strongly suggest that what is typically labeled "schizophrenia" in our society has a great deal to do with sex-role rejection or alienation, and that Scheff's theory of mental illness as labeled deviance may explain the "psychopathology" of schizophrenia in women better than theories of intrapsychic causation. This labeling process also extends to sociocultural inhibition of expression of certain feelings, attitudes, or behaviors in women which may result in them being labeled as "symptoms" of psychopathology when they are expressed. Thus, assertion in women is labeled "aggressiveness" and anger becomes pathological. Rawlings and Carter (1977), for instance, give a detailed analysis of how such judgments colored the treatment of an angry woman, as reported by a traditional male therapist.

Although feminist therapy avoids the negative "labeling" of traditional psychotherapies, it concurs with them in viewing many of the traditional diagnostic categories as signs of less than optimal functioning in some way. The discussion presented here is not intended to be exhaustive of all categories of psychiatric disturbance; rather, the points listed are illustrative of feminist therapy's approach to redefining the concept of individual psychopathology.

This interpretation of psychiatric symptoms is not intended to replace completely the traditional intrapsychic interpretations of psychopathology, but to augment them with a socioculturally based theory. This alternative view of the etiology of emotional distress will not explain all symptoms but will certainly be applicable to a great many women in therapy. The purpose is to avoid overpathologizing clients' problems and to offer a broader view of why women suffer psychological distress.

The full implications of this position await the formulation of more complete theoretical statements on the psychology of women. It may be that feminist therapy will concur in its views of the psychodynamics of many of the current diagnostic categories, or it may not. What is clear, however, is that feminist therapy is unique in its insistence that social and cultural factors—sex roles, socialization, social status, and social values—must be an integral part of the way in which psychiatric symptoms are defined and interpreted. Therefore, feminist therapy assumes that therapeutic interventions must focus on the interaction between society and the individual.

■12
The Focus of Therapeutic Interventions

We have no insight into our own culturally learned ideas and values. They sit within us quietly, unconsciously providing the baseline against which we make value judgments, but never themselves coming into judgment. . . . Freud taught us how important childhood relationships with our parents are in forming an unconscious mold shaping later relationships. What needs to be stressed equally is how important our culturally learned ideas and values are in forming an unconscious mold shaping later ideas and values. When we fully realize this as therapists, then we will realize that we are indeed culture-bound.

Torrey (1973, p. 83)

The preceding chapter details the assumption that women in our society are prevented from realizing their full human potential and in fact are placed at risk for psychological disturbance through the female sex role, which results in high anxiety, low self-esteem, poor ego-strength, lack of autonomy, and a failure to develop adequate (androgynous) adult living skills. In addition, we have seen that women's lesser status in our society results in the development of manipulative, passive-aggressive, hysterical, and "helpless" modes of relating to others, which in turn generate symptoms of psychological disturbance. We have also seen that, despite the obvious undesirability of the female role, both in terms of social values and in living skills, women who deviate from it run the risk of being labeled "mentally ill" and of consequently adopting the career of "mental patient."

Personality, Behavior, and Social Context

> (Culture is defined as) a system of interrelated socio-cultural premises that norm or govern the feelings, the ideas, the hierarchization of the interpersonal relations, the stipulation of the type of roles to be fulfilled, the rules for the interaction of individuals in such roles, the where's, when's and with whom and how to play them. All of this is valid for interactions within the family, the collateral family, the groups, the society, the institutional superstructures . . . and for such problems as the main goals of life, the way of facing life, the perception of humanity, the problems of sex, masculinity and femininity, economy, death, etc.
>
> Diaz-Guerrero (1967, p. 81)

The evidence of the psychological effects of the female sex role and of women's subordinate personal, economic and social status in our society leads feminist therapy to question the assumption that the person is driven by unconscious forces deeply embedded in her mental apparatus. Instead, feminist therapy assumes that personality and behavior are more a function of cultural expectations and social context than of an individual inner dynamic determined by biology, childhood experiences, or simply a relatively stable set of personality "traits" that cause a person to act with relative consistency across situations.

This assumption is based in large part on the social psychology research of the last 20 years, which, if it has taught us anything, has revealed that human beings are changeable creatures who adapt to suit the demands and expectations of their situations. Weisstein (1972) summarizes the research of Milgram (1965a; 1965b); Rosenthal and Pode (1960); Rosenthal (1966); and Schachter and Singer (1962) and the implications of their findings as follows:

> If subjects under quite innocuous and noncoercive conditions can be made to kill other subjects and under other types of social conditions will positively refuse to do so; if subjects can react to a state of psychological fear by becoming euphoric, because somebody else around is euphoric, or angry

because somebody else around is angry; if students become intelligent because teachers expect them to be intelligent, and rats run mazes better because experimenters are told the rats are bright, then it is obvious that a study of human behavior requires, first and foremost, a study of social contexts within which people move, of the expectations about how they will behave, and of the authority that tells them who they are and what they are supposed to do. (p. 217)

Similarly, Chodorow (1971) discusses evidence from cross-cultural studies of socialization which indicates that personality and behavior are determined by the requirements of the role that society expects of them and that roles, in turn, are determined by the type of economy that society is based upon and requirements for its continuity.

Based on research such as this, feminist therapy concludes along with Weisstein (1972) that the mounting evidence indicates that what a person does and who she believes herself to be generally will be a function of what people around her expect her to be and what the overall situation in which she is acting implies that she is. Weisstein concludes that, "Compared to the influence of the social context within which a person lives, his or her history and 'traits' as well as biological makeup may simply be random variations, 'noise' superimposed on the true signal which can predict behavior" (p. 210).

Therefore, while feminist therapy concurs with psychotherapy in viewing "symptoms" as signals of internal conflict and distress, it has no model of intrapsychically caused "psychopathology." Instead, feminist therapy concludes that it is society—as manifested in the female sex role and the oppression of women—that is pathological, not the individual women who struggle with adapting to or departing from the role. While this is not a unique position—Halleck, Laing, Szasz, and others have reached similar conclusions—feminist therapy is unique in its focus on sex role as one vehicle by which this malaise is transmitted to individual members (women) of society and in its integration of this position into the therapy process.

Scheff (1966) points out that, while role playing is usually thought of as an individual playing his role by articulating his behavior with the cues and actions of other persons involved in the transaction, this proposition may also be reversed, i.e., having an audience that acts toward the individual in a uniform way may lead the actor to play the expected role, even if he is not particularly interested in doing so. To the degree that alternative roles are closed off, the proffered role may come to be the only way the individual can cope with the situation. Verification of this hypothesis comes unintentionally but irrevocably from the autobiography of Jan Morris (1974). After living more than 40 years as a man—being a member of the Royal Guards, a mountaineer, writer, diplomat, athlete, and father of five—James Morris became Jan Morris through transsexual surgery. Writing of others' responses to him after he became a woman, he says,

> Men treated me more and more as a junior—my lawyer, in an unguarded moment one morning even called me "my child"; and so, addressed every day of my life as an inferior, involuntarily month by month I accepted the condition. I discovered that even now men prefer women to be less informed, less able, less talkative, and certainly less self-centered than they are themselves; so I generally obliged them. . . . The more I was treated as a woman, the more woman I became. I adapted willy-nilly. If I was assumed to be incompetent at reversing cars or opening bottles, oddly incompetent I found myself becoming. If a case was thought too heavy for me, inexplicably I found it so myself. (p. 64)

Surely there can be no better testimony than this to the powerful effects that social pressure has on a person's acceptance of an assigned sex role.

An Interactional Model of Behavior

Feminist therapy addresses itself to both individual and social problems of living, rather than focusing solely on "deviant" personality traits or "maladaptive" behavior without regard for the social context within which they arise. It utilizes an interactional model of human behavior in which social structure, culture, and the individual are assumed to be dynamically interrelated, with role being the mediating link between society and the individual. This model assumes three levels of human functioning—emotional, cognitive, and social—which interact to produce "personality" and behavior. The emotional level is assumed to consist of feelings, impulses, drives, needs, motives, and value-conclusions; the cognitive level is described as thoughts, ideas, and basic premises about people and life. These factors interact with the current social context, previous social conditioning, and cultural norms to determine behavior. The assumption is that initiation and direction of behavior comes primarily from the continual interaction between the person and the situation she encounters.

Endler and Magnusson (1976) describe the interactive effect in this way: "The individual's behavior is influenced by meaningful aspects of the situation and, in addition, the individual selects and interprets the situations in which behavior occurs. Subsequently, the person's behavior affects these situations and their meaning" (p. 960). This represents a social learning model that emphasizes reciprocal influence between psychological situations and social learning variables. It is in distinction to a trait model of personality that assumes that behavior is primarily determined by latent, stable dispositions and is initiated solely from within the individual.

Figure 12–1 is a schematic representation of how personal variables, situation, culture, and socialization interact to generate attitudes and behaviors. This model reflects the interdependence of all factors in generating both personality and behavior and also outlines the processes involved in translating the cultural myths into personal attitudes and aspirations. It shows how women acquire, through a process of socialization (B) a set of attitudes, beliefs, and feelings (C) and a set of choices and behaviors (E) that are consistent with the sex roles they are expected to play in society. Although therapy typically focuses its intervention on (C), "Personal attitudes and values," this model points out the necessity for awareness of how cultural norms, socialization practices, and current situational factors, as well as sex differences, influence both personality and behavior.

For women, the available range of choices and behaviors (E) is further defined and constricted by current situational practices such as job discrimination, peer pressure to fill traditional roles or behave in traditional ways, limited educational opportunities, lack of information that would expand role options, and lack of alternative role models—women who have adopted alternative roles successfully. These factors, in turn, may influence the woman's attitudes and beliefs about what is possible for her, as well as engender anxiety when she considers alternatives outside the role usually offered to women.

Cultural norms and economic and political realities (A) influence attitudes, values, and feelings, both through reflection in current situational factors (D) and through agents of the socialization process (B), such as parents, teachers, and other authority figures or role models. Within this model, the family is viewed as an interpreter of cultural

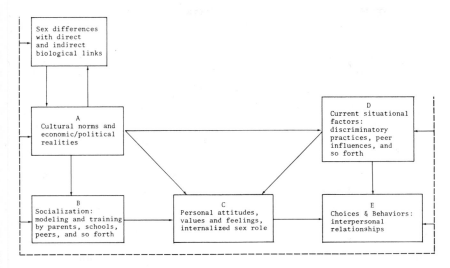

FIGURE 12–1. Interactional model of personality. Adapted from Parsons, Frieze, and Ruble, "Introduction." *Journal of Social Issues*, 1976, *32* (3): 1–5.

norms and values—an arena for conflicts that arise from the inequities sanctioned by the larger society. Rawlings and Carter (1977) suggest that the portion of "pathology" in a woman that is internal—as opposed to being caused by (D) current external factors—has been conditioned by her parents, who have themselves been conditioned and shaped by a sexist society. Thus, the family is seen as the most important—but certainly not the only—agent of socialization, rather than as an isolated unit whose ties to the larger society are relatively unimportant in interpreting psychopathology.

Parsons, Frieze, and Ruble (1976) point out that, given a thorough socialization experience, a woman may never consider roles other than traditional ones of wife and mother, since socializing agents do not typically present alternative attitudinal-behavioral models and, in fact, discourage the child from questioning the validity of these beliefs and roles. Therefore, this ideology is internalized by a woman nonconsciously, as fact rather than as opinion, and the restrictions it places upon her self-development may be accepted as normal and irrefutable. In this manner, society controls not only women's alternatives but their motivation to choose any but one (the traditional female role) of the alternatives.

Sherman (1976) has also suggested that sex differences that have either direct or indirect biological links may both influence cultural norms and be influenced by them. She maintains that biologically based sex differences influence both cultural norms and economic realities, but that cultural developments or values can also affect the actual biological sex differences—at least their influence and importance. For example, she points out, the impact of women's reproductive capacity has been lessened by modern birth control, the availability of abortion, bottle feeding, and better health care. Further changes could be effected by better understanding of female menstrual cycle changes, pregnancy, childbirth, menopause, and by better childcare provision. On the other hand, aggression in males, which has been seriously considered as possibly biologically based (Maccoby and Jacklin, 1974; Sherman, 1971) can be either augmented and developed by cultural influence (as in our culture) or diminished, as in such other cultures as the Arapesh.

Such a social-learning model of human behavior is congruent with the feminist view of human nature as being diverse and of human beings as being flexible, adaptable, capable of change, and capable of choice. If personality is not seen as a relatively inflexible set of traits, then change in both behavior and personality is made possible. For women, this opens the possibility not only of changing many of their negatively valued personality characteristics, but of changing their role in society as well.

This model implies that the problems of women occur on two levels. The first is the level of personal discomfort, the level at which therapy has traditionally felt most comfortable in intervening. The second level is the impact of sociocultural factors on women's lives; feminists assume that women have personal problems because they live in a society that encourages and produces the circumstances that allow this personal discomfort to exist.

Feminist therapy assumes that both internal and external sources of distress must be remediated in order to effect therapeutic change. Therefore, women's problems are dealt with on two levels in feminist therapy: 1) the intrapsychic and interpersonal level that emphasizes relevance to the individual client's personal life, and 2) the social level that interprets one woman's personal feelings and problems as significant manifestations of larger social phenomena, such as discrimination, internalization of sex roles, oppression of minority groups, and power struggles between the sexes.

How Therapy Facilitates Change

> Understanding the connections between objective conditions, the myths that support them, and personal experience is *psychology*. Sharing these understandings is *therapeutic*.
>
> Krakauer (1972, p. 33)

Common to all modes of therapy are assumptions about how the process of therapy effects personality and behavioral change and alleviates emotional distress, as well as assumptions about what facilitates this process.

Frank (1975) discusses five ways in which therapies influence patients; these may also be understood as agents or processes that facilitate change. Within this context, we may assume that therapeutic benefit is produced in the following ways:

1. By providing the patient with new opportunities for both cognitive and experiental learning.
2. By enhancing the patient's hope of relief.
3. By providing opportunities for success experiences that "enhance the sufferer's sense of mastery, interpersonal competence, or capability," thus implicitly or explicitly changing the patient's image of herself as a person who is overwhelmed by her symptoms and problems to that of one who can master them.
4. By helping the patient to overcome her "demoralization and sense of alienation" from others, so that she discovers that her problems are not unique and that others can understand her and care about her welfare.
5. By arousing the patient emotionally. Emotional arousal is assumed by Frank to be a prerequisite for attitudinal and behavioral change.

Following from the assumption that the female sex role and female socialization play a primary role in the etiology of emotional distress in women, feminist therapy assumes that therapeutic change is facilitated by helping women to break their psychological maintenance of sex roles and by providing a resocialization process. In the remainder of this chapter, we shall see how the therapeutic encouragement of these processes also helps a woman to develop the five factors described by Frank (1975).

Breaking Psychological Maintenance of Sex Roles

> Women's liberation is, finally, only personal. It is hard to fight an enemy
> who has outposts in your head.
>
> Gornick (1972, p. 130)

Successful oppression of any group relies on the subordinate group internalizing the value system of the dominant group, including beliefs about their own inferiority and hence in cultural justification for their oppression. For women, this means that, in order to maintain psychological sex roles, they must have internalized the dominant (male) definition of female personality and women's role in society. Successful maintenance of the status quo is thus dependent on women internalizing this role without examination of its source and without analysis of its impact on them. Such internalization becomes the primary mechanism of psychological maintenance of sex roles.

Maintenance of sex roles is also facilitated by women's reliance on male approval, which increases their isolation from one another and prevents them from forming a group identity. It is further supported by women continuing to individualize and personalize their problems so that they do not recognize the common social roots of similar problems in other women. With the advent of the women's movement, however, women have begun to realize that broader social problems often have been mistakenly identified and disguised as individual ones. Expressed in the feminist slogan that the "personal is political," they have begun to realize that there is not "something wrong" with each of them as a person or with women as people; rather, there is something wrong with a society that gives women no real choice.

Becker (1968) has said that neurosis (or deviance, or whatever we choose to call human distress) is at heart a social problem, a "problem of what society will allow people to know and to do" (p. 165). As we have seen, what society will allow women to know and to do is severely limited by their role and status in our society. Feminist therapy responds by assuming that, in order for change to occur in individual women, they must develop a critical awareness of how social and cultural factors collude to inhibit them from "knowing and doing." This awareness can help them to cease their cooperation in their own oppression.

To this end, feminist therapy focuses on helping women to identify and differentiate "internal from external" sources of distress. It helps women to differentiate between what is accepted as socially appropriate and what actually may be appropriate for an individual woman; between the reality of their situation and their feelings about it; between socially prescribed feelings, attitudes, and behaviors and their actual feelings and attitudes; and between external sources of oppression and internal sources of collusion with that oppression—including internalized sex roles, devaluation of their own and other women's abilities, and so forth.

This kind of awareness might be expressed by an individual woman as follows: "The problem is that women are often discriminated against in the job market (social level) and when I don't get a job or a promotion I want (personal level), I feel (scared, angry, depressed) and I (question my abilities, quit the job, give up)." Because female socialization teaches women to be intropunitive and to internalize blame for failures, it is especially important that they learn to recognize external sources of emotional distress and to externalize part of the blame when appropriate.

A necessary precondition for developing this kind of awareness would seem to be identification of oneself as a part of a minority group that is oppressed on the basis of sex. In order to be able to sort out internal from external causes of distress, women must have some awareness of themselves as being treated differentially by society because of their sex. Yet, as Hacker (1976) points out, few women consciously believe themselves to be members of a minority group and subsequently are largely unaware of the extent to which their group membership influences the way that others treat them. Consequently, women continue to interpret others' behavior toward them solely in terms of their own personal characteristics and so they internalize the blame for any negative responses they get from others. Most women seem to be aware of themselves as members of a certain group (women) but to be unaware of or to deny the general disesteem with which this group is generally regarded. Others seem to recognize that they are differentially treated because of their group membership, but believe that this treatment is warranted by the distinctive characteristics of their group (identification with the aggressor).

Another consequence of this failure to identify women as a minority group is a lack of a sense of group "belongingness." Hacker (1976) notes:

> . . . the minority-group person does not suffer discrimination from members of his own group. But only rarely does a woman experience this type

of group belongingness. Her interactions with members of the opposite sex may be as frequent as her relationships with members of her own sex. Women's conceptions of themselves, therefore, spring as much from their intimate relationships with men as with women. (p. 159)

This fact makes it even more difficult, and thus even more important in feminist therapy, for women to form a group identity. Identification of oneself as a member of an oppressed group prepares women to widen their cognitive field and to develop a critical awareness of how social and cultural expectations impinge on them, both as individuals and as women. Feminist therapy assumes that, in order for women in therapy to resolve their emotional distress, they must broaden their awareness to include not only awareness of internal feeling states and personal circumstances but awareness of women's place in the social and economic structure of our society. It is assumed that, by identifying cultural expectations and proscriptions for women, we gain power over their influence upon us as well as expanded options for creating new identities.

To this end, feminist therapy relies heavily on the use of sex-role analysis and differential-power analysis as cognitive tools to help women differentiate between internal and external sources of distress. The following list is summarized from the work of Polk (1974), who has detailed the components of each of these analyses. According to her, a sex-role analysis of society states that:

1. Each society arbitrarily views a wide variety of personality characteristics, interests, and behaviors as the virtually exclusive domain of one sex or the other. The fact that societies vary in their definition of feminine and masculine roles is proof that sex roles are based on social, rather than on biological, factors.
2. The parceling up of human characteristics into feminine and masculine categories deprives all people of full humanness.
3. Sex roles are systematically inculcated in individuals, beginning at birth, by parents, the educational system, peers, the media, and so forth; and are supported by the economic, political, and legal structures of society. Individuals learn appropriate roles through role models and differential reinforcement.
4. Sex roles form the core of an individual's identity. Because self-evaluation is closely linked to sex and to adequacy of sex-role performance, the propriety of the role to which one was socialized becomes difficult to dislodge in adulthood, when it is seen as dysfunctional.

5. Sex roles are basic roles and thus modify expectations in virtually all other roles. Differential expectations by sex in other roles lead to differential perceptions of the same behavior in a woman and a man. . . . Differential expectations and selective perceptions limit the extent to which individuals can step outside their sex roles and are major mechanisms for the maintenance of sex roles.

6. Female and male roles form a role system in which the expectations for behaviors of each sex have implications for the definitions of and behaviors of the other sex.

7. The male role has higher status. This status is directly rewarding and provides access to other highly valued statuses and rewards.

8. Males have power over females because of role definitions. Being powerful is itself a part of the masculine role definition.

Polk's (1974) differential-power analysis states that:

1. Men have power and privilege by virtue of their sex. They may and do oppress women in personal relationships, in groups, and on the job.

2. It is in men's interest to maintain that power and privilege. There is status in the ability to oppress someone else, regardless of the oppression one suffers oneself.

3. Men occupy and actively exclude women from positions of economic and political power in society. Those positions give men a heavily disproportionate share of the rewards of society, especially economic rewards.

4. Marriage is an institution of personal and sexual slavery for women, who are duped into marrying by the love ethic or economic necessity.

5. Although most males are also oppressed by the system under which we live, they are not oppressed, as females are, *because* of their sex.

6. Feminine roles and cultural values are the product of oppression. Idealization of them is dysfunctional to change.

7. Males have greater behavioral and economic options. Where individuals have wider options, they are responsible for their choices. In this way, men are responsible, individually and collectively, for their oppression of women.

8. Men oppress women through the use of brute force, by restricting options and selectively reinforcing women within these options, through control of resources and major institutions, and through expertise and access to the media.

These points form a core of basic assumptions and beliefs about the nature of sex roles and about male power. Feminist therapy employs these in the service of cognitive restructuring of women's beliefs and assumptions about themselves, about women as a group, and about their position in society. Within this framework, women's newly legitimized objective is to change or reject detrimental social environments, instead of internalizing all of the blame for failure to achieve desired goals and consequently focusing exclusively on personal change.

Endler and Magnusson (1976) maintain that the most influential situational factor affecting an individual's behavior is the meaning she assigns to a situation. It is assumed that by utilizing both sex-role analysis and power differential analysis to understand their lives, women will change the meaning they assign to their life situations, understanding them in terms of social forces and cultural expectations as well as personal context. Conversely, it is assumed that, without making this kind of analysis, women cannot truly understand or solve their emotional distress since they will, at least partially, be attempting to find individual solutions to what are actually social problems.

It is further assumed that, by applying these analyses to life situations common to all women (such as menstruation, childbirth, rape, menopause, motherhood, name changes with marriage, and widowhood), as well as to individual life situations, women will begin to see both themselves and other women in a different and more positive light. As they begin to have some awareness of how society constricts their choices as well as their development, they will restructure their thinking about themselves and their lives, and they will broaden their arena of choices.

As an example, within this framework, women may come to see rape as a tool of male oppression of women, rather than as the result of women "asking for it" in some way. Failure to achieve vocationally may be seen as the result of discrimination against women, rather than as personal ineptitude or inadequacy. Lesbianism may be seen as an alternate choice to living with one's oppressor; feelings of personal insecurity, low self-esteem, and lack of self-confidence may be understood as being inculcated by the female sex role, rather than as springing exclusively from personal deficits.

This expanded awareness is assumed to bring with it responsibility for both personal and social change. It is assumed that, once a woman's cognitive understanding of her situation has been expanded through learning sex-role and power analyses, she then is responsible for taking charge of her life, for solving personal problems, for changing the way in which she relates to both men and women in interpersonal relationships, and for participating in social action. The process by which these changes occur in feminist therapy is best understood in terms of resocialization.

Recalling Frank's (1975) factors which facilitate change, we see that recognition of women's minority-group status helps them to overcome their "demoralization" and sense of alienation from other women through development of a group identity. Feminist therapy assumes that recognizing commonalities with other women leads to the intensely felt realization that what had always been taken for symptoms of personal unhappiness, dissatisfaction, or frustration is so powerfully and so consistently duplicated among women that perhaps these symptoms may just as well be ascribed to cultural causes as psychological ones. Thus, in addition to alleviating alienation, identification of personal problems as due to minority-group status affords women a hope for relief, since labeling the cause of a problem brings with it the possibility of change, as well as implied strategies for doing so.

The sex-role analysis utilized by feminist therapy affords an opportunity for new cognitive learning advocated by Frank. The remaining factors—experiential learning, opportunity for success experiences and improving self image, and emotional arousal—are provided in feminist therapy by the process of resocialization.

Resocialization

If it is true that much of women's emotional and psychological problems result from their socialization, it seems reasonable to assume that, in order to alleviate these problems, women must experience a resocialization process.

Eastman (1973) distinguishes resocialization from primary socialization in that the latter "is understood to occur as a result of affectual attachment to significant others during the early course of development. The child assumes the roles and attitudes of significant others, internalizes them, and thus makes them his own" (p. 154). She goes on to point out that, in the early phases of this experience, the child is unable to differentiate between objective facts and social roles (such as sex roles) because there is such widespread cultural agreement on the definition of this aspect of "reality." She says,

Society establishes the means of categorizing people and the spread of attributes felt to be ordinary and natural for members of each of these categories. The same body of knowledge is transmitted to the next generation, learned as objective truth in the process of socialization, and thereby internalized as subjective reality. (pp. 154–155)

As it is assumed that the individual shapes her self-definition from the responses of others, the importance of other people in this process cannot be underestimated. Eastman (1973) says,

> . . . the entire experience of socialization teaches him that others' perceptions and judgments are reliable sources of evidence about reality, with the consequence that a thin line exists between what is real because the physical events of nature are convincing; that which is real because it is subjectively experienced as such; and that which is real because others say it is real. Thus the ability to experience, to decide and to control personal behavior through decision-making, is dependent in subtle and involuntary ways on relationships and interactions with others. (p. 154)

She goes on to point out that, as an individual experiences the loss of the world as she once embraced it (as, for example, through learning to think of experiences and situations in terms of sex-role and power analyses), it becomes necessary for her to accept counterexplanations of her own or those of a group. This leads her to conclude that, " . . . radical individual change after primary socialization may rest on the availability of an alternative effective plausibility structure, a social base, to function as a laboratory of transformation mediated by means of significant others" (p. 155). Within feminist therapy, this structure is provided by the all-female therapy group. It is assumed that change is facilitated by the alternate frame of reference created in the therapy group, with its different expectations for women's attitudes and behaviors within the group.

All-female groups convey to women important messages not conveyed by mixed-sex groups: that women exist apart from men and are persons within themselves; that it is permissible and even desirable for women to bond strongly to each other and not to be chiefly defined by their bonds to men; that women are worthwhile and have valuable contributions to make to one another; and that men have no monopoly on power and importance.

In discussing her rationale for choosing all-female groups for working with women, Bernardez-Bonesatti (1975a) cites as advantages the greater ease of women exploring and dealing with their sexuality and sexual feelings; the freedom to express and deal with anger and assertiveness without fear of male disapproval; and the opportunity to explore mother-daughter conflicts. She also points out that, by reducing women's isolation from one another, all-female groups facilitate women discovering their commonalities. Following this, they can more readily identify and deal with the ways in which they have internalized sex-role expectations. She also points out that, in an all-female group, women are forced to learn to take leadership roles, since the usual male authority figure is not present to do so; this facilitates women's learning to rely on their own judgment, rather than complying to men's expectations in order to gain male approval.

The feminist therapy group holds more positive expectations for group members than the larger culture holds for women generally. Specifically, the primary assumption is that women are capable of taking charge of their lives and of knowing what they want (whether this corresponds to the traditional role or not) and that, with the support of other women in the group, they will take steps to solve their problems and attain their goals. It is assumed that women can and will think for themselves, set goals, and make decisions; in other words, that they will function as adult human beings moving toward self-actualization.

The feminist therapy group thus serves as a reference group for creating new identities, as well as a "legitimating body" for the cognitive changes brought about through sex-role and power analyses. It serves to validate and give legitimacy to women's new perceptions of themselves and their environment, and to offer support and encouragement for personal changes. Figure 12–2 presents a model for how this process occurs.

The role of others in facilitating this resocialization process is essential. Feminist therapy assumes, along with Eastman (1973, p. 157) that " . . . change occurs after the frame of reference (the system of functional relations made of the extant influences operative at the time) [is] not only internalized by each individual member but [is] communicated to and shared with other persons." Thus, it is assumed that changes in frames of reference (that is, resocialization) occur not because the person "sees the error of her ways" but because the frame of reference that she has shared with others has been modified by the group.

Furthermore, it is axiomatic that one person cannot effect social change. Since so much of women's "personal" problems are assumed to

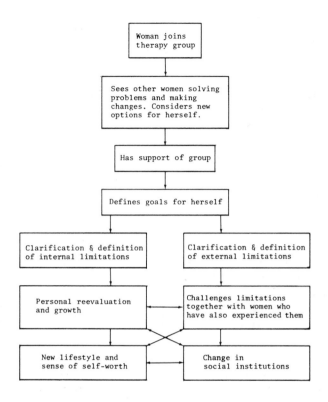

FIGURE 12–2. Role of the group in resocialization. Adapted from Gluckstern, "Beyond therapy: Personal and Institutional Change." In Edna Rawlings and Dianne Carter, eds., *Psychotherapy for Women*, pp. 429–444. Springfield, Ill.: Charles C Thomas, 1977.

be social in origin, it becomes essential for women to work together in solving their individual problems if they are also to effect changes in the source of those problems. Wyckoff (1973b) has expressed this in the following formula:

$$\text{Awareness} + \text{Contact} = \text{Action} \qquad \text{Liberation}$$

Within this context, we see that either awareness (such as that provided by sex-role analysis) or contact with others alone is not sufficient to initiate change; but that together, they generate action that results in liberation from the oppression that women experience both individually and collectively.

Feminist therapy assumes that relationships among various group members are as important as any individual member's relationship with the therapist. It is assumed that the curative factors in the group are mediated not only by the therapist but by other members who provide validation, support, and feedback. Both therapist and group members are assumed to act as role models. Feminist therapy assumes that women in the therapy group will experience ego growth and an enhanced sense of self to the extent that women with better self-concepts are available as models and to the extent that they can internalize new experiences.

The primary result of the resocialization experience in feminist therapy groups is that women become identified with other women as a group, and become emotionally involved with other women. In contrast to the dislike of one's own sex that results from traditional female socialization, feminist therapy results in women learning to love one another as well as themselves. In addition, the shift produced by resocialization from identification with the male-defined social system to a female-oriented social system helps women to further the individuation process and to complete unfinished developmental tasks such as adolescent independence, assertiveness, and autonomy. As a consequence of this shift, women also become more supportive and loving to other women and begin to make more selective use of their psychological resources. David (1975a) says,

> . . . when women are the recipients of the warmth, understanding, and support they have given to others, they come to value these functions more fully. In addition, when they begin to contrast the appreciation they are accorded when they give support to other women with the lack of response frequently experienced from the men with whom they have been involved, there is an almost overwhelming recognition of their interpersonal oppression. (p. 176)

Summary

Feminist therapy assumes that the process of change in therapy is facilitated by removal of internalized cultural and societal barriers to self-actualization, such as internalized sex roles; by the cognitive restructuring of basic ideas and assumptions about oneself, women, and society; and through group support and validation for behavioral and attitudinal change. These processes represent preparation for the social changes advocated by feminist therapy. It is assumed that, by removing internalized barriers to self-actualization, and by helping women to solve specific individual problems, they will have more energy and motivation to participate in social change.

If there are priorities in the process of feminist therapy, they are as follows:

1. Removal of socially conditioned, internalized barriers to optimal functioning through cognitive restructuring of the way in which a woman perceives herself, women as a group, and the political and economic structure of society.

2. Identification and resolution of individual, soluble problems, with the support of other women in the feminist therapy group.

3. Facilitation of self-actualization through the resocialization process, which provides positive role models, affords opportunities for experiential learning and practice of new behaviors, and gives validation of feelings and perceptions by other women.

4. Support and encouragement for participation in action to change the societal causes of women's distress.

■13
The Role of the Therapist

All therapies have implicit in them beliefs about the role of the therapist in the therapeutic process: what constitute criteria for competence or effectiveness in a therapist; what the function of the therapist is and in what manner these functions should be carried out; and what characterizes an effective relationship between therapist and client.

Three basic assumptions shape the feminist viewpoint of these beliefs. First, it is assumed that the therapist as a person, and particularly her values, have an important impact on the process and outcome of therapy. Secondly, the therapist's role is viewed more in terms of a facilitator than as an "expert"; and third, therapy is viewed as a consumer service in which the therapist facilitates the client's reaching of her goals.

Traditional psychotherapy seems to assume that it is primarily therapeutic procedures or techniques that effect change in the client, with the role of the therapist being characterized as a relatively passive conductor of these techniques. Feminist therapy, however, recognizes the importance of the therapist variables in therapy and assumes that the therapist as a person and her involvement with the client are integral parts of the change process. This viewpoint is supported by recent research on therapeutic outcome as a function of the client adopting the therapist's value system (Landfield and Nawas, 1964; Rosenthal, 1955) and research on the effect of the sex of the therapist on therapy outcome, (Orlinsky and Howard, 1976).

149

Criteria for Feminist Therapists

In addition to the traditionally valued qualities of warmth, empathy, and cognitive understanding, feminist therapy advocates the following traits as criteria for effective feminist therapists: 1) the therapist must be a woman, 2) she must be aware of her own values and be willing to make these values explicit to her clients, 3) she should be involved in social action for women, and 4) she should be working toward optimal functioning in her own life.

Although there continues to be debate as to whether or not men should treat female patients, with many feminist therapists taking the position that they should not (Chesler, 1972; Leidig, 1976), the majority agree that the most *effective* feminist therapy is done by female therapists. This is supported by Fabrikant's (1974) findings that male therapists often espouse more "liberated" and egalitarian attitudes and values than what they transmit to their female patients. This study, as well as Tavris's (1973) study on differences between attitude and behavior in "liberal" men suggests that men, and particularly male therapists, are under a great deal of social pressure to espouse "liberated" ideas which they may not actually hold and which they do not translate into behavior.

This data, in conjunction with the phenomenon of female passivity in the presence of males, indicates that female therapists may do more to facilitate female clients' growth than male therapists. Proponents of this position also point to the other advantages of the female therapist, including the ability to serve as a role model for clients, greater ability to empathize with women because of shared experiences of being a woman in this society, and potentially greater sensitivity to women's issues because they are more personally relevant for her. Feminists also point out that having a female therapist does not perpetuate the usual power hierarchy of male "expert" and female "patient," and thus gives women a chance to develop peer-relationship skills.

As discussed in the literature on feminist therapy, another important criterion for a feminist therapist is that she be aware of her own values and be willing to share them with her clients in order to give the client an opportunity to consciously accept or reject them, and to minimize the possibility of covert persuasion. Women in Transition (1975) suggest that clients interview prospective therapists regarding their values and policies and publish a list of questions to use in doing so.

Rawlings and Carter (1977) go further, stating that the feminist therapist has an "obligation" to make her values explicit to her clients during the first three interviews.

Another personal criterion for the feminist therapist is that she herself be involved in social action on behalf of women. Rawlings and Carter call this an "essential professional responsibility" of therapists. They state,

> Since the focus of feminist therapy is upon the cultural and social oppression of women, it would be inconsistent and shortsighted, indeed, for therapists to focus all their energies upon the treatment of individuals. To do so would make them . . . guilty of treating the symptom (the client) rather than the disease (society). (p. 63)

This represents a sharp departure from traditional psychotherapies, which have tended to limit the therapist's sphere of influence to the therapy setting.

Finally, the feminist therapist should be working in her personal life toward the optimal functioning previously outlined, with her personal relationships being based on equality, mutual understanding, and respect; in other words, she should be working to forge her own individual identity, apart from the traditional female stereotype.

With regard to criteria for professional competence and training, feminist therapy looks more for technical competence in doing therapy, for skill and expertise, than for formal degrees. Rawlings and Carter (1977) state,

> Feminists believe that skill, expertise, and a commitment to feminist philosophy are more important credentials than formal degrees and titles. . . . Therefore, having a professional degree is not a sufficient qualification, nor is believing that men and women should be equal. Commitment to the principles of feminism is suspect if a therapist does not apply feminist principles to her/his personal as well as her/his professional life. (pp. 70–71)

In fact, it seems logical, in view of how male-dominated our graduate and medical schools are, to assume that having a formal degree and traditional training is likely to hamper the acquisition of a feminist philosophy of treatment. Thus, if a therapist has been traditionally trained, she must overcome the sexist attitudes presumed to be a part of such training, as well as other traditional psychological ideologies such as the need to be "scientific" and "objective" and to view clients as "patients" or "cases" rather than as whole persons.

This implies another criterion—that the feminist therapist should herself have been through the consciousness-raising process in order to thoroughly familiarize herself with the feminist analysis of society. As discussed by Thomas (1975) and others, feminist therapy means that the therapist brings a feminist awareness to the therapy process. This functions as a filter that affects how the therapist listens to what the client says, what issues she hears as crucial, how she interprets symptoms, and so forth. It is assumed that, in order to develop this kind of cognitive filter, the therapist must have been through consciousness raising herself. In addition, she should have read, studied, attended seminars, and made all possible efforts to become an expert on the psychology of women and on women's problems. Without this kind of expertise in these areas, a therapist might be nonsexist, but not feminist. Feminist therapists' professional conduct is also marked by a willingness to slide their fees for women who cannot pay full fee and, in fact, many feminist therapists consider suspect anyone who does not do so.

Other criteria for the feminist therapist as a person have to do with her attitude toward her client. It is assumed that she will have adopted the feminist image of women and so will believe that there is no single "proper" role for women, either traditional or "liberated." Carter (1977) says, "A woman's (person's) place is wherever she is most happy and comfortable. For some women, that happy place is in the home, for others it is not. Neither choice should impose a penalty in terms of limited personal growth or the critical regard of the other" (p. 96). Thus, feminist therapists assume that clients should make decisions about their behavior based on what they want for and from themselves, and not on what is expected of them because of their sex. For instance, homosexuality is not considered to be a sign of psychological disturbance solely on the basis of sexual preference; and alternative sexual lifestyles are accepted by the therapist as healthy, provided they are chosen with conscious consideration of possible consequences for oneself and others.

The feminist therapist views her clients as basically competent people and assumes that the client is her own best expert on herself. David (1975b) says, "Successful therapy with women requires a fundamental belief in their abilities to function well in all situations and to take on and fulfill responsibilities in all the same areas as men with equal competence. Even women who may be currently floundering can learn to function more effectively and it is our job to help them do so" (p. 172). Thus, the therapist's attitude is that clients are people who are having problems in living but who, with help, can overcome these problems to take charge of their lives.

The Function of the Therapist in Feminist Therapy

The assumption that the client is basically a competent person leads logically to the view of the therapist as a facilitator rather than as an "expert." Therefore, it is assumed that the appropriate function of the feminist therapist is to facilitate personal problem solving, growth toward self-actualization, and the resocialization process.

Part of the therapist's function is to teach clients the sex-role and power analyses previously discussed, with the assumption that problem solving will be facilitated by analysis of personal problems within this framework. To this end, the feminist therapist will reinforce women for actively seeking solutions and for changing the system that oppresses them, instead of taking the victim role. She will encourage women to become "more curious about but less critical of their behavior" (David, 1975b) so that they can get on with problem solving; and she will help women to examine the particular ways in which they discount their importance or diminish their self-esteem, without implying or without allowing them to infer that they are being criticized or blamed. A feminist therapy client states;

> . . . my feminist therapy was a road where "madness" did not exist, where my pain was acknowledged and where responsibility became a social and political issue, not just my individual problem. . . . Its process was one of strengthening me, not of defining me. It supported my change, not my adjustment. I was validated without judgments. I was nurtured without guilt.
>
> Joyce (1975, p. 184)

The feminist therapist facilitates both personal problem solving and personal growth by encouraging the female client to trust her own intuitions, feelings, and perceptions, both in defining problematic areas and in formulating solutions. It is most helpful in this regard that both the female therapist and other group members can offer validation of the client's perceptions from the standpoint of their shared experience of being female in our society. Personal growth is also facilitated by the therapist helping and encouraging clients to focus on their strengths. Women have focused for so long on their inadequacies that they forget about their strengths and, to the extent that they lose sight of genuine skills and abilities, they will not use them. Growth toward self-actualization is also facilitated by the therapist encouraging clients to practice new skills (such as assertiveness, self-confidence, self-reliance, expression of anger, and confrontation) and to voice newly formulated attitudes and beliefs in the therapy group.

The feminist therapist facilitates the resocialization process previously described in several ways. By setting the expectation of competence and personal power from each client, the therapist immediately begins a reversal of the usual socialization process, which views women as incompetent, powerless semi-persons. Another part of the therapist's function with regard to resocialization is to help the group develop into a cohesive unit that will function as an alternative socialization system for its members. This is facilitated by the therapist's functioning as a "model-setting participant," rather than as a "technical expert." Yalom (1970) says that by demonstrating or modeling certain types of behavior the leader helps to develop therapeutic group norms; by offering a model of nonjudgmental acceptance and appreciation of others' strengths as well as their problem areas, the leader may help to form a health-oriented group. Since feminist therapy assumes that active emotional involvement on the part of the therapist is appropriate and desired to effect therapeutic change, the concept of the therapist as group participant is congruent not only with the therapist's function as facilitator, but with the view of the therapist as role model.

In this capacity, the therapist functions as a model of women relating intimately to other women. By operating honestly and spontaneously with clients, the therapist models an image of women as both potent and fallible. Hogie Wyckoff (1977) frequently stresses this viewpoint. She says, for instance,

> As group facilitator, I want to be real and intimate with the people in the group and not hold myself back or be professionally cool. I want to share myself as a person and answer any questions that people have about my life, assuming, of course, that I have the same right to confidentiality that

everyone else in the group has. . . . I explain to group members that I want to struggle with them in the same manner I do with people with whom I am intimate. I tell them how I feel about them and what they are doing: I do not hold back or censor. (p. 393)

Although this attitude represents a radical departure from the traditional model of the therapist as a dispassionate observer/expert, feminist therapy seems to recognize that this same "objectivity" separates the therapist not only from her own feelings, but from those of her client. Deflecting questions back to the client [see, for example, Wolberg's (1954) advice to therapists in this regard], or otherwise avoiding answering them honestly and directly, not only discounts the client and her question but models avoidance of feelings and interpersonal dishonesty for the client. Thus, feminist therapy clearly values the therapist's emotional involvement with the client as much as the cognitive analysis of content. This is in contrast to the masculine definition of the therapist's role as being objective, instrumental, rational, distant, and performance oriented.

Another aspect of a model of women relating intimately to other women is the concept of women nurturing both themselves and other women. Feminist therapy recognized this traditionally "female" quality as a valuable emotional resource that women have usually reserved for their husbands, lovers, and children, leaving little for themselves. Feminist therapy encourages women to use their psychological resources (such as the ability to nurture) more selectively, so that they get more in return and are not drained by their caring for others. In addition, the feminist therapist provides an example of a woman who nurtures herself as well as others (clients) and who encourages the free exchange of nurturing among women. Schultz (1977) says,

A women's group should be led by a woman who is able to be a role model, providing strength, compassion, and competence: a woman who can say that the primary ingredient of therapy is the capacity of the therapist to love her patient and to say to her, "Here is a second chance to organize your life. If you are angry, and aggressive, that's okay. If you must ventilate your anger, use me. I can take it. If you must cry, I will not treat you as a little girl, but as a woman in pain who needs nurturing and acceptance. If you are afraid of being alone I will share my own loneliness with you and together we will support each other's solitude. If you want to use your aggressiveness, your talents, your competence, DO! It will not threaten me. I will do anything to help you be what you want to be and can be." (p. 358)

By providing such a role model of nurturance, the therapist helps group members to realize that a need for nurturance and support is a valid human need and not a sign of weakness or selfishness. Following this, the therapist can work with individual women to help them develop their own appropriate ways in which to ask others (and particularly other women) for support and nurturance, as well as help them learn appropriate ways to nurture themselves so that their needs do not become overwhelming to others. Then, when support is not forthcoming from the environment, as it often is not for women, they can provide it for themselves.

Finally, the overall role model of the therapist as a competent—yet human, and thus fallible—woman will teach group members that assertiveness and independence do not preclude asking others for help and that, in fact, it can be a strength to trust others enough to ask for their help. The therapy group can provide a forum not only for women to practice these nurturing skills but also an experience of support, trust, and nurturance among women.

The feminist therapist also serves as a model of an androgynous woman working toward full actualization of her potentials. The candor advocated by Wyckoff and others gives women an example of how one woman deals with her own personal growth toward optimal functioning and balancing of the complex combination of roles that modern women face. She also models for group members specific personal qualities such as assertiveness, self-confidence, competence, warmth, honesty, and emotional responsiveness. By taking the role of model-setting participant, the therapist provides both a model of a woman in a leadership role and a model of a group member who is cooperative rather than competitive. Such a mode of interacting makes it possible for (and, in fact, almost requires) group members to at times assume the leadership role themselves. The social activism desired of feminist therapists also provides a model for group members of a woman who takes an active role in the community and in changing social institutions oppressive to women. This provides for them a model of women as active, assertive, and effecting change.

The final function of the feminist therapist is to act as an advocate for her clients. This may entail raising objections to discriminatory practices such as including "sexual promiscuity" as a symptom of psychiatric disturbance for women but not for men, or protesting against demeaning remarks about women in professional meetings. Carter (1977) discusses specific ways in which she acted as an advocate for a female client by sharing the contents of confidential reports from the client's previous therapist, sharing the results of personality testing (and, in fact, giving her a copy of her MMPI profile), and discussing openly the client's dissatisfaction with her previous treatment. What this amounts to, then, is that the feminist therapist always functions to serve the client and to help her reach her goals, rather than to serve some third party whose goals may not correspond to those of the client or even to her best interests.

Krause (1969) discusses several different types of people who may have an interest in a given therapy situation and its outcome. In addition to the therapist and the person receiving the therapy (the patient), he mentions persons whose complaints will be remedied by the therapy (the clients) and persons whose planning and material support are responsible for the provision of the therapy (the sponsors). He points out that, although in some cases these are all the same person, such as the affluent self-referral for psychotherapy, in other cases they may all be different people. For example, take the case of the husband (the client) who commits his wife (the patient) to a state mental hospital (the sponsor). Krause points out that the therapists who actually deliver the therapeutic services are almost always selling their services as means to someone else's ends, as well as applying their own professional norms concerning means and ends. Therefore, he says, as responsible vendors, they should subscribe to the values of their sponsors; as honest contractors, to the values of their clients; and as humanitarians, to the values of their patients. In a situation where these are not all the same person, the feminist therapist will *always* place the interests of the "patient" first.

The Therapist-Client Relationship

Every school of psychotherapy makes assumptions about the nature of the relationship between therapist and client. Virtually every writer on feminist therapy mentions the egalitarian relationship between therapist and client as a hallmark of feminist therapy. This emphasis is based on a view of therapy as a consumer service and on concern about the unilateral control exercised by the therapist in traditional psychotherapy models.

To combat the latter, Rawlings and Carter (1977) suggest the adoption of Argyris' (1975) model of reciprocal influence as a model for therapy. They outline the essential points of this model, which seem to form a body of assumptions about how therapy should be conducted. These points are translated into this form and summarized as follows:

1. Goals and values should be clearly and precisely articulated.
2. The therapist should invite confrontation of her views.
3. Each person should make the maximum possible contribution to the group, in order to assure the widest possible exploration of views.
4. Power should be shared with anyone who has competence and who is relevant in deciding or implementing the action.
5. The therapist should not make decisions for clients.
6. The therapist should avoid competition or the use of "one-upmanship" ploys with clients.
7. If new concepts are created, the meaning given them by the creator and the inference processes used to develop them are open to scrutiny by those expected to use them.
8. Evaluations and attributions should be minimized.
9. If evaluations and attributions are used, they should be coupled with the observable behavior that led to their formulation.
10. If evaluations and attributions are used, they should be presented in such a way as to encourage open and constructive confrontation.

It is assumed that adoption of this model for the conduct of therapy would serve to equalize power between client and therapist. This has several specific implications for the nature of the relationship between therapist and client, including responsibilities and powers of each party. In viewing therapy as a consumer service, it is assumed that the client has both the power and the responsibility to "shop" for a therapist as she would for any other service. The therapist, in turn, must assume responsibility for being willing to reveal personal and professional values that relate to the therapy situation and to her philosophy of treatment. The client is also responsible for participating in setting goals for treatment; to facilitate this process and articulate goals clearly, many feminist therapists use verbal contracts that specify the content, length of the therapy, fees, and, at times, behavioral or attitudinal goals to be achieved. As a consumer, the client is also responsible for assisting in evaluating treatment outcomes and, to this end, the feminist therapist often solicits feedback from the client about the progress and efficacy of the therapy.

To counteract the traditionally greater power of the therapist in psychotherapy, feminist therapists eschew the use of expert, coercive, and legitimate power in favor of reliance on reward and informational and referent power (see Seidler-Feller, 1976). This means that they do not use diagnostic labels or patronizing jargon and that they ask questions instead of making interpretations. They do not presume to tell the client about herself, diagnose her, or "prescribe" treatment. It is assumed that the therapist's opinions do not have any greater weight than those of the client. In turn, the client is responsible for being the "expert" on her wants and feelings and for accurately reporting them to the therapist.

Feminist therapists also advocate sharing their skills with their clients, in essence teaching them what they know so that they will have the tools to be their own therapists. Women in Transition (1975) emphasize that the therapist should be willing to share her skills rather than trying to impress the client with them. Wyckoff (1977) says,

> The goal is not to build dependency relationships or admiration for the facilitator's skills but rather to work on a constant transfer of power and expertise in the process of self-transformation. In return, the client must be willing to take responsibility for making her own decisions regarding what direction the therapy will take and for doing her own problem solving with the therapist's guidance rather than looking to the therapist to give her "answers." (p. 394)

There are several benefits that may be assumed to result from this type of egalitarian approach. Most obviously, it is assumed that through this approach the therapist and client will share equal control of the therapy process. It is assumed that the artificial dependencies often created by therapy will thereby be avoided, as well as the problems of resistance" and transference, which occupy much therapeutic time in traditional models. Lerman (1974) says, "If the therapist is a real person . . . and is consonant with humanist principles, there is little room for transference and it becomes an irrelevant concept. If the client is competent and knows her own wishes, that essentially disposes of the concept of resistance" (p. 11). Instead, it is assumed that a therapy of equals will have a greater generalization of effects to real life than conventional therapy, because it affords the client a chance to learn egalitarian interaction between peers rather than to see human relationships in terms of parent and child, or expert and supplicant. Brodsky (1975), for instance, notes that, "If one goal for these women [clients] is to free them to be adults, capable of acting independently and autonomously, then the therapeutic role permitted of the client by the therapist is important to the corrective experience they need" (p. 6). In contrast, much of traditional psychotherapy hinges on the idea of transference of feelings to the therapist as an authority figure of some type and, therefore, serves as a hierarchal model for relating and perhaps even encourages the client to see all human relationships as hierarchal. In addition, it is assumed that, by fostering an egalitarian relationship between therapist and client, the social control aspects of therapy will be reduced.

■14
Goals of Feminist Therapy

Is the object of the therapeutic intervention to make clients feminists? . . . yes in the sense that what I have said so far is certainly all related to issues of feminist consciousness, by which I mean awareness of the external oppression and the attempt to gain self-definition within it. If that is the sole meaning of feminist, yes, indeed, I want my clients to become feminists. If you mean that they have to shift their life patterns and goals and espouse the specific tenets of feminism, there my answer is no. . . . The goal is to help them become the best person they can be, within the limits of their personal circumstances and the patterns of society in general. If that means they need to become active feminists, fine; if not, fine, too.

Lerman (1974, pp. 9–10)

Goals in psychotherapy are typically nebulous and ill-defined, conceptualized most often as the alleviation of "symptoms" or the acquisition of "insight." Often, there is an implicit assumption that the purpose of psychotherapy is to free the patient of "mental illness," although mental health is seldom clearly defined. In discussing the goals of feminist therapy, it is important to remember that, while feminist ideology has been essential in the development of this philosophy of treatment, conversion of clients to political feminism is not necessarily a goal of feminist therapy.

161

This is verified by Thomas (1975), who found that, for the therapists she interviewed, cultural feminism was more important than political. While some of the therapists she interviewed were politically radical, many were not, and *all* clearly placed a higher priority on meeting the clients' needs and on reaching therapy goals than on reaching political goals. Therapy issues were consistently considered more important than feminist issues and client self-actualization was seen to be as critical a part of feminist therapy as social awareness and social action.

It may seem contradictory in some ways to discuss the "goals" of feminist therapy in light of previous discussions of feminist therapy as dedicated to serving the client's needs and goals. Too often, therapists speak and write about "primary goals" and "mediating goals" of therapy (for example, Mahrer, 1967), with seeming disregard for the values or wishes of the client. If optimal functioning is presumed to be a desirable state for women, however, it seems logical that it also implicitly represents a desired therapy outcome. In addition, the obvious discrepancies between descriptions of this state and the female sex role in our society clearly imply specific changes that feminist therapists value as desirable. Therefore, it seems necessary, as part of the process of making values explicit, to discuss what feminist therapists see as desirable outcomes of therapy and how they evaluate those outcomes in conjunction with their clients.

Optimal Functioning

Applying feminist ideology to determination of treatment goals means rejection of the social conformity goals, adopted by "adjustment" models of mental health, in favor of goals representing personal self-definition and self-determination. According to the feminist/humanist view, the central task of growth is individuation—the process through which an individual actively shapes his/her identity by choosing roles and adapting them to fit personal needs, rather than by passively accepting roles and role definitions and then living them out. Although this means running the risk of being labeled a nonconformist, feminists consider the lack of a sense of self to be worse than suffering the label. Klein (1976) says, "The pain and hazards of this individual struggle may equal the cost of conformity to traditional values . . . but the payoff in terms of human dignity, freedom, and potential for personal meaning is infinitely greater" (p. 94).

Thus, the purpose of feminist therapy might best be described as being to bring women closer to a state of individually defined optimal functioning. This state is described as an optimal mode of relating to self, others, and environment; as including a set of attitudes and behaviors that are a function of personality and situation and through which an individual may further actualization of her human potentials.

Such a model assumes neither perfection nor equanimity. It takes into account the adversity of social realities for women, negative as well as positive emotions, self-doubt, and human imperfection. There is, however, a basic assumption that it is possible for women to make a place for themselves and to develop living skills for surmounting difficulties, as well as learning from them. Within this framework, it is assumed that the optimally functioning woman has access to herself, accepts herself, and works toward androgynous realization of her potentials; that she will find some work outside herself in which to invest much of her energy and which will further her sense of self-identity; that she is capable of having intimate relationships that are characterized by openness and spontaneity and are based on mutuality, rather than need and dependence; and that she has a sense of her community with other women and connection with all humanity.

Criteria for Therapeutic Effectiveness

Within the framework of feminist therapy, there seem to be two criteria for therapeutic effectiveness: change and integration.

Since feminist therapy rejects the adjustment model of mental health, it instead presumes that therapy must effect behavioral, affectual, and attitudinal change. This reflects the influence of radical therapy ideology, which asserts that therapy means change, not adjustment (Agel, 1971). To varying degrees, feminist therapists also adopt the goals of social and political change advocated by radical therapists. Within this framework, however, personal change is always primary and there is a clear and often-stated assumption that this change, whatever its content, should be in the direction of increased autonomy and self-determination. For instance, Barrett, Berg, Eaton, and Pomeroy (1974) state:

> The major goal of therapy should be to facilitate the development of autonomous individuals who are valued in their own right. For many women, this means radically altering the process by which their identity is known, raising their self-esteem, and increasing their ability to function independently. It also means deliberately fostering the freedom to choose and

rechoose alternative life styles, providing education as to consequences and support during crises. (p. 14)

This implies that "insight" and "understanding" are meaningless criteria for therapeutic effectiveness unless they compel the client to some type of observable change.

The second criterion of therapeutic effectiveness is the androgynous integration of personality characteristics. Barrett et al. (1974) state: "The goal of psychotherapy should be to integrate and establish harmony between . . . polarities, not to nurture one as 'female' and one as 'male' " (p. 140).

Block (1973) uses Bakan's (1966) concepts of agency and communion to conceptualize the duality represented by current sex roles and their consequent synthesis. Bakan defines *agency* as being concerned with the organism as an individual, which manifests itself in self-protection, self-assertion, and self-expansion. Culturally, this represents the masculine mode of interacting with the environment. *Communion* is defined as being concerned with the individual organism as it exists in some larger organism of which it is a part and manifests itself in a sense of being at one with other organisms; this is the "feminine" mode.

Bakan (1966) maintains that the fundamental task of the organism is to mitigate agency with communion. Unmitigated agency, he asserts, represents evil, whereas viability—both for the individual and for society—depends on successful integration of agency and communion. This view has been adopted as a general goal of feminist therapy, expressed in the model of the androgynous personality and in a desire for integration of masculine and feminine modes of "being-in-the-world." For women, integration of communion with agency requires that communion—the concern for harmonious functioning of the group, the submersion of self, and the importance of the consensus characteristic—be integrated with agenic qualities of self-assertion, self-expression, and a sense of being centered in one's self.

These goals mean that feminist therapy evaluates the outcome of therapy very differently from traditional therapies and may at times even hold as desirable certain outcomes labeled as negative in traditional therapy. Klein (1976) points out,

There are instances where a "favorable" treatment outcome from a traditional perspective—"What is good for society must be good for the women"—seems unhealthy from the feminist viewpoint. There are other occasions where negative or questionable outcomes from a traditional standpoint are positively valued by the feminist perspective—"What is good for the woman may not always be good for society." (p. 89)

Desired Treatment Outcomes

With these points in mind, let us turn to an examination of the desired treatment outcomes implied by the discrepancies between self-actualization for women and optimal functioning on the one hand, and the constraints of the female sex role on the other. I am indebted to Klein's (1976) excellent discussion of goals of feminist therapy, which provided the outline and much of the material discussed here.

Symptom Removal

One of the widest divergencies between traditional and feminist viewpoints occurs on the issue of the role of "symptoms" of emotional distress in treatment outcome. Klein (1976) maintains that both traditional and feminist views share the ultimate goal of alleviating suffering; however, she stresses that the difference between the two lies in the way pain or distress is interpreted in the first place, and in the recognition that certain kinds of conflict or distress may accompany the steps an individual must take to define a personally satisfying lifestyle and role pattern.

She notes that conceptions equating pain with pathology and equating removal of pain with therapeutic progress will reinforce traditional stereotypes unless they deal with the life circumstances in which symptoms arise. Feminist therapy is concerned, therefore, with the functional significance of pain; pain in response to a bad situation is seen as adaptive, not pathological. Within this framework, pain may at times be seen as healthy or as "growing pain," insofar as it represents an increased awareness of oppressive or constrictive external conditions. For example, anger arising from a greater awareness of sexism may be viewed as a healthy response to oppression. To avoid or remove this discomfort without recognizing and dealing with its social significance is to destroy a potential source of motivation for change. Thus, feminist therapy maintains that working to help a client disperse her anger and alleviate pain globally may be merely a way of adjusting the woman to her situation, rather than of allowing her to grow as a person.

Another example of pain as being functional rather than pathological is that of role conflict. Klein (1976) points out that the traditional view of role conflict has tended to stress acceptance of or adjustment to role demands, assuming that maximizing performance will minimize unhappiness. Feminist therapy, on the other hand, acknowledges the authenticity and legitimacy of this distress and assumes that the therapeutic goal is change in role expectations. By this definition, a reduction in pain is healthy only when accompanied by a change in role definition. Klein concludes that concern with the functional significance of pain (symptoms) will help us to make a meaningful distinction between neurotic and social conflict.

Even when the source of conflict has been defined, feminist therapy does not assume that removal of all conflict is good or even desirable. Jahoda and Havel (1955) point out that, "Women are often written of as though, because they have conflicts, something were radically wrong with them; or that life should be so ordered for them that they would be free of conflict." Since a feminist analysis of society tells us that role conflict and the resultant emotional distress will continue for women until societal changes occur, it seems unrealistic to think that women can or will be completely without conflict, at least not for some time to come. For this reason, feminist therapy assumes that the desirable and realistic treatment outcome for women is not complete freedom from distress but, rather, an increased ability to tolerate and deal effectively with conflict and greater confidence in one's ability to do so. In this light, Jahoda and Havel point out that conflict may be a positive experience in that, as women face conflict and deal with it successfully, they will experience gratification and increased confidence in their abilities.

This view of pain and conflict reflects a dialectic view of the therapy process (Adams and Durham, 1977), which defines the natural state for human beings as one in which the individual is in a constant state of disruption, though not necessarily in pain. This model assumes that it is natural for individuals to be full of contradictions and in a constant process of synthesizing these contradictions into new behaviors and attitudes. Pain, according to this view, is assumed to be caused by the alienation of the individual from this synthesizing process. Attempts to remove all conflict in women in therapy are not only doomed to failure, but alienate the individual from her own constructive processes.

Self-Esteem

Increase in self-esteem is frequently used as a measure of successful therapy outcome. Klein (1976), however, points out that if self-esteem is measured by the number of desirable qualities in the self-image, women are placed at a disadvantage in that there are fewer desirable traits in the traditional female ideal than in the male ideal. She also cites evidence that both the client's ideal image of a woman and a consensual ideal of women are heavily contaminated by sexist stereotypes. Thus, if self-esteem is equated with realization of an idealized self-image based on sex-role stereotypes, then successful therapy outcome is in danger of being defined in terms of increasing sexism. A successful feminist therapy outcome would be more likely to involve reexamination of sex-role stereotypes and redefinition of the "ideal self," rather than redefinition of the individual woman's self-image. For example, a woman might begin to see herself as attractive, regardless of whether or not she measured up to societal standards of "beauty." Or, she might redefine her idealized self-image to include qualities and attributes outside the traditional female role model, so that strength, competence, or self-assurance become part of her concept of an "ideal" woman.

Klein points out that "Women traditionally have been taught and expected to anchor their self-definition and esteem externally, usually in the achievements and expectations of the men in their lives" (p. 91). Thus, the source of women's self-esteem has been largely external and dependent on the evaluation and judgments of others, often to the exclusion of the woman's own judgments and values. Feminist therapy, therefore, assumes that a desirable treatment outcome for women would be represented by a shift from reliance on external sources of self-esteem to more autonomous self-definition. This would mean that self-esteem would be based more on internal processes and evaluations than on external (and usually male) sources of approval. Perlstein (1976) says, "A healthy woman sustains herself, gives some meaning to her own existence, and looks to others for added meaning and support, but not for basic survival . . . because she can fulfill her own needs . . . others merely add to her central core" (pp. 387–388). The content of the self-image is as important as the process by which it is formed. Klein suggests that characterization of the self in terms such as degree of autonomy, openness to realistic appraisal of capabilities and potential, flexibility, freedom from stereotypes, or insulation from negative social evaluations is compatible with feminist philosophy and thus would represent a desirable treatment outcome in feminist therapy.

In addition, the emphasis of feminist therapy on resocialization as a part of the therapy process suggests that changes in the reference group through which a woman obtains validation of her self-image are desirable treatment outcomes. The reference group becomes female, instead of male. Thus, the process by which a woman defines herself is validated by other women's experiences and perceptions, rather than by male perceptions of a woman's role.

Quality of Interpersonal Relationships

Klein (1976) says, "Few would argue with the view that, following successful psychotherapy, patients will show enhanced relationships with others, be warmer, more expressive, facilitative, supportive, and nurturant. The problem from a feminist point of view is that change in these directions may result in too much of a good thing" (p. 91). Since a great deal of women's role and of their self-esteem has traditionally been based on facilitation of harmonious interpersonal relationships, change in these directions may represent simply increased role performance, rather than significant personal change. Klein points out that the personal cost to the woman for functioning in this traditional role is great: "Bearing the responsibility for the harmonious functioning of husband and children, for whose emotional health she is often held accountable, almost inevitably requires a personally painful deference, vigilance, and often acquiescence to others' demands and needs" (p. 91). Thus, greater warmth, support, and nurturance in interpersonal relationships would represent a favorable treatment outcome from a feminist viewpoint only if it were not at the expense of the woman meeting her own needs, and only if the woman were equally supportive and nurturant to herself. In fact, a decrease in these qualities in interpersonal relations could in some cases represent a desirable treatment outcome in feminist therapy if the woman had previously extended them at the expense of her own emotional needs.

Because of this aspect of the traditional female role, feminist therapy views increased assertiveness in women as a desired and, in fact, essential treatment outcome. Klein says, "Having relied on dependent, indirect or manipulative devices to influence others, many women need support, practice, and even direct training in expressing their needs and wishes directly and working assertively . . . for what is important to them" (p. 92). While assertiveness in women is often labeled aggressiveness or dominance by traditional psychotherapists and hence considered an undesirable treatment outcome, feminist therapy assumes that development of these skills is essential to the goal of autonomy and optimal functioning for women. In addition, increased assertiveness serves to equalize personal power in relationships—also assumed to be desirable. Thus, it is assumed that successful feminist therapy will result in a balance of autonomy and interdependence in interpersonal relationships, of nurturing and supporting others while assertively asking for reciprocal emotional support.

Klein (1976) notes that, in the process of growing and expanding her roles, a woman may "severely threaten her marriage and upset the family so that things may look shakiest at the point where the woman has changed most favorably from a feminist point of view" (p. 92). She urges, however, that the conflict generated by this "interpersonal risk taking" not be mistaken for continued pathology or registered as an unsuccessful treatment outcome, as is done in many marital adjustment ratings.

Finally, feminist therapy is concerned with the quality of women's relationships with other women in assessing treatment outcomes. Traditional therapy has generally been more concerned with women's relationships with men than with their relationships with other women. Feminist ideology, however, stresses the importance of women learning to seek nurturance and support from other women; learning to like, trust, and respect other women; and placing equal value on their relationships with other women as on male relationships. As Klein notes, "Coming to terms with one's own gender and developing a workable sex role must take account of woman-woman as well as man-woman relationship patterns" (p. 92). Thus, a desired treatment outcome of feminist therapy, particularly in its resocialization aspects, is that women form bonds with other women, discover their commonalities, and value these relationships as important and mutually supportive.

Role Performance

Competence in work, social, and family roles are important aspects of health in our complex, achievement-oriented society." (Klein, 1976, p. 92). Here, as in other areas, however, traditional measures of therapy outcome are biased in evaluating women's competence. Pointing to ways in which evaluations of occupational ability and role performance have been divided according to sex, Klein concludes that rigid conformity has been both more rewarded and more highly regarded. She notes that men are generally evaluated with regard to their occupational roles, while women are judged in housewifely and parental functions. Frequently, homemaker roles are unrealistically equated with occupational roles and judged by inappropriate criteria, such as "dissatisfaction with household tasks." This represents one type of bias in this area; however, Klein also warns against the opposite, that of assuming that working per se is equal to "liberation" for women. She warns that, "working is not automatically evidence of progress in personal growth for a woman, especially if her position is in a secondary or dead-end status, or (simply) an extension of previous dependent domestic functioning (1976, p. 93). She advises evaluating therapeutic effectiveness in this area by process criteria: the way an individual has chosen and defined roles; whether they have been freely chosen or prescribed by tradition; how role conflicts are resolved; and how well roles are integrated into the self.

Target Problems and Problem Solving

Using the extent to which target problems are resolved as a measure of therapeutic success also requires certain qualifications in the cases of female patients. First, concern with problem resolution alone may ignore the functional aspects of the problem, as has been discussed with regard to symptom removal. Klein (1976) notes that, since women have traditionally been responsible for the happiness of the family unit, "many women seek treatment for problems that they perceive as their own but that actually involve the whole family and which cannot be solved by the woman alone" (p. 93). In addition, she cautions against using the number of problems resolved as criteria for treatment outcome, unless a distinction is made between soluble and insoluble problems. Many problems presented by women are intertwined with their social and economic position in society and thus cannot be resolved in therapy.

Clarification of target problems may in itself represent a treatment goal. Once clarified, they can be subjected to problem-solving techniques. Klein stresses choice and decision making as important steps in personal growth; these should show change in any patient at the resolution of successful therapy. Since women traditionally have been viewed as indecisive and reliant upon others (men) for advice and guidance, many women have internalized this view of themselves and have little confidence in their abilities to solve problems or make decisions. She concludes, therefore, that one of the most important gains a woman may make in feminist therapy is learning to trust her own decision-making and problem-solving skills and to give up accepting others' decisions.

Body Image and Sensuality

As previously noted, female socialization results in women having extremely ambivalent feelings about their bodies. On the one hand, young girls growing up are taught that women are weak, sick, and unclean, especially in relation to menstruation. On the other hand, society places great stress on external attractiveness for women, with the current image of the "glamor girl" consistently receiving approval. Therefore, Klein suggests that an important therapeutic change in feminist therapy is represented by the resolution of this conflict, with the client coming to terms with her own body and liking herself as she is, regardless of whether she measures up to the stereotyped image. Other feminist therapists stress as a therapeutic goal women increasing their physical coordination and body awareness, in order to become more "centered."

The extent to which a woman knows and accepts her body and takes responsibility for knowing and managing both her sexual and reproductive processes is also a criterion for successful treatment. Here, as elsewhere, feminist therapy stresses the importance of women taking charge of their own lives, including fulfillment of their sexual and sensual needs, instead of relying on men for fulfillment. The right and ability to be orgasmic is seen as a legitimate therapeutic goal for women and, to this end, special programs have been developed to help women get in touch with their sexuality and take charge of their sexual selves (Barbach, 1975).

Political Awareness and Social Action

All of the treatment outcomes discussed thus far represent the application of feminist ideology to what are essentially traditional and conventional areas of therapeutic goals. Feminist therapy is unique, however, in its emphasis on political awareness and social action as desirable and necessary treatment goals, and it is in this respect that feminist therapy most clearly shows its alliance with the women's movement in general and with consciousness raising in particular.

If society is partially to blame for inducing psychopathology, alteration of society becomes a legitimate and necessary treatment goal. Feminist therapy is based in large part on the feminist assertion that, insofar as women's problems are generated by a sexist society, there are no individual solutions for women. Therefore, feminist therapy, like consciousness-raising groups, stresses the importance of social action measures, that is, cooperative, group solutions to what appear to be individual problems.

Jessor (1956) has suggested that social change should be a major goal of psychotherapy. He points out that, whereas psychotherapy usually focuses on intrapsychic goals and social conformity goals, " . . . much personal conflict is due to objective conflicts, contradictions, and shortcomings in the socioeconomic organization in which the patient lives. Therapy, then, ought to influence the patient to work toward the elimination of objective social conflicts or toward cultural reorganization, in order to escape his own personal conflicts" (p. 102). Feminist therapy, however, also stresses the importance of social change as being necessary not only to alleviate individual suffering but to change the social conditions that generate distress, conflict, and pain for all women. This seems to represent what Jessor calls a "broad social philosophy" that includes cooperative work for the benefit of the whole group or society.

While it is true that each individual woman must define for herself how she can contribute to society and how she can participate in alleviating injustices that affect all women, there is an implicit assumption that some sort of action is necessary and expected as a treatment goal. There seems to be an assumption by feminist therapy that, although social conditions may be dealt with in one's own way and according to one's own priorities, they must not be ignored, and action must be taken. Thus, a sense of community with female humanity results in social action that involves cooperative rather than competitive efforts and generates new and viable patterns of behavior and relating.

Evaluating Treatment Outcome

The areas just discussed represent developments that feminist therapy considers to be desirable as treatment outcomes, yet, within an egalitarian model, true treatment effectiveness can only be evaluated in conjunction with the client; it is, after all, the client's goals that feminist therapy seeks to serve. Therefore, the process of evaluating treatment outcome is a cooperative one between therapist and client, not a unilateral one.

Listed below are questions developed by Klein (1976) to be used conjointly by the feminist therapist and her client in assessing treatment outcome; they might also be used to advantage, in the initial stages of therapy, to identify problem areas and set goals for treatment. The value system of feminist therapy, its image of women, and its hopes for its clients are clearly reflected in these questions:

1. What is the connection between the client's pain, her symptoms, and her life situation? Is she reacting to role conflicts or frustrating, unsatisfying roles?

2. Are some of her pains "growing pains," resulting from decisions to change her life, break out of old patterns, and take risks?

3. Is her self-esteem dependent on others' evaluations and reactions, or based on her own judgments and values?

4. Are her ideals and role choices influenced by traditional sexist stereotypes?

5. Does her interpersonal style allow a full range of behavior, including direct expression of anger and power needs and a balance between autonomy and interdependence? Does she need to please others all the time, or can she challenge and confront them as well?

6. Can she relate to both sexes as people? Does she feel good about herself and other women and draw support from women's shared experiences?

7. Is her role pattern her own free choice and personal blend, responsive to her needs, including her need for competence and recognition?

8. Does she use and trust her own decision-making and problem-solving skills? Can she decide which problems are soluble and which are not?

9. Does she accept and like her body, enjoy her sensuality, and take responsibility for knowing and managing her sexual and reproductive life?

In the final analysis, the goals of feminist therapy may not appear to be all that different from the espoused goals of traditional psychotherapy. What is radical about feminist therapy is that it insists that these goals be extended to women as readily as they are to men. It recognizes the particular difficulties women face in attaining these goals and takes them into account in formulating treatment techniques. This position has profound implications, not only for psychotherapy as a profession, but for the whole structure of female-male relationships in our society.

■ four
CONCLUSIONS

█ 15
The Impact of Feminist Therapy

The philosophy of treatment presented here is based on a political, sociological, and psychological analysis of women's position in our society. Politically, women have, until the last fifty years, been disenfranchised and, until recently, were openly barred from holding positions of power in the political and economic structure of American society. Feminists hold that this discrimination still occurs, both overtly and covertly. A sociological analysis of women's position reveals that women have been socialized differently than men and have been reinforced for behaviors and attitudes that maintain the patriarchal structure of society. Our culture has glamorized and mythologized acceptable female roles in order to encourage women to follow these roles, and has imposed harsh economic and social sanctions against adoption of nontraditional or "unacceptable" roles by women. On a psychological level, women have internalized dominant (sexist) beliefs and attitudes about themselves and their roles and have adopted characteristic modes of feeling and interacting with others that support the roles assigned to them by society as a means of emotional and economic survival. These internalized beliefs and attitudes serve to maintain the sexist status quo.

This book represents an integration of these analyses with the structures and conceptual dimensions of traditional psychotherapy, in order

177

to create a feminist model for the treatment of psychological disturbance in women. Although it is clearly related to both philosophy and sociology, its focus is always on the definition of a treatment model of clinical psychology. Because of the heterogeneous sources from which this model was developed, it is expected to have impact on diverse areas of our society. The most important, however, will obviously be the two areas from which it draws most heavily: the feminist movement and the profession of psychotherapy.

Impact on the Feminist Movement

This conceptualization of treatment for women is expected to further the goals of the larger feminist movement by facilitating change in the internalized psychological oppression of women and by increasing personal understanding in individual women of the effects of sexist social programming.

In addition, it integrates feminist ideology (particularly the tenet that the "personal is political") and practices (from consciousness-raising groups) into an important professional area, one that has vast potential for helping women to reshape their lives. It goes beyond the rhetoric of feminist ideology to give a comprehensive conceptualization of feminist therapy, thus furthering the process of "legitimization" that must occur in order for feminist therapy to be given credence by mental-health professionals. It also expands the feminist movement to attract and include an important group of professional women who previously have not been active in the movement. It is hoped that, by articulating a feminist philosophy of treatment within the familiar framework of traditional dimensions of psychotherapy, female psychologists will be led to discover previously unrecognized (or unlabeled) feminist sympathies and to rethink their approach to treating women.

Impact on the Psychotherapy Profession

Every model of human nature contains two explanatory models of human personality. On the one hand, it implies a desired constellation of personality traits that is presumed to occur in the course of normal human development. This results in a growth model of counseling that focuses on personal discovery and development. On the other hand, it also holds implications for how psychopathology occurs when things go wrong developmentally, with a resultant remediation model of psychotherapy.

The revised image of women developed by feminist therapy affects both of these models of treatment. It offers an alternative explanation, via sex-role and sociocultural conditioning, of why things may go wrong for women developmentally, with corresponding implications for the interpretation of psychopathology. In addition, it offers a much wider range of possible growth for women and defines some new ways in which therapy can help women grow and develop themselves as people.

For those who do not agree with this feminist conceptualization of treatment, it invites reexamination of some of their cherished beliefs about crucial aspects of the treatment process. For example, what do we, as therapists, believe about the capacities and limitations of women? Is there a bias against women in one's favorite theoretical position? What is the role of the therapist vis-à-vis the client? Must the therapist always be in control of the therapeutic relationship? Does psychotherapy facilitate change in women, or does it simply "adjust" them to their social roles? What are the political and social implications of psychotherapy for women? These questions challenge therapists to examine their own socially programmed sexist biases and how these biases affect their treatment of female clients.

By expanding the focus of psychotherapy to include the social context of human behavior, feminist therapy forges a conceptualization of therapy-as-process, in which the philosophy, theory, and techniques of treatment are constantly being influenced by the culture, as well as constantly changing to meet the needs and demands of the social milieu. This challenges the implicit assumption underlying most psychotherapy that there is an immutable body of truth about human nature and behavior which, once known, may be universally applied in treating psychological distress in all people. There are in fact few, if any, "truths" about human personality and behavior. Rather, there are conceptualizations of human nature that are either useful or not useful in explaining why people think, feel, and behave as they do.

For example, Freud lived in a Victorian culture epitomized by sexual repression. Recognizing that a crucially important part of human nature was thus being culturally denied, he found that adopting a conceptualization of people as sexual beings actually did explain more of human life than the Victorian conceptualization. Freud's conceptualization in turn shaped cultural views of what people were like. As his views gradually came to be accepted and integrated into the culture, new conceptualizations began to form. Once the sexual nature of human beings and the phenomenon of unconscious motivation were accepted, a new image of human nature evolved as the neo-Freudians emphasized the importance of ego functioning and the development of autonomy.

I could list many other examples of the dialectic process between culture and schools of psychotherapy in the development of conceptual explanations of what people are like. The central point here, however, is this: feminist therapy has grown from an awareness that the old conceptualizations about women inherent in traditional models of therapy are no longer useful for explaining women's thoughts, feelings, and behavior. For this reason, feminist therapy has developed new conceptualizations that are based directly on women's experience of life, rather than on men's ideas of what women are like. These views seem to describe more accurately the nature of modern women in American society and to be more useful in explaining their feelings and behavior. These conceptualizations should be used as long as they remain useful, but we must recognize that, in time, they, too, may become outmoded as cultural images of women change.

Feminist therapy also refines previous criticisms of psychotherapy as being a means of social control. It defines the particular ways in which women are controlled and restricted by traditional psychotherapy and offers an alternative model of therapy in which client and therapist work in partnership to achieve the client's goals. In this respect, feminist therapy also represents an extension of the recent trend of consumerism into the realm of therapy.

The philosophy of treatment outlined here clearly implies recommendations for the treatment of women in therapy, regardless of the therapist's theoretical stance. The broader view of psychological distress outlined here, in which social as well as individual factors are recognized, suggests that therapists should first consider the possibility that female clients' problems may be due to role conflict or to social factors such as sexual discrimination, economic oppression, and so forth. They should not automatically assume individual psychopathology to be the sole source of emotional distress. This, in turn, stresses the necessity for therapists to be educated on women's issues, not only current social and political issues arising from the women's movement, but also recent research on sex roles, female psychology, and female development. The therapist should actively encourage the female client to examine the female role and to be honest with herself in selecting those aspects of it that suit her needs and in rejecting those that do not.

This model of treatment also stresses the necessity for increased awareness of how values and attitudes operate in the therapy setting and on the therapist's awareness of his/her own values regarding women. The philosophy presented here is firm in its insistence that the sexual and emotional exploitation of female clients by male therapists must stop. Remembering the research on nonverbal communication of values and attitudes in therapy, as well as the feminist emphasis on women's need for strong female role models and the phenomenon of female passivity in the presence of males, male clinicians should be candid in discussing with themselves whether they can offer the most effective treatment to female clients.

The feminist emphasis on women learning to be supportive and caring toward one another implies the superiority of all-female therapy groups for women. In addition, it implies that, if women are seen in mixed-sex groups, support and noncompetitiveness among the women in the group should be openly encouraged and facilitated by the therapist. Competition among the women in the group for attention from male group members should be openly confronted and discouraged. This model of treatment also suggests that the therapist should become aware of community resources for women and make referrals to women's centers, consciousness-raising groups, and action organizations such as NOW, WEAL, and others, when appropriate.

Perhaps one of the clearest and most important recommendations that might be made from this framework is the necessity for accepting women's anger as appropriate and necessary to their psychological growth. This means that the female therapist must have worked through her own anger and the male therapist must have worked through his guilt and fear of retaliation, in order for either of them to be able to effectively facilitate female clients in expressing and moving through their own anger.

This model also recommends assertiveness training as essential for female clients, regardless of the therapist's theoretical orientation. At the same time, the therapist should be aware of the social and political realities for women and has a duty to give women a realistic view of the external barriers that they may face in achieving their goals.

A final recommendation deals with the relationship between therapist and client: it should be an egalitarian relationship and may include open contractual agreement about the various parameters of the therapy. It must reflect an orientation toward achieving the client's goals, rather than the therapist's.

■16
New Directions

Feminist views of the treatment of emotional and psychological distress point to several new avenues for research, as well as to needed innovations in research methodology in feminist therapy.

The most obvious direction suggested by any philosophical or theoretical study such as this is testing for consensual validation. In this case, this would mean surveying feminist therapists regarding their degree of agreement or disagreement with the philosophy of treatment presented here. Although Thomas (1975) and Poverny (1976) have done some work in this area, they surveyed only attitudes and practices, without offering a conceptual framework in which to place them. It seems necessary, therefore, to obtain some degree of agreement among feminist therapists regarding this conceptual framework, before further theoretical developments can take place.

A central assumption of feminist therapy is that cultural factors play an important part in the etiology of psychological distress in women, so it seems crucial that research be devised to factor out how much of women's psychological distress is due to cultural programming and how much due to intrapsychic factors. Research should also examine the interaction between these factors and might further define the concept of resocialization as a part of the change process in therapy; it could test the correlation between successful resocialization and treatment outcome.

A central question in looking at any type of therapy is, of course,

182

does it do what it purports to do? This suggests further directions for research in feminist therapy that might be conducted through a predictive-outcome study, in which predictions regarding treatment outcome would be made from the philosophy of treatment presented here and pre- and post-tests administered to gauge the accuracy of the predictions. Specific predictions suggested by this model might include increased assertiveness, increased agreement with feminist ideology, more positive female identification, increased self-confidence, increased androgyny and/or role defiancy, increased problem-solving ability, and increased political awareness.

Another area is the emphasis placed by this model on the effect of attitudes and values in therapy. This strongly points to the need for further research on the verbal and nonverbal transmission of attitudes and values in all types of therapy, as well as their influence on the process and outcome of therapy.

There is a need for innovations in research methodology in studying feminist therapy. The whole issue of researcher bias, feminists' observed reluctance to be studied by nonfeminists (Thomas, 1975), and feminist ideology itself all suggest that feminist therapy should be studied by feminist researchers. Stricker (1977) suggests that, "If one wished to discover how females are treated in psychotherapy, the methodology of choice would be to observe the therapy, describe it in a systematic way, and then draw conclusions" (p. 14). The consumerism expressed in the feminist philosophy of treatment, however, suggests the need to involve the client/consumers of feminist therapy in evaluating and describing their own treatment in feminist therapy—as in Dorothy Tennov's (1975) cocounseling model.

The whole question of how philosophy of treatment affects the treatment process, as well as the specific concepts presented in this model, point to the need to go beyond traditional psychological instrumentation in studying feminist therapy. Additional tools and/or new instruments are necessary in order to study the broadened conception of therapy presented by this model, which includes social and cultural factors as well as intrapsychic ones. For instance, the description of the goals of feminist therapy presented here suggests that many of the constructs traditionally used to measure treatment outcome (such as self-esteem, role performance, and symptom removal) need to be redefined for women and new instruments need to be designed to measure these constructs. In general, it appears that sociological or anthropological methods might be more appropriate than traditional psychological methods and instrumentation for examining the content, process, and outcome of feminist therapy.

REFERENCES

References

Abramowitz, Stephen; and Abramowitz, Christine. 1973. "The politics of clinical judgment: What nonliberal examiners infer about women who do not stifle themselves." *Journal of Consulting & Clinical Psychology, 41* (3): 385–391.

Adams, Harold; and Durham, Leona. 1977. "A dialectical base for an activity approach to counseling." In Edna Rawlings and Dianne Carter, eds., *Psychotherapy for Women*, pp.411–428. Springfield, Ill. Charles C Thomas.

Adams, Margaret. Nov. 1971. "The compassion trap—Women only." *Psychology Today:* 71–72 & 100–103.

Agel, Jerome, ed. 1971. *The Radical Therapist*. New York: Ballantine Books.

Albin, Rochelle. 1976. "Depression in women: A feminist perspective." *APA Monitor, 7:* 9–10 & 27.

Alexander, Franz; and Selesnick, Sheldon. 1966. *The History of Psychiatry*. New York: Harper & Row.

Allport, Gordon. 1954. *The Nature of Prejudice*. Garden City, N.Y.: Doubleday.

Angrist, Shirley; Dinitz, Simon; Lefton, Mark; and Pasamanick, Benjamin. 1961. "Rehospitalization of female mental patients." *Archives of General Psychiatry, 4:* 363–370.

Angrist, Shirley; Dinitz, Simon; Lefton, Mark; and Pasamanick, Benjamin. 1968. *Women After Treatment*. New York: Appleton-Century-Crofts.

Anthony, Nicole. 1970. "Open letter to psychiatrists." *Radical Therapist, 1:* 8.

APA Task Force on Sex Bias and Sex Role Stereotyping in Psychotherapeutic Practice. 1975. "Report of the task force on sex bias and sex role stereotyping in psychotherapeutic practice." *American Psychologist, 30* (12): 1169–1175.

April. Sept. 1972. "Covert sexual discrimination against women in psychological contexts: As clients." Paper presented at American Psychological Association Convention, Honolulu, Ha.

Argyris, Chris. 1975. "Dangers in applying results from experimental social psychology." *American Psychologist, 30*: 469.

Aslin, Alice. 1977. "Feminist and community mental health center psychotherapists' expectations of mental health for women." *Sex Roles: A Journal of Research, 3* (6): 537–544.

Bakan, D. 1966. *The Duality of Human Existence*. Chicago: Rand McNally.

Barbach, Lonnie. 1975. *For Yourself*. Garden City, N.Y.: Doubleday.

Barrett, Carol; Berg, Pamela; Eaton, Elaine; and Pomeroy, Lisa. 1974. "Implications of women's liberation and the future of psychotherapy." *Psychotherapy: Theory, Research and Practice, 11* (1): 11–15.

Bart, Pauline. 1971. " The myth of a value free psychotherapy". In Wendell Bell and James Mav, eds., *Sociology and the Future*. New York: Russell Sage Foundation.

Bart, Pauline. 1975. "Unalienating abortion, demystifying depression, and restoring rape victims." Paper presented at American Psychiatric Association meeting, Anaheim, Calif.

Baruch, Grace; and Barnett, Rosalind. 1975. "Implications and applications of recent research on feminine development." *Psychiatry, 38* (4): 318–327.

Barwick, Judity. 1971. *Psychology of Women: A Study of Bio-cultural Conflicts*. New York: Harper & Row.

Becker, Ernest. 1968. *The Structure of Evil*. New York: George Braziller.

Belote, Betsy. 1976. "Masochistic syndrome, hysterical personality, and the illusion of a healthy women." In Sue Cox, ed., *Female Psychology: The Emerging Self*, pp. 335–348. Palo Alto: Science Research Associates.

Bem, Sandra. 1975. "Sex role adaptability: One consequence of psychological androgyny." *Journal of Personality and Social Psychology, 31* (4): 634–643.

Benston, Margaret. Sept. 1969. "The political economy of women's lib." *Monthly Review, 21* (5): 3–4.

Bernard, Jessie. Sept. 1976a. "Sex role is major factor in depression of women." *Behavior Today*, p. 7.

Bernard, Jessie. 1976b "Homosociality and female depression." *Journal of Social Issues, 32* (4): 213–238.

Bernardez-Bonesatti, Teresa. 1974. "Feminist and non-feminist outpatients compared." Paper presented at American Psychiatric Association meeting, May 7, Detroit, Mich.

Bernardez-Bonesatti, Teresa. 1975a. "Therapeutic groups for women: Rationale, indications, and outcome." Paper presented at American Group Psychotherapy Association meeting, February, San Antonio, Tex.

Bernardez-Bonesatti, Teresa. 1975b. "Psychotherapists' biases towards women: Overt manifestations and unconscious determinants." Paper presented at the American Psychiatric Association meeting, May, Anaheim, Calif.

Bettelheim, Bruno. 1965. "The commitment required of a woman entering a scientific profession in present day American society". *Woman and the Scientific Professions*. Paper presented at the MIT Symposium on American Women in Science and Engineering.

Block, Jeanne. 1973. "Conceptions of sex role: Some cross-cultural and longitudinal perspectives". *American Psychologist, 28* (6): 512–526.

Bonetti, Deborah; Hai, Sandra; Perl, Harriet; and Wagner, Jane. 1974. *CR Handbook*. Los Angeles: Los Angeles NOW Consciousness Raising Committee.

Brodsky, Annette. March 1975. "Is there a feminist therapy?" American Psychological Association symposium on "Issues in Feminist Therapy." Presented at Southeastern Psychological Association, Atlanta, Ga.

Broverman, I.K.; Broverman, D.M.; and Clarkson, F.E. 1970. "Sex role stereotypes and clinical judgment of mental health." *Journal of Consulting and Clinical Psychology, 34* (1): 1–7.

Carter, Dianne. 1977. "Counseling divorced women." *Personnel and Guidance Journal, 55* (9): 537–541.

Cheek, F. 1964. "A serendipitious finding: Sex role and schizophrenia." *Journal of Abnormal and Social Psychology, 69*: 392–400.

Chesler, Phyllis. 1972. *Women and Madness*. Garden City, N.Y.: Doubleday.

Chessick, Richard. 1969. *How Psychotherapy Heals*. New York: Science House.

Childs, E.K.; Sachnoff, E.A.; and Stocker, E.S. 1976. "Women's sexuality: A feminist view." In Sue Cox, ed., *Female Psychology: The Emerging Self*, pp.309–313. Palo Alto: Science Research Associates.

Chodorow, Nancy. 1971. "Being and doing: A cross-cultural examination of the socialization of males and females." In V. Gornick, and B. Moran, eds., *Women in a Sexist Society*, pp. 259–291. New York: Basic Books.

Cox, Sue, ed. 1976. *Female Psychology: The Emerging Self*. Palo Alto: Science Research Associates.

David, Sara. 1975a. "Emotional self-defense groups for women." In Dorothy Smith and Sara David, eds., *Women Look at Psychiatry*, pp. 173–181. Vancouver, B.C.: Press Gang Publishers.

David, Sara. 1975b. "Becoming a non-sexist therapist." In Dorothy Smith and Sara David, eds., *Women Look at Psychiatry*, pp. 165–174. Vancouver, B.C.: Press Gang Publishers.

de Beauvoir, Simone. 1961. *The Second Sex*. New York: Bantam Books.

Dejanikus, Tacie; and Pollner, Fran. 1974. "Feminist counseling." *Rough Times: A Journal of Radical Therapy, 4*: 10–12.

Diaz-Guerrero, Rogelio. 1967. "Socio-cultural premises, attitudes and cross-cultural research." *International Journal of Psychology, 2*: 79–87.

Dixon, Marlene. Dec. 1969. "Why women's liberation?" *Ramparts*, 58–63.

Dreifus, Claudia. 1973. *Woman's Fate*. New York: Bantam Books.

Earnhart, Beth. 1976. "A conceptual framework for the process of feminist therapy." Unpublished working paper, July 13.

Eastman, Paula. 1973. "Consciousness-raising as a re-socialization process for women." *Smith College Studies in Social Work, 43* (3): 153–183.

Edwards, Gwenyth; Cohen, Dale; and Zarrow, Marla. 1975. "Feminist therapy conference, 1975." *Rough Times: A Journal of Radical Therapy, 4* (7): 18–19.

el Sendiony, M.D. 1975. "The status of Egyptian women and psychoneurotic symptoms." *International Mental Health Newsletter, 17* (3): 14–16.

Endler, Norman; and Magnusson, David. 1976. "Toward an interactional psychology of personality." *Psychological Bulletin, 83* (5): 956–974.

Erikson, Erik. 1973. "Inner and outer space: Reflections on womanhood." In Stephen Berg and S.J. Marks, eds., *About Women*, pp. 127–145. Greenwich, Conn.: Fawcett Publications.

Fabrikant, Benjamin. 1974. "The psychotherapist and the female patient: Perceptions, misperceptions and change." In Violet Franks and Vasanti Burtle, eds., *Women in Therapy*, pp. 83–110. New York: Brunner/Mazel.

Ferson, Jean. 1973. "The feminist therapy collective of Philadelphia." Unpublished manuscript.

Fields, Rona. 1972. "Psychotherapy: The sexist machine." Pittsburgh: Know.

Fine, Reuben. 1974. "Psychoanalysis as a philosophical system." *Journal of Contemporary Psychotherapy, 6* (2): 103–107.

Firestone, Shulamith. 1970. *The Dialectic of Sex: The case for Feminist Revolution*. New York: William Morris.

Frank, Jerome. 1975. *Persuasion and Healing: A Comparative Study of Psychotherapy*. New York: Schocken Books.

Freeman, Jo. 1971. "The women's liberation movement: Its origins, structures, and ideas." Pittsburgh: Know.

French, J.R.; and Raven, B.H. 1959. "The bases of social power." In D. Cartwright, ed., *Studies in Social Power*. Ann Arbor, Mich.: Institute for Social Research.

Friedan, Betty. 1963. *The Feminine Mystique*. New York: Dell.

Gardner, Jo-Ann. 1971. "Sexist counseling must stop." *Personnel and Guidance Journal, 49* (9): 705–713.

Gluckstern, Norma. 1977. "Beyond therapy: Personal and institutional change." In Edna Rawlings and Dianne Carter, eds., *Psychotherapy for Women*, pp. 429–444. Charles C Thomas.

Gordon, Suzanne. 1976. "What's come over the women's movement?" *Mother Jones, I* (4): 27.

Gornick, Vivian. 1972. "Woman as outsider." In Vivian Gornick and Barbara Moran, eds. *Woman in Sexist Society,* pp. 126–144. New York: New American Library.

Gornick, Vivian; and Moran, Barbara, eds. 1972. *Woman in Sexist Society,* New York: The New American Library.

Gove, Walter. 1972. "The relationship between sex roles, marital status and mental illness." *Social Forces, 51* (1): 34–44.

Gove, Walter; and Tudor, Jeanette. 1973. "Adult sex roles and mental illness." In Joan Huber, ed., *Changing Women in a Changing Society,* pp. 50–73. Chicago: University of Chicago Press.

Greenspan, Miriam. Feb. 1976. "Psychotherapy and women's liberation." Paper presented at the First Annual Conference on Feminist Therapy, Boulder, Colo.

Greer, S.; and Morris, T. 1975. "Psychological attributes of women who develop breast cancer: A controlled study." *Journal of Psychosomatic Research, 19* (2): 147–153.

Grinker, Roy. 1957. *Toward a Unified Theory of Human Behavior.* New York: Basic Books.

Gump, Janice. 1972. "Sex role attitudes and psychological well-being." *Journal of Social Issues, 28* (2): 79–91.

Hacker, Helen. 1976. "Women as a minority group." In Sue Cox, ed., *Female Psychology: The Emerging Self,* pp. 156–170. Palo Alto: Science Research Associates.

Halleck, Seymour. 1971. *The Politics of Therapy.* New York: Science House.

Hammer, E. 1964. "Creativity and feminine ingredients in young male artists." *Perceptual and Motor Skills, 19:* 414.

Hare-Mustin, Rachel. 1976. "Women's experience: The half-known life." *Voices, 12* (3): 4–5.

Harlow, H. F. 1958. "The nature of love." *American Psychologist, 13:* 673–685.

Harrison, Barbara Grizzuti. 1974. "Is romance dead?" *Ms., III* (1): 39–43 & 95.

Heide, Wilma Scott. 1969. "The reality and challenge of the double standard in mental health and society." Pittsburgh: Know.

Helson, Ravenna. 1966. "Personality of women with imaginative and artistic interests; the role of masculinity, originality and other characteristics in their creativity." *Journal of Personality, 34:* 1.

Henley, Nancy. 1970. "The politics of touch." Pittsburgh: Know.

Horney, Karen. 1963. "The problem of feminine masochism." In Jean Baker

Miller, ed., *Psychoanalysis and Women*, pp. 21–38. Baltimore, Md.: Penguin Books.

Houck, John. 1972. "The intractable female patient." *American Journal of Psychiatry, 129*: 27–31.

Hunter, Jean. 1976. "Images of woman." *Journal of Social Issues, 32* (3): 7–17.

Hurvitz, Nathan. 1973. "Psychotherapy as a means of social control." *Journal of Consulting and Clinical Psychology, 40* (2): 232–239.

Jacobson, Aileen. 1973. The feminist therapists. *Washington Post*, September 9.

Jahoda, M.; and Havel, J. 1955. "Psychological problems of women in different social roles: A case history of problem formulation in research." *Educational Record, 36*: 325–333.

Jaynes, Julian. 1978. *The Origins of Consciousness in the Breakdown of the Bicameral Mind*. Boston: Houghton-Mifflin.

Jessor, R. 1956. "Social values in psychotherapy." *Journal of Consulting Psychology, 20* (4): 264–266.

Johnson, Marilyn. 1976. "An approach to feminist therapy." *Psychotherapy: Theory, Research and Practice, 13* (1): 72–76.

Jong, Erica. 1973. *Fear of Flying*. New York: New American Library.

Jourard, S.M.; and Laskow, P. 1958. "Some factors in self-disclosure." *Journal of Abnormal and Social Psychology, 56* (1); 91–98.

Jourard, S.M.; and Rubin, S.E. 1968. "Self-disclosure and touching: A study of two modes of interpersonal encounter and their interactions." *Journal of Humanistic Psychology, 8* (1): 38–48.

Joyce, Barbara. 1975. "I'm not crazy after all." In Dorothy Smith and Sara David, eds., *Women Look at Psychiatry*, pp. 183–194. Vancouver, B.C.: Press Gang Publishers.

Kaplan, Alexandra. 1976. "Eight stages in the 9-month life span of a feminist therapy training group." *Voices, 12* (3): 41–45.

Kardener, Sheldon.; Fuller, Marielle; and Mensh, Ivan. 1976. "Characteristics of 'erotic' practitioners." *American Journal of Psychiatry, 133* (11): 1324–1325.

Kaschak, Ellyn. 1976. "Sociotherapy: An ecological model for therapy with women." *Psychotherapy: Theory, Research and Practice, 13* (1): 61–63.

Kasten, Katherine. 1972. "Toward a psychology of being: A masculine mystique." *Journal of Humanistic Psychology, 12* (2): 23–43.

Kay, Jane. 1974. "Local therapists: They accentuate women's strengths to restore psyches." *Arizona Daily Star*, April 26.

Keller, Suzanne. 1974. "The female role: Constants and change." In Violet Franks and Vasanti Burtle, eds., *Women in Therapy*, pp. 411–434. New York: Brunner/Mazel.

Kellerman, Johnathan. 1973. "Sex role stereotypes and attitudes toward parental blame for the psychological problems of children." Unpublished paper.

Kerr, Carmen. 1972. "Women's orgasms." *Rough Times: A Journal of Radical Therapy, 2* (1): 3–4.

Klein, Marjorie. 1976. "Feminist concepts of therapy outcome." *Psychotherapy: Theory, Research and Practice, 13* (1): 89–95.

Kluckhohn, Florence. 1956. "Value orientations." In Roy Grinker, ed., *Toward a Unified Theory of Human Behavior*, pp. 83–93. New York: Basic Books.

Koedt, Anne. 1976. "The myth of the vaginal orgasm." In Sue Cox, ed., *Female Psychology: The Emerging Self*, pp. 127–138. Palo Alto: Science Research Associates.

Koedt, A.; Levine, D.; and Rapone, A. 1973. *Radical Feminism*. New York: Quadrangle Books.

Krakauer, Alice. 1972. "A good therapist is hard to find." *Ms., I* (Oct.): 33–35.

Krause, Merton. 1969. "Construct validity for the evaluation of therapy outcomes." *Journal of Abnormal Psychology, 74*: 524–530.

Kravetz, Diane. 1976. "Consciousness-raising groups and group psychotherapy: Alternative mental health resources for women." *Psychotherapy: Theory, Research and Practice, 13* (1): 66–71.

Kreiger, Mari. 1974. "Consciousness-raising and gestalt for women: A synthesized approach." Unpublished master's thesis. Sonoma, Calif.: California State College.

Kronsky, B. 1971. "Feminism and psychotherapy." *Journal of Contemporary Psychotherapy, 3*: 89–98.

Kuhn, Thomas. 1970. *The Structure of Scientific Revolutions*. Chicago: University of Chicago Press.

Kwitney, Ziva. 1975. "Living without them. Three who've tried it and like it." *Ms., IV* (4): 68–71.

Landfield, A.W.; and Nawas, M.N. 1964. "Psychotherapeutic improvement as a function of communication and adoption of therapist's values." *Journal of Counseling Psychology, 11*: 336–341.

Lasky, Ella. 1974. "A feminist psychotherapist's view of a healthy person." Paper presented at American Psychological Association meeting, September 2, New Orleans, La.

Leidig, Margie. 1976. "Feminist therapy." Unpublished paper, January.

Lerman, Hannah. 1974. "What happens in feminist therapy?" Paper presented at American Psychological Association meeting, September, New Orleans, La.

Letailleur, M.; Morin, J.; and LeBorgne, Y. 1958. "Autoscopie hétérosexuelle et schizophrénie [The self-induced heterosexual image and schizophrenia]." *Annales Medico-Psychologiques*, Vol. 2.

Levine, Saul; Kamin, Louisa; and Levine, Eleanor. 1974. "Sexism and psychiatry." *American Journal of Orthopsychiatry, 44* (3): 327–336.

Lifton, Robert J. 1976. *The Life of the Self.* New York: Simon & Schuster.

Lindsey, Karen. 1974. "On the need to develop a feminist therapy." *Rough Times: A Journal of Radical Therapy, 4*: 2–3.

Liss-Levinson, Nechama. 1976. "AWP feminist therapy roster: Therapist criteria, past use and future suggestions." Association for Women in Psychology.

London, Perry. 1964. *Modes and Morals of Psychotherapy.* New York: Holt, Rinehart, and Winston.

McCartney, J. 1966. "Overt transference." *Journal of Sex Research, 2*: 227–237.

McClelland, David; and Watt, Norman. 1968. "Sex role alienation in schizophrenia." *Journal of Abnormal Psychology, 73* (3): 226–239.

McKeachie, Wilbert. 1976. "Psychology in America's Bicentennial year." *American Psychologist, 31* (12): 819–933.

McKee, J.P.; and Sherriffs, A.C. 1957. "The differential evaluation of males and females." *Journal of Personality, 25*: 356–371.

Maccoby, Eleanor, 1963. "Women's intellect." In Seymour Farber and Roger Wilson, eds., *The Potential of Woman*, pp. 24–39. New York: McGraw-Hill.

Maccoby, Eleanor, ed. 1966. *The Development of Sex Differences.* Palo Alto: Stanford University Press.

Maccoby, Eleanor; and Jacklin, C. 1974. *The Psychology of Sex Differences.* Palo Alto: Stanford University Press.

MacLeod, Robert. 1975. *The Persistent Problems of Psychology.* Pittsburgh, Pa.: Duquesne University Press.

Mahrer, Alvin. 1967. *The Goals of Psychotherapy.* New York: Appleton-Century-Crofts.

Mannes, Marya. 1963. "The problems of creative women." In Seymour Farber and Roger Wilson, eds., *The Potential of Women*, pp. 116–130. New York: McGraw-Hill.

Mannes, Marya. 1964. "The roots of anxiety in modern woman." *Journal of Neuropsychiatry, 5*: 412.

Maracek, Jeanne. 1976. "Powerlessness and women's psychological disorders." *Voices, 12* (3): 50–66.

Marmor, J. 1972. "Sexual acting out in psychotherapy." *American Journal of Psychoanalysis, 22*: 3–8.

Martin, Del. 1976. *Battered Wives.* San Francisco: Glide Publications.

May, Rollo. 1967. *Psychology and the Human Dilemma.* Princeton, N.J.: Van Nostrand.

Mead, Margaret. 1968. *Male and Female.* New York: Laurel Edition.

Merriam, G. & C. Co. 1965. *The New Merriam-Webster Pocket Dictionary*. New York: Merriam-Webster Co.

Milgram, Stanley. 1965a. "Some conditions of obedience and disobedience to authority." *Human Relations, 18*: 57–76.

Milgram, Stanley. 1965b. "Liberating effects of group pressure." *Journal of Personality and Social Psychology, 1*: 127–134.

Miller, Jean Baker; and Mothner, Ira. 1971. "Psychological consequences of sexual inequality." *American Journal of Orthopsychiatry, 41* (5): 767–775.

Millet, Kate. 1969. *Sexual Politics*. New York: Avon Books.

Mitchell, Juliet. 1974. *Psychoanalysis and Feminism*. New York: Random House.

Morgan, Robin. 1970. *Sisterhood is Powerful: An Anthology of Writings from the Women's Liberation Movement*. New York: Vintage Books.

Morgan, Robin. 1972. "Revolucinations." In *Monster: Poems by Robin Morgan*, New York: Random House.

Morris, Jan. 1974. *Conundrum*. New York: Harcourt, Brace, Jovanovich. Excerpted in *Ms.*, 1974, *III* (1): 57–64.

Mueller, Karen; and Leidig, Margie. 1976. "Women's anger and feminist therapy." Presented at Feminist Therapy Conference, Boulder, Colo.

Mundy, Jean. 1974. "Feminist therapy with lesbians and other women." *Homosexual Counseling Journal, 1* (4): 154–159.

New York Narcotic Addiction Control Commission. 1971. "Differential drug use within the New York state labor force: An assessment of drug use within the general population." Albany, New York.

Nowacki, C.M.; and Poe, C.A. 1973. "The concept of mental health as related to sex or person perceived." *Journal of Consulting and Clinical Psychology, 40*: 160.

O'Neill, William. 1969. *Everyone Was Brave: The Rise and Fall of Feminism*. Chicago: Quadrangle Books.

Orlinsky, D.; and Howard, K. 1976. "The effects of sex of therapist on the therapeutic experience of women." *Psychotherapy: Theory, Research, and Practice, 13* (1): 82–88.

Ornstein, Robert. 1972. *The Psychology of Consciousness*. San Francisco: W.H. Freeman.

Parsons, Jacquelynne; Frieze, Irene; and Ruble, Diane. 1976. "Introduction." *Journal of Social Issues, 32* (3): 1–5.

Perl, Harriet; and Abarbanell, Gay. 1976. *Guidelines for Feminist Consciousness Raising*. Los Angeles: NOW.

Perlstein, Marcia. 1976. "What is a healthy woman?" In Sue Cox, ed., *Female Psychology: The Emerging Self*, pp. 385–389. Palo Alto: Science Research Associates.

Pheterson, Gail; and Moed, Lillian. Jan. 1976. "A feminist therapy training program in Holland." Unpublished paper.

Pincus, Cynthia; Radding, Natalie; Laurence, Roberta. 1974. "Professional counseling service for women." *Social Work, 19*: 187–195.

Polanyi, Michael. 1974. *Personal Knowledge*. Chicago: University of Chicago Press.

Polk, Barbara. 1972. "Women's liberation: Movement for equality." In Constantina Safilios-Rothschild, ed., *Toward a Sociology of Women*, pp. 321–330. Lexington, Mass.: Xerox College Publishing.

Polk, Barbara. 1974. "Male power and the women's movement." *Journal of Applied Behavioral Science, 10* (3): 415–431.

Poverny, Linda. 1976. "Feminist therapists." Unpublished master's thesis. Los Angeles: University of California.

Radloff, Lenore. In press. "Sex differences in helplessness with implications for depression." In L.S. Hansen and R.S. Rapoze, eds., *Career Development and Counseling for Women*. Springfield, Ill.: Charles C Thomas.

Raffini, Mary. 1975. "A feminist alternative: The Elizabeth Stone House." *Rough Times: A Journal of Radical Therapy, 4*: 12–15.

Rawlings, Edna; and Carter, Dianne, eds. 1977. *Psychotherapy for Women: Treatment Toward Equality*. Springfield, Ill.: Charles C Thomas.

Rebecca, Meda; Hefner, Robert; and Oleshansky, Barbara. 1976. "A model of sex role transcendence." *Journal of Social Issues, 32* (3): 197–206.

Reiff, Robert. 1974. "The control of knowledge: The power of the helping professions." *Journal of Applied Behavioral Science, 10*: 451–461.

Rickles, Nathan. 1971. "The angry woman syndrome." *Archives of General Psychiatry, 24*: 91–94.

Riesman, Frank; and Miller, S.M. 1964. "Social change vs. the 'psychiatric world view.' " *American Journal of Orthopsychiatry, 34* (1): 29–38.

Robertiello, R. 1975. "Iatrogenic psychiatric illness." *Journal of Contemporary Psychotherapy, 7*: 3–8.

Roche Psychiatric Viewpoints. 1971. "Report XIII: Women's liberation." Roche Pharmaceuticals, *1* (1): 8.

Rose, Clare. 1975. "Women's sex role attitudes: A historical perspective." *New Directions for Higher Education, 11*: 1–31.

Rosenthal, David. 1955. "Changes in some moral values following psychotherapy." *Journal of Consulting Psychology, 19* (6): 431–436.

Rosenthal, R. 1966. *Experimenter Effects in Behavioral Research*. New York: Appleton-Century-Crofts.

Rosenthal, R.; and Pode, K.L. 1960. "The effect of experimenter bias on the performance of the albino rat." Unpublished manuscript. Cambridge, Mass.: Harvard University.

Rossi, Alice. 1972. "The roots of ambivalence in American women." In Judith Bardwick, ed., *Readings on the Psychology of Women*, pp. 125–127. New York: Harper & Row.

Rotter, Julian. 1963. "A historical and theoretical analysis of some broad trends in clinical psychology." In Sigmund Koch, ed., *Psychology: A Study of a Science. Vol. 5: The Process Areas, The Person and Some Applied Fields: Their Place in Psychology and in Science*, pp. 780–830. New York: McGraw-Hill.

Rubins, Jack. 1975. The relationship between the individual, the culture, and psychopathology." *American Journal of Psychoanalysis, 35*: 231–249.

Saleebey, Dennis. 1975. "A proposal to merge humanist and behaviorist perspectives." *Social Casework, 56* (8): 468–479.

Schachter, S.; and Singer, J.E. 1962. "Cognitive, social, and physiological determinants of emotional state." *Psychological Review, 63*: 379–399.

Schafer, Roy. 1974. "Problems in Freud's psychology of women." *Journal of the American Psychoanalytic Association, 22*: 459–485.

Scheff, Thomas. 1966. *Being Mentally Ill: A sociological theory*. Chicago: Aldine Press.

Schickel, Richard. 1975. "Gillooly doesn't live here anymore." *Time*, February 17, p. 67.

Schlossberg, Nancy; and Pietrofesa, John. 1973. "Perspectives on counseling bias: Implications for counselor education." *Counseling Psychologist, 4* (1): 44–53.

Schultz, Ardelle. 1977. "Radical feminism: A treatment modality for addicted women." In Edna Rawlings and Dianne Carter, eds., *Psychotherapy for Women*. Springfield, Ill.: Charles C Thomas.

Sedney, Mary Anne. Sept. 1976. "Complexities in conceptualizing clients' problems in androgynous terms." Paper presented at American Psychological Association meeting, Washington, D.C.

Seiden, Anne. 1976. "Overview: Research on the psychology of women. II. Women in families, work and psychotherapy." *American Journal of Psychiatry, 133* (10): 1111–1123.

Seidler-Feller, Doreen. 1976. "Process and power in couples psychotherapy: A feminist view." *Voices, 12* (3): 67–71.

Seligman, Martin. 1975. *Helplessness: On depression, development and death*. San Francisco: W.H. Freeman.

Shepard, M. 1971. *The Love Treatment: Sexual Intimacy between Patients and Psychotherapists*. New York: Wyden.

Sherman, Julia. 1971. *On the Psychology of Women: A Survey of Empirical Studies*. Springfield, Ill.: Charles C Thomas.

Sherman, Julia. Sept. 1975. "Freud's 'theory' and feminism: A reply to Juliet Mitchell." Paper presented at American Psychological Convention, Chicago, Ill.

Sherman, Julia. 1976. "Social values, femininity and the development of female competence." *Journal of Social Issues, 32* (3): 181–196.

Silveria, Jeanette. 1972. "The effect of sexism on thought: How male bias hurts psychology and some hopes for a woman's psychology." Pittsburgh: Know.

Simon, Leonard J. 1970. "The political unconscious of psychology: Clinical psychology and social change." *Professional Psychology,* (Summer): 331–341.

Simonton, O. Carl; Matthews-Simonton, Stephanie; and Creighton, James. 1978. *Getting Well Again*. Los Angeles: J.P. Tarcher.

Singer, Erwin. 1970. *Key Concepts in Psychotherapy*. New York: Random House.

Singer, June. 1976. *Androgyny: Toward a New Theory of Sexuality*, 2nd ed. New York: Doubleday.

Smith, Dorothy; and David, Sara, eds. 1975. *Women Look at Psychiatry*. Vancouver, B.C.: Press Gang Publishers.

Spitz, Rene. 1945. "Hospitalism: An inquiry into the genesis of psychiatric conditions in early childhood." *The Psychoanalytic Study of the Child,* 1: 53–74.

Spitz, Rene. 1946. "Hospitalism: II." *The Psychoanalytic Study of the Child,* 2: 113–117.

Spitz, Rene. 1957. *No and Yes*. New York: International Universities Press.

Stevens, Barbara. 1971. "The psychotherapist and women's liberation." *Social Work, 11*: 12–18.

Stricker, George. 1977. "Implications of research for psychotherapeutic treatment of women." *American Psychologist, 32* (1): 14–22.

Sundland, Donald; and Barker, Edwin. 1962. "The orientations of psychotherapists." *Journal of Consulting Psychology, 26* (3): 201–212.

Szasz, Thomas. 1961. *The Myth of Mental Illness*. New York: Hoeber-Harper.

Tavris, Carol. 1973. "Who likes women's liberation—and why. The case of the unliberated liberal." *Journal of Social Issues, 29* (4): 175–198.

Tedeschi, James; and O'Donovan, Denis. 1971. "Social power and the psychologist." *Professional Psychologist,* (Winter): 59–64.

Tennov, Dorothy. 1973. "Feminism, psychotherapy, and professionalism." *Journal of Contemporary Psychotherapy, 5* (2): 107–111.

Tennov, Dorothy. 1974. "An alternative to therapy." *Aurora,* (4): 5–8.

Tennov, Dorothy. 1975. *Psychotherapy: The Hazardous Cure*. New York: Abelard Schuman.

Thomas, Susan Amelia. 1975. "Moving into integration: A study of theory and practice in feminist therapy." Unpublished master's thesis. Portland: Portland State University.

Thompson, Clara. 1963. "Cultural pressures in the psychology of women." In Jean Baker Miller, ed., *Psychoanalysis and Women*, pp. 69–84. Baltimore: Penguin Books.

Tooley, Kay. 1977. "Johnny, I hardly knew ye: Toward revision of the theory of male psychosexual development." *American Journal of Orthopsychiatry, 47* (2): 184–195.

Torrey, E. Fuller. 1973. *The Mind Game*. New York: Bantam Books.

Walstedt, Joyce. 1971. "36-24-36: Anatomy of oppression: A feminist analysis of psychotherapy." Pittsburgh: Know.

Weissman, M.M.; and Klerman, G.L. In press. "Sex differences and the epidemiology of depression." *Archives of General Psychiatry*.

Weisstein, Naomi. 1969. "Woman as nigger." *Psychology Today, 20*: 22 & 58.

Weisstein, Naomi. 1972. "Psychology constructs the female." In Vivian Gornick and Barbara Moran, eds., *Woman in Sexist Society*, pp. 207–224. New York: New American Library.

Wesley, Carol. 1975. "The women's movement and psychotherapy." *Social Work, 20* (2): 120–124.

Whitbeck, Caroline. 1976. "Theories of sex difference." In Carol Gould and Marx Wartofsky, eds., *Women and Philosophy*, pp. 54–80. New York: G.P. Putnam's Sons.

Williams, Elizabeth Friar. 1976. *Notes of a Feminist Therapist*. New York: Praeger.

Wolberg, L. 1954. *The Technique of Psychotherapy*. New York: Grune & Stratton.

Wolowitz, Howard. 1972. "Hysterical character and feminine identity." In Judith Bardwick, ed., *Readings on the Psychology of Women*, pp. 307–313. New York: Harper and Row.

Women in Transition. 1975. *Women in Transition: A Feminist Handbook on Separation and Divorce*. New York: Charles Scribner's.

Women's Institute of Alternative Psychotherapy. 1976. *Women's Institute of Alternative Psychotherapy Newsletter*. May 4, No. 22.

Wyckoff, Hogie. 1970. "Radical psychotherapy and transactional analysis in women's groups." *Transactional Analysis Bulletin, 9* (36): 128–133.

Wyckoff, Hogie. 1971. "The stroke economy in women's scripts." *Transactional Analysis Journal, 1* (3): 16–20.

Wyckoff, Hogie. 1973a. "Between women and men." *Issues in Radical Therapy, 1* (2).

Wyckoff, Hogie. 1973b. "Problem solving groups for women." *Issues in Radical Therapy, 1* (1): 6–12.

Wyckoff, Hogie. 1975. "Power sources." *Issues in Radical Therapy, 4* (1): 4–9.

Wyckoff, Hogie. 1977. "Radical psychiatry techniques for solving women's problems in groups." In Edna Rawlings and Dianne Carter, eds., *Psychotherapy for Women,* pp. 392–403. Springfield, Ill.: Charles C Thomas.

Yalom, Irvin. 1970. *The Theory and Practice of Group Psychotherapy.* New York: Basic Books.

INDEX

Index

All-female therapy groups, 144–145, 181
  as legitimating body, 145
  expectations in, 145
  rationale for, 144–145
  See also Resocialization
American Psychological Association, Psychology of Women, (Division 35), 72
Androcentrism, 55–60, 87
Androgyny, 77–78, 100–104, 164
  androgynous model of personality, 102, 164
  advantages of, 102
  versus sex roles, 101–103
Anger in women, 58, 79, 128–129, 165, 181
APA Task Force on Sex Bias and Sex Role Stereotyping in Psychotherapeutic Practice, Report of, 52–53, 57–60
  See also Sex role analysis
Assertiveness, 168–169, 181
Association for Women in Psychology, 72–80
  on characteristics of feminist therapy, 80–81
Attitude change, 12

Attitudes towards women, history of, 90
Autonomy, 163, 167, 169

Basis for feminist therapy, 3
deBeauvoir, Simone
  on feminist image of women, 91–94
Behavior, interactional model of, 133–136
"Being-in-Becoming," 8–9, 15–16, 18, 84, 100
Belief systems, 11, 24–26, 27–28
  American behaviorist, 26
  cognitive restructuring of, 142–143, 147
  effect on women in therapy, 27–28, 179
  feminist, 5–6
  Freudian, 26
  Humanistic, 27
  limitations of, 11, 24–25
  therapy and, 3–4, 23–27
Biological determinism, 44, 50, 94
Bisexuality, 78
Black movement compared to feminism, 6

Body image of women, 171
Body politics, vii

Change, 34–35, 84, 137, 138, 182
  as goal of therapy, 163–164
  factors facilitating, 137
  personal, 142, 163–164
  social, 142, 147–148
Chesler, Phyllis, 55, 56
  on physical beauty, 59
  on therapy and marriage, 64–65
Collateral mode of relations, 16, 33–34
Consciousness raising, 45–48, 80, 172
  and feminist therapists, 80, 152, 178
  feminist therapy and, 48, 68
  origins of, 46
  purposes of, 47–48
Consumerism in mental health services, 68, 149, 157–158, 183
Costs of feminist therapy, 152
Criteria for feminist therapists, *see* Feminist therapists
Cultural feminism, 42, 25
Culture, defined, 131
Culture and therapy, 14–18

Depression, 110, 123–124
  sex role as factor in, 123
  See also Female sex role
Diagnostic categories, 129
Dialectic view of therapy, 166
Differential power analysis, 141
Doctor-patient relationship
  exploitation of, 59
  sexual relations in, 59–60, 181
  See also Therapist-client relationship
Dominant mothers, 125
Dominant/subordinate relationship between the sexes, 113–115
Double standard of mental health,
  see Mental health, double standard

Egalitarianism in feminist therapy, 80–81, 158–160, 181

Fees for feminist therapy, 152
Female friendships, viii, 169
Female inferiority, myth of, 92–93
Female passivity in presence of males, 150
Female schizophrenics, 127–128
Female sex role
  and schizophrenia, 127–128
  breaking psychological maintenance of, 138–143
  conflict generated by, 78–79, 108–109, 111, 116
  definition of, 106–107
  depression and, 111, 123–124
  deviation from, 27, 127–129, 131
  emotional results of, 107–110, 142
  identity and, 28, 108–109
  impact of, 116, 177
  mental health and, xi, 14, 56, 106
  mental illness and, 111–112, 116, 132
  psychological effects of, 110–112, 131
  rejection of, 77, 168–169
  self-actualization and, 107
  social context and, 132–133
  symptoms of psychological distress and, 119–121, 137
Female sexuality, redefined, 78, 93, 171
Female socialization, viii, 23, 109, 126–137
Female world, defined, viii
Feminine Mystique, The, 40
Feminist criticism of psychotherapy, 3, 5, 54–66, 70–71, 80–84, 180
  double standard of mental health, 55–60

exploitation of female clients, 59–
60, 181
social control issues, 60–65, 80,
180
See also Psychotherapy
Feminism
as advocacy system, 6
commonality of female experience,
6
definition of, 4–5, 6, 43–44
impact of practice of psychotherapy, 5, 54–60
Feminist consciousness, 77
Feminist critique of society, 44
Feminist humanism, 77, 88–89
Feminist image of women, 89–94,
152
See also Human nature
Feminist movement, 39–48
consciousness raising and, 45–48
critique of Freudian theory and,
49–53
feminist therapy and, 45, 178
goals of, 44–45
groups within women's movement, 40–43, 45
history of, 39–40
19th century compared with today, 39, 45–46
reemergence of American feminism, 40
Feminist therapists, 150–160
consciousness raising and, 152
criteria for, 150–153
fee scale of, 152
female, advantages of, 150
functions of, 153–160
client advocate, 156–157
facilitator of resocialization process, 154
role model, 80, 82, 154–156
teacher, 153, 159
validation, 154
image of women held by, 152
involvement in social action, 150,
151

personal qualities of, 150–151
professional competence and training, 151–152
relationship with clients, 80–81,
84, 157–160, 181
power equalization and, 81–82,
128–160
research with, 76–77, 78, 83
role of, 81–83, 149–160
view of clients, 152–153
Feminist therapy, ix, 67–72, 75–84,
87, 147–174
and social action, 151, 163, 171–
172
basis of, 3
client as "expert" in, 82
collectives, 69–70
consumerism in, 68, 157
criteria for effectiveness, 163–165
definition of, 76, 80–81
equalization of power in, 158–160
future research directions in, 182–
184
gender of therapist in, 150
goals of, ix, 161–174, 183, *see also*
Goals of Feminist therapy
growth of, 67–68, 70–72
impact of, 177–181
male therapists and, 83, 150
need for, ix, 69
outcome evaluation in, 164–165,
170, 172–174, 183
philosophy of, ix, 5
power-sharing strategies in, 82
priorities of, 148, 162
reciprocal influence model and,
157–158
resocialization in, 142–147, 168
responsibilities of client and therapist in, 158
role of change in, 137, 143, 163–
164
role of therapist in, 81–83, 149–
160, *see also* Feminist therapists
steps of, 77

Feminist therapy (*cont.*)
  symptom interpretation in, 117–
    129, *see also* Symptoms of
    psychological distress
  therapeutic interventions in, 130–
    148
  therapy groups in, 144–147, 181
  views on women's anger, 79, 165,
    181
Feminist value system, 5, 75–84
  androgyny and, 77–78
  congruency among therapists
    about, 76
  egalitarianism in, 81–82
  feminist consciousness, 77
  feminist humanism, 77
  in feminist therapy, 75–84
  rejection of traditional female role
    by, 77
Freud, Sigmund
  biological determinism of, 50
  concept of unconscious, 26
  cultural influences on theories of,
    179–180
  feminist critique of, 50–51
  on nature of man, 31
  origins of modern psychotherapy
    and, 7–9
  phallocentric view of human de-
    velopment, 90
  psychoanalysis, 52
  theory of human nature, 8
  on women, 50, 51, 90
  women's movement and, 49–53
Friedan, Betty, 40
Functions of a therapist, 153–157
  See also Feminist therapists

Goals of feminist therapy, 161–174
  androgyny, 164
  autonomy as, 163, 167, 169
  body image and, 171
  cultural feminism, 162
  interpersonal relationships and,
    168–169

optimal functioning, 162–163
  political awareness and social ac-
    tion, 171–172
  role performance and, 169–170
  self-esteem, 167–168
  social change as, 163, 172
  symptom removal as, 165–166
  target problems, 170–171

Horney, Karen, 51, 95–96
Housewife role, 109
Human nature, 7–9, 30–35,
    179
  and etiology of psychological dis-
    tress, 32
  feminist view of, 87–89
  Freudian model of, 7–8
  and goals of therapy, 34–35
  Hobbes' view of, 31
  Humanistic model of, 88–89, 104
  Jungian view of, 104
  nature of, 30–32
  Rogerian model of, 8–9
  Rousseau's view of, 31
  and social context, 179–180
  and symptom interpretation, 32–
    33
  therapeutic relationship and, 33
Hysterical personality, 120–121

Id, 8
Impact of feminist therapy, 177–
    181
  on feminist movement, 178
  on psychotherapy profession, 178–
    181
"Insight," 12
Institutional power, 112–113
Interactional model of behavior,
    133–136
  social learning theory and, 134,
    136
  socialization and, 134–135
  in treatment of women, 136

Jaynes, Julian, 25–26
Jungian view of women, 90–91

Kluckhohn, Florence, 15
Koch, Sigmund, xii
Kuhn, Thomas, 24–25

Learned helplessness, 123–124
Lesbianism, 78, 99–100, 142
Liberal feminism, 41

Male dominance, rationale for, vii
Male therapists in feminist therapy,
    83, 150
    See also Doctor-patient relation-
        ship
Marriage, 64–65, 111, 141, 169
Masochism in women, 119–120
Masculine value system, 17
    compared with female system,
        17–18
Mead, Margaret, 101
Media portrayal of women, 124
Mental health
    adjustment model of, 163
    conceptualizations of, 4, 61, 63
    counselor bias and, 56
    double standard of, 13–14, 55–60
    feminist definition of, 103–104
    marital status and, 111–112
    masculine standards of, 57
    sex role and, 57–60
Mental illness
    etiology of, 32, 105–106
Minority group status of women,
    112–116, 139–140, 143
    and dominant/subordinate rela-
        tionship of sexes, 113–114
    ego defenses and, 115–116
    personality distortion as a result
        of, 115
    psychological effects of, 112–116
    recognition of, 139–140, 143

Narcissism, 120
National Organization for Women
    (NOW), 40, 41
    use of consciousness raising in, 46
Nature of Woman, 85–104, 120
    androgyny and, 100–104
    deBeauvoir, Simone on, 91–94
    female value system and, 87
    feminist view of, 87, 89–94
    Freudian view of, 50, 51, 90, 120
    Humanistic view of, 87–89, 91
    Jungian view of, 90
    male definitions of, 91–92, 94
    nature of human nature and, 86–87
    self-actualization and, 95–100
    women's view of, 31
Neurosis, 122
    as social problem, 138
Neurotic symptomatology, *see* Role
    conflict
Nonverbal communication in ther-
    apy, 65
Normative power, 112

Oedipal complex, 51
Oppression of women, 44, 132
Optimal functioning, 150, 151, 162–
    163
Other-directedness, 108

Passivity in women, 120, 128, 150
Penis envy, 50, 53
"Personal is political," 47, 79, 138,
    178
Personality
    behavior and social context and,
        131–133
    cross-cultural studies of, 132
    role playing and, 132–133
Philosophy
    and therapy, 18–23
    assumptions of, 23
    compared with psychotherapy and
        psychology, 20–23

Philosophy (*cont.*)
  defined, 3
  history of, 18–19
Philosophy of treatment, xii, 3–9, 35
  assumptions of, 10–29
  based on female value system, 17
  defined, 9
  importance of, 7–9
  reasons for, 3–4
  values and, 10–14, 15
Politics of psychotherapy, 60–65
Power
  differential power analysis of society, 141
  differentials between men and women, 112–113, 141
  equalization of, in therapy, 81–82, 158–160
  erotic, of women, 125
  of expertise, 113
  personal, women and, 125
Powerlessness, 112, 123
Power sharing strategies in feminist therapy, 81–82
Pseudoscientism, 8
Psychoanalysis, 16, 33
Psychological distress in women, 32
  causes of, 32, 79–80, 105–116
  cultural factors and, 182
  interpretation of symptoms, 32–33
  levels of, 136, 138–139
  role conflict and, 110–112, 116
  view of human nature and, 32–33
Psychological effects of female sex role, 110–112, 131
  See also Female sex role
Psychological effects of minority group status of women, 112–116
  See also Minority group status of women
Psychological maintenance of sex roles
  breaking of, 138–143
  See also Female sex role
Psychological power, 113

Psychology
  compared with philosophy and psychotherapy, 20–23
  definition of, 19, 137
  history of, 18–19
  problems of, 19
Psychopathology
  causes of, 32
  feminist definition of, 116, 129, 132
  interpretation of symptoms of, 32–33, 117–129
Psychosomatic symptoms, 125–126
Psychotherapy
  as social control agent, 60–66, 159, 180
  belief system of, 8
  compared with psychology and philosophy, 20–23
  criticism of, 3, 5, 54–66, 70–71, 80, 84
  goals of, 34–35, 162
  historical roots of, 11
  impact of feminist therapy upon, 178–180
  models of, 80, 84, 178
  origins in Freud, 7–9
  reciprocal influence model of, 157–158
  role of therapist in, 33–34, 149, 157
  sexism in, 54–60, 91
  shift in attitudes and emphasis, 7
  social context of, 179–180
  techniques, defined, 9
  theory of, defined, 10
  See also Feminist criticism of psychotherapy

Radical Feminists, 41
Rape, 142
Redstockings, 41
Resocialization, 143–147, 168, 182
  comparison with primary socialization, 143

cooperative effort in, 145–146
in feminist therapy groups, 144–147
results of, 147, 168
role of others in, 145, 147
See also All-female therapy groups
Reward power, 113
Role conflict in women, 121–122, 166, 169
emotional distress as a result of, 121
neurosis and, 122
Role definition
culture and, 132
social context and, 131
Role deviancy theory, 126–127
Role of psychotherapist, 33–34, 149, 157
See also Feminist therapists

Schizophrenia and sex roles, 127–129
Self-actualization, 95–100, 107
androgyny and, 102
autonomy and, 97
female sex role and, 107, 122
self-consciousness and, 95
self-definition and, 96–97
sexuality and, 98–100
Self-esteem, 167–168, 169
Sex differences, 101, 136
Sexism in psychotherapy, 54–66, 70–71, 87–88
Sex role
alienation, 128
analysis of society, 140–141
culture and, 131–133
fostered by psychotherapy, 57–58
humanistic theory and, 87
maintenance of, 115
mental health and, xi, 14, 56–60, 111–112
psychological maintenance of, 138–143

sociocultural factors and, 44
symptoms of psychological distress and, 116
transcendence of, 102–103
value judgments in therapy, and, 13–14
value systems and, 17
See also Female sex role
Sexuality, 78, 93, 171, 179–180
Social control and psychotherapy, 60–66, 180
examples of, 61, 64
political aspects of, 62
Social learning theory, 80, 134, 136
Socialist feminism, 43
Socialization, female, 23, 123–124, 143–144
depression and, 123
powerlessness and helplessness and, 112, 123
Sociobiology, vii–ix
Status of women
minority group, 112–116, 139–140, 143, *see also* Minority group status of women
subordinate, 28, 113–115, 125, 130–131
Superego, 8
Symptoms of psychological distress, 117–129, 165–166
as role conflict, 121–122
as role deviancy, 126–129
as survival tactics, 124–126
cultural factors and, 121, 182
definition of, 117
female role and, 119–121
female socialization and, 123–124
interpretations of, 32–33, 119
feminist view of, 119–132
humanistic view of, 118
psychoanalytic view of, 118
neurotic symptoms, 118–119
psychosomatic, 125–126
removal of, 165–166
sex role and, 116

Therapeutic effectiveness, 163–165
Therapeutic interventions, 130–148
Therapist attitudes
  communication of, 14
  impact on therapy, 5, 27–28
  personal philosophy of life and, 9
  sexism in, 55–59
  values and, 11
Therapist-client relationship, 33–34,
    157–160, 181
  in feminist therapy, 157–160, 181
  selection of therapist, 68, 158
  sexual contact in, 59–60, 181
Therapy collectives, 69–70
  Feminist Counseling Collective,
    Washington, D.C., 70
  Feminist Therapy Collective,
    Philadelphia, 70, 83
  IRT Collective, Berkeley, 70
Therapy groups, all-female, 144–145
  See also All-female therapy groups
Thompson, Clara, 51
Time orientation
  cultural value orientation and, 15
  of traditional psychotherapy, 17
Training of feminist therapists, 151–
    152
Treatment outcomes in feminist
    therapy
  comparison with psychotherapy,
    173–174
  evaluation of, 164–165, 172–174,
    183
  questions for assessing, 173
  See also Goals of feminist therapy

Value conflict in women, 23
Value systems, 11–14
  American behaviorist, 16
  definition of, 15
  Humanistic, 16
  internalization of, 138
  male and female compared, 17
  of feminist therapy, 17–18
  psychoanalytical, 16

relation to psychotherapy, 16, 181
values and therapy, xii, 8–9, 11–
    14, 16, 181, 183

Women
  anger and, 79, 128–129
  as minority group, 112–116
  as sex objects, 59
  as wives and mothers, 125, 128,
    135
  biological determinism and, 44,
    50, 94
  body image of, 171
  deBeauvoir, Simone on, 91–94
  defined by women, 92
  defined in male terms, 91–92, 94–
    96, 107–108
  emotional problems of, 78–79, 136
  feminist image of, 89–94
  Freudian theory and, 50, 51, 90
  historical views of, 90
  in media, 124
  mental health of, 103–104
  nature of, 85–104
  negative images, 90
  other-directedness in, 108
  personal power and, 125
  powerlessness and, 112, 123, 125
  self-actualization of, 95–100
  socialization of, 23, 123–124, 143–
    144
  subordinate status of, 28, 125,
    130–131
Women's liberation movement, 4–5,
    39–48
  critique of Freudian theory, 49–53
  goals of, 44–45
  history of, 39–40, 40–43
  left-wing groups in, 42–43, 45
  liberal feminist groups in, 40–41,
    45
  psychotherapy and, 3, 28–29
  Roche Report on, 57, 61
Wyckoff, Hogie, 146